Knitting in the Old Way

Knitting in the old way means knitting by thinking, not by following.

This book guides you to discover a way of knitting. It unfolds a process that connects you to centuries of textile wisdom and helps you invent and create designs of your own.

Knitting in the old way involves working each sweater from a plan based on proportions, instead of from a line-by-line pattern.

It's what you do that makes your soul.

Barbara Kingsolver
in *Animal Dreams*

Although
I am passionate
in my pursuit of
handcrafting textiles of all sorts
(especially knitting), that is not what I
do. What I *do* is bear witness to the work of
spinners and knitters of other times and places.
I acknowledge the accomplishments of these artisans,
who built the foundations for all that we do today. Now,
if that is not my soul, it is certainly soul-satisfying!

—P G-R

Knitting
in the Old Way

Designs & Techniques
from Ethnic Sweaters

by

Priscilla A. Gibson-Roberts
and Deborah Robson

illustrations by
Priscilla A. Gibson-Roberts

Nomad Press expanded edition

Nomad Press
Fort Collins, Colorado

Corrections: We have worked extremely hard to ensure the accuracy
of this book's contents, yet we are human (or, in some cases, feline or
canine) and computers are inscrutable. If you find an item that needs
to be corrected, please let us know by way of the addresses below. We'll
post any critical changes on our web site and we'll improve the next
printing.

Drawings and charts: Priscilla Gibson-Roberts
Scanning and image preparation: Rebekah Robson-May
Editorial, design, and production: Deborah Robson
Index and proofing: Katie Banks

Nomad Press expanded edition.

This is a fully revised and expanded edition of *Knitting in the Old Way,*
published in 1985 by Interweave Press in Loveland, Colorado.

Cataloging-in-Publication data

Gibson-Roberts, Priscilla A.
Knitting in the old way : designs & techniques from ethnic sweaters / by Priscilla
A. Gibson-Roberts and Deborah Robson ; illustrations by Priscilla A. Gibson-
Roberts — Nomad Press expanded ed. — Fort Collins, Colo. : Nomad Press, 2004.
   p. cm.
Includes bibliographical references and index.
ISBN 0-9668289-2-5
1. Sweaters. 2. Knitting. 3. Knitting—Patterns.
I. Robson, Deborah. II. Title.
TT825 .G53 2004   2003091924
746.432—dc21   CIP

10 09 08 07 06 05 04
10 9 8 7 6 5 4 3 2

Printing: McNaughton and Gunn

Nomad Press
PO Box 484
Fort Collins, CO 80522-0484 USA

www.drobson.info/nomad.htm

This book is a labor of love.
May it bring each reader joy.

Priscilla Gibson-Roberts and Deborah Robson share the values, spirit, and sense of adventure embodied in knitting in the old way. The voice and experience at the core of this book are Priscilla's. Deborah is the technical editor, print designer, and asker-of-questions. She devised the presentation of Priscilla's information, and in the process wrote supplementary sections. This book has been made like a sweater produced by two knitters who have matched their gauges.

Priscilla Gibson-Roberts has dedicated her passion and intelligence to discovering the secrets of ethnic knitting styles and techniques. She supplements her studies of the textiles themselves with large doses of written and oral history. In addition to serving as the spinning editor for *Knitter's* for thirteen years, she has published articles in many other periodicals, including *Interweave Knits* and *Spin-Off*. Her books include:

> *Knitting in the Old Way:*
> *Designs and Techniques from Ethnic Sweaters* (2004)
>
> *Simple Socks: Plain and Fancy* (2001)
>
> *High Whorling:*
> *A Spinner's Guide to an Old-World Skill* (1998)
>
> *Ethnic Socks and Stockings: A Compendium*
> *of Eastern Design and Technique* (1995)
>
> *Salish Indian Sweaters:*
> *A Pacific Northwest Tradition* (1989)
>
> *Knitting in the Old Way* (1985)

At last count, **Deborah Robson** had edited or been a consultant on the development and production of more than seventy-five books, more than a third of which involved textile crafts. For fourteen years, she was a book and magazine editor at Interweave Press, including twelve years as editor of *Spin-Off: The Magazine for Handspinners*. She also edited *Shuttle Spindle & Dyepot* for the Handweavers Guild of America and has published articles, essays, and short stories.

Contents

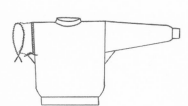

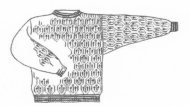

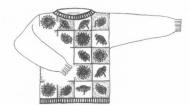

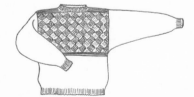

How to use this book

Knitting in the Old Way represents many lifetimes of knowledge, beginning with the contributions of the knitters who invented the craft out of necessity and an adventurous spirit. They and those who followed them have wrought marvels with exquisitely simple tools and materials. It's amazing what you can do with a loop of yarn.

And it's amazing what *you* can do with a loop of yarn, if you take one loop, one idea, one technique at a time. Start where you are—beginner or adept—and add one new possibility at a time. Approach some knitting days with utility in mind. On others, experiment with mathematical precision. At still other times, go for artistic expression.

Mix and match. The basic plans, cardigan and neckline variations, and sweater designs have all been drawn and reproduced to the same scale. You can make tracings that combine elements from different garments, and then you can knit what you have envisioned. Keep notes—even rudimentary ones—so that you will remember what you did in the past. Keep your gauge swatches, marked with needle sizes and comments.

Make discoveries and make sweaters.

What is needed for dramatic change is an accumulation of acts—adding, adding to, adding more, continuing.

Clarissa Pinkola Estés
in *The Bloomsbury Review*

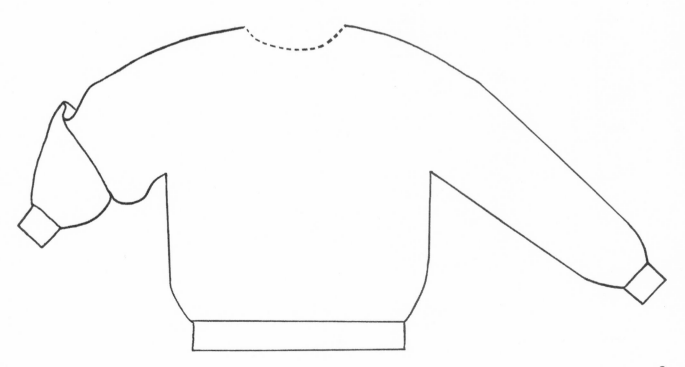

List of quick summaries and special topics

Chance favors the
prepared mind.

*Louis Pasteur
(1822–95)*

Quick summary of shapes

See Chapter 7 for detailed information on each of these shapes. The sweaters in Chapters 9 through 13 build on, but are not limited to, these ideas. For example, the Folk Art Vests (pages 196–98) combine the vest concept of Plan 14 with square armholes, like those of Plan 7.

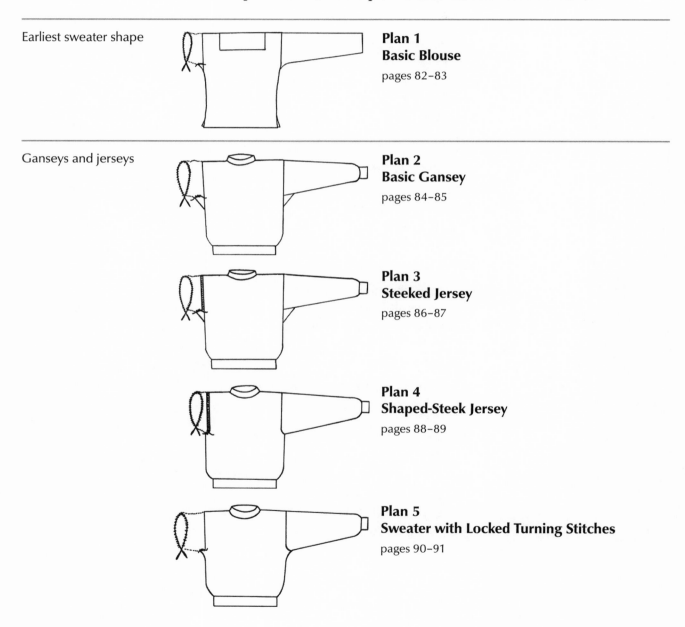

Earliest sweater shape

Plan 1
Basic Blouse

pages 82–83

Ganseys and jerseys

Plan 2
Basic Gansey

pages 84–85

Plan 3
Steeked Jersey

pages 86–87

Plan 4
Shaped-Steek Jersey

pages 88–89

Plan 5
Sweater with Locked Turning Stitches

pages 90–91

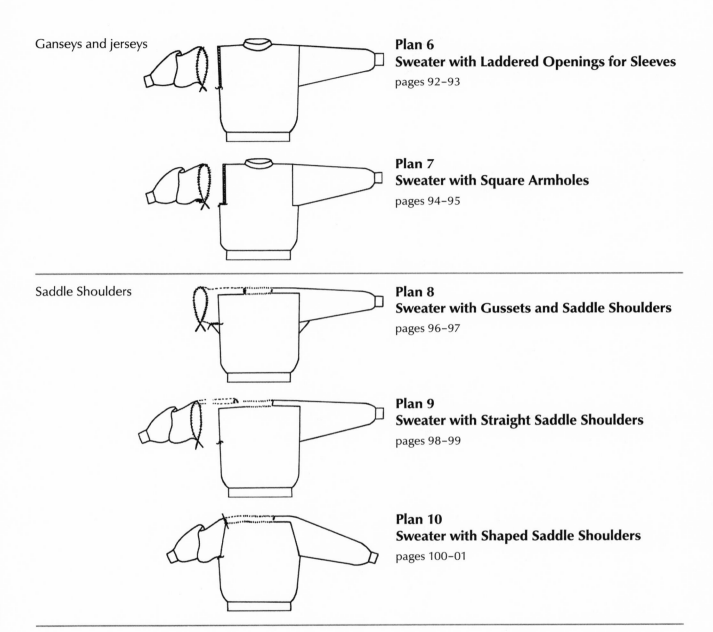

Ganseys and jerseys

Plan 6
Sweater with Laddered Openings for Sleeves

Plan 7
Sweater with Square Armholes

Saddle Shoulders

Plan 8
Sweater with Gussets and Saddle Shoulders

Plan 9
Sweater with Straight Saddle Shoulders

Plan 10
Sweater with Shaped Saddle Shoulders

Raglans

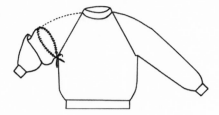

Plan 11
Sweater with Raglan Sleeves

page 102

Round yokes

Plan 12
Sweater with Full Yoke

pages 103–07

Plan 13
Sweater with Shoulder Yoke

pages 108–09

Shaped sweaters

Plan 14
Shaped Vest

pages 110–11

Plan 15
Shaped Sweater

pages 112–15

Cardigan variations

pages 116–21

Neckline variations

pages 122–30

Acknowledgments

First and foremost, I wish to acknowledge the legions of knitters who believe that *Knitting in the Old Way* is a "classic" and must remain available for present and future generations of knitters. Your encouragement means more to me than words can express. I hope that you find this revision worthy of your faith.

Closer to home, a heartfelt "Thank you, Jack," for realizing that I need uninterrupted time and space to write. At its best, writing is a chore for me—leaving me be so I can tackle the job is the best possible gift.

Next, a special "Bless you, dear friend," for Noel Thurner, who provided both spiritual and practical support on many occasions.

And most importantly, "Thank you, Deb and Rebekah," for everything this mother-daughter team has done to make this revision possible. Rebekah, you are an *imagician*—your magic superbly transformed my pen-and-ink illustrations into computer images. Deb, you have more than earned the inclusion of your name in shared authorship of this version. Every step of the way has been "with Deborah Robson" at my side.

And finally: thank you to those who willingly assumed the task of cheering us through the final stages of production and finding gremlin-induced problems in the text and illustrations: Joanne Clark (who has joyfully shared her bag of tricks with me through the years), Robin Grace, Kris Paige, Deborah Pulliam, and Noel Thurner.

—Priscilla A. Gibson-Roberts

Ours is not the task of fixing the entire world all at once, but of stretching out to mend the part of the world that is within our reach.

Clarissa Pinkola Estés
in *The Bloomsbury Review*

Many more people helped than I can name here. The following folks gave me huge boosts when I really needed them: Sharon Altergott, Miriam Bass, Judy Fort Brenneman, Daryl Burkhard, Dorine Burkhard, Robin Grace, Lynn Humphries, Kris Paige, Deborah Pulliam, Allene and Bill Robson, Jean Scorgie, Suzanne Taylor, Jonathan Taylor, Noel Thurner, Lorrie Wolfe, and Steve Wolfe. Group support came from the Colorado Authors' League, Sage Writers' Cache, and WriterL— special thanks there to Lynn Franklin, Jon Franklin, and Lisa Kartus. Tempest's Ariel Miranda, CD, CGC, reminded me several times a day to check what was going on in the outside world.

Rebekah Robson-May: without you, we wouldn't have made it.

—Deborah Robson

Preface 1

When *Knitting in the Old Way* was first published nearly twenty years ago, I had no idea so many knitters shared my passion for ethnic design and technique. And as I look back over that time span I am amazed by the increase in the number of knitters and by their interest in the technicalities of the craft. For these reasons, this edition of *Knitting in the Old Way* incorporates major revisions. The material related to knitting remains intact, and there is even more of it—including a unit on intarsia techniques that originated in South America, as well as information about an Old World crochet technique that was utilized in Finnish sweaters and yet had roots in Central Asia. This edition contains many more sweaters and charts than its predecessor, and even the basic material has been completely revised.

Because information on making good handspun yarn has grown far beyond anything I can present within the confines of a book that emphasizes knitting, I decided to delete the basic spinning information that appeared in the previous edition. For those interested in spinning, I suggest you seek out one of the many excellent books now available, including my own *High Whorling: A Spinner's Guide to an Old-World Skill.*

In writing this book, I've assumed that you understand the basic knitting stitches. Regardless of your skill level, I highly recommend that you read the book through, because the techniques described often build on each other. This is especially important in this revised edition, in part because I have added information about the importance of understanding the vagaries of the knit loop—specifically, how the current loop can be entered, how the new loop can be wrapped, and the resultant stitch mount. You may be surprised to find ways to improve simple stockinette knitting, especially important for sweaters made with a combination of circular and flat sections! You will also discover compelling reasons to develop increased dexterity in holding and managing the yarn and your needles. Working in only the standard Western manner, while holding the yarn in either the English/American (right hand) or Continental/German (left hand) way, is no longer sufficient for the modern repertoire of design techniques, including many methods detailed in this revision.

The idea was to eliminate everything unnecessary, to make the whole as direct and simple as possible but always with the beautiful in mind as the first goal.

Henry Mather Greene
1870–1954

16

Every effort has been made to accurately portray the history of the folk sweaters that I so dearly love. Because there are many conflicting theories about the origins of these garments, I've attempted to provide information based on sound research and common sense, some of which may in time be revised again in light of new information and understanding. Likewise, I have not attempted to reproduce any specific old sweater. Instead I've chosen to present composites that capture the essence of each style.

My admiration of the knitting developed in different regions of the world is boundless. As I have studied I have become, heart and soul, a part of each generation and every ethnic group—a source of endless personal pleasure.

But I have come to realize that this book is not about the past. It is about the present and about the future, a future built on a solid foundation of skills proven and improved by generation upon generation of knitters around the world. May your heart sing along with mine as you master the "real stuff" of knitting, working in the old ways!

—Priscilla A. Gibson-Roberts

"Life is a stocking," grandma says,
"And yours has just begun.
But I am knitting the toe of mine,
And my work is almost done."

Nineteenth-century rhyme

. . . beauty is beauty
twice over
and good things are doubly
good
when you're talking about a pair of wool
socks
in the dead of winter.

Pablo Neruda
from "Ode to a pair of socks,"
translated by Ken Krabbenhoft

Preface 2

By chance and good fortune, I knitted my first-ever sweater "in the old way." What a gift! I was a freshman in college. Terry Rittenhouse and I walked along the quiet streets of Northfield, Minnesota, to a shop located in the basement of a home. The room, probably ten feet by fifteen feet, held an abundance of paper and fiber, of color and potential: still my favorite things.

Among the shop's collection of printed designs, I discovered a five-color ski sweater with bands of patterning all over the body and sleeves. The yarns I chose did not match the photograph: I selected a light sage green for the dominant color, then added a dark sage green, a chocolate brown, and a dusty gold, plus off-white for single-stitch accents. Thanks to Terry and the shop's owner, I never doubted that the sweater I imagined would come into being through the work of my hands, even though the instructions were written in a language I don't know. I could read the pattern charts. That was all that mattered.

My mentors must have helped me work and measure a gauge swatch. They must have told me how many stitches to cast on for the body, how to work the ribbing on smaller needles, how to start and then to shape the sleeves. I learned from the beginning to read the growing fabric, not a set of instructions. Thirty-five years and much fiber later, my fingers remember the feel of those smooth, durable wool yarns.

Terry and the yarn-shop owner made sure I loved the vision in my head, that I had good materials, and that I cast on the correct number of stitches. Then they launched me into discovery. I thought that was how everyone began to knit. After many more years and sweaters (also scarves, vests, hats, shawls, and bags—even a fiber-related career), I still knit by "bushwhacking." It's enormously enjoyable.

By the time the 1985 edition of Priscilla Gibson-Roberts' *Knitting in the Old Way* was published, I could knit anything I wanted and had become an editor of textile publications. Knowing and working with Priscilla has allowed me to refine my skills and increase my already substantial pleasure in exploring the world of yarn and needles.

I'm delighted to be so closely involved with bringing Priscilla's approach to the craft to more knitters. It's the only way to go!

—Deborah Robson

Freedom is not worth having if it does not include the freedom to make mistakes.

Mohandas K. Gandhi (1869–1948)

Introduction

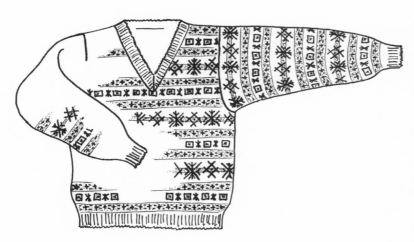

E vents of the twentieth century—the two World Wars and similar conflicts between nations, the revival of the Olympic Games, many migrations of peoples, populations with sufficient wealth for world travel, national pride, globalization, and so on—have all played a part in bringing the ethnic or folk knitting of many cultures to the world at large. The study of sweaters from other times and other places has accelerated in recent years, with knitwear designers looking around the globe for inspiration. More and more handknitters have followed the designers' lead, seeking to express themselves instead of being limited by the fashions of the moment.

Masterfully handcrafted sweaters from many regions show us, however, that knitting skills have been badly neglected for generations in the parts of the world where industrialization occurred early, most especially in the United States. Printed patterns and incomprehensible written instructions (i.e., "knitter-ese") replaced intuitive design skills and a thorough understanding of technique. A once simple and delightful craft has become shrouded in elaborate line-by-line instructions—enough to daunt the most skillful knitter while thoroughly intimidating the novice.

But today's knitters can once again be in control of the craft without struggling to translate "knitter-ese" into knitting knowledge. Armed with a general overview of sweater construction and some basic sweater formulas, they can become proficient at knitting in the old way.

It's only a short step back to the era of beautiful folk sweaters, because sweaters as we know them today date from no earlier than

Fair Isle sweater shaped with steeks (page 167).

the seventeenth century and are largely the product of the nineteenth century, with some acknowledged traditional styles as young as the early twentieth century. True, many garments were made from knitted fabric before sweaters came on the scene: the fabric was knitted in the round, felted, cut, and tailored to make jackets and trousers. But sweaters themselves most likely evolved from undergarments, and as they came out from "under" they quickly became glorious expressions of their respective cultures. Often the designs utilized in folk sweaters had been perfected much earlier, through the craft of sock knitting.

Most knitters today are familiar with sweaters whose roots lie in traditional European folk knitting. There are, for example, the Guernsey (or gansey), with its knit-and-purl designs and simple cables covering the chest and upper arms; the Fair Isle, banded with designs in ever-changing color combinations; the Aran, with its bold embossed texture of intricate cables, bobbles, and interlaced stitches; the classic Nordic garment, with its color-stranded stars and flecks; and the Icelandic yoked sweater, in an undyed spectrum of colors of luxurious native wool.

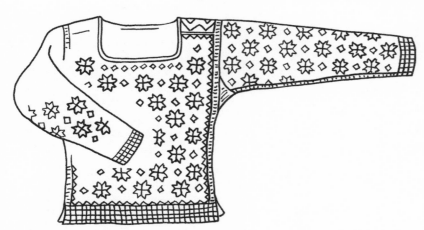

But what of the history of, and the many variations within, these general styles? And what of the less familiar styles? These include the Bavarian, with its intricate crisscrossing of traveling twisted stitches on a purl ground; the Tyrolean, sprinkled with gay, embroidered alpine flowers; the elaborate Hebridean, with panels of varied designs; the Swedish Bohus, with subtle color shadings and textures on delicately designed yokes; the Danish brocade blouse, patterned after damask weaving; the red-and-black fishermen's sweaters of Sweden; and the robust Cowichan sweaters of Canada's Northwest coast. Part of the excitement of studying folk knitting is the realization that unique styles evolved in many small pockets of the world.

Many knitters begin with an interest in recreating a folk sweater in modern yarns. Then they want to go beyond this, and to work with traditional-style yarns spun from the appropriate wools. Yet there is little information available on the yarns used in traditional sweaters, much

Danish brocade blouse, long version (page 238).

20

less on how to select the most appropriate alternatives from today's many styles. Meanwhile, a growing number of knitters want to interpret the traditional patterning in natural fibers other than wool, because they want to have sweaters for all seasons. To succeed in this, they need to understand how the properties of those fibers differ from the properties of wool, and how their designs need to accommodate those differences.

This book will help today's handknitters select yarns and draw upon folk designs and construction techniques to create garments of their own design. Bear in mind that these techniques, which have served so well for so long in traditional knitting around the world, were passed from one generation to the next by word of mouth, supplemented perhaps by simple graphs and samplers. As a result, many styles and variations evolved and their actual origins were lost in time. Furthermore, traditions change; new ways develop and become incorporated into the old, making handknitting the dynamic craft so many of us enjoy. Without clinging to the past just for the sake of tradition, we must preserve what is good, adapting it to meet today's needs.

Why no mention of any traditional folk sweaters developed in the United States? Because there are none. This book includes two vests and a sweater decorated with American folk motifs. They are hybrids. Our ancestors were busy birthing a nation when sweaters, as such, first appeared. That nation was destined to become one of mixed nationalities. Traditional folkwear develops as part of group identity. Our claim to fame in the world of folkwear is blue jeans! Ah, but our melting-pot nature allows us to cross cultural lines and draw on all the old ways, wantonly using modern adaptations of old techniques.

My goal is to help knitters create freely from the many styles and designs of knitted folk sweaters, returning to the old way of simply understanding what to do rather than duplicating a printed pattern (which often presents design *sans* technique). This path leads to greater self-expression through unique, one-of-a-kind creations of enduring quality.

Cowichan cardigan
with pictorial motifs
(page 193).

21

Chapter

1

Origins

Knitting, a venerable craft, is young compared to spinning and weaving. In fact, most textile historians now believe that knitting is among the youngest of all the basic textile techniques. One reason we have trouble deciding when knitting began is the difficulty in determining which methods were used to construct ancient fabrics. Knotless netting, sprang, and certain types of embroidery can look enough like knitting to confuse even the experts.

Mary Thomas, in her classic work, *Mary Thomas's Knitting Book,* discusses in detail a fragment dating to about 200 A.D. She describes its construction as a crossed-stitch knitting technique. Yet subsequent research has indicated the piece was actually made with a single-needle technique practiced in many parts of the world in various forms. Magnificent textiles of this type were made by highly skilled workers in places as far apart as Peru and northern Europe. Even today, a similar technique called *nålbinding* is practiced in some Scandinavian countries.

Why did a knowledgeable knitter, steeped in history, think that this fragment had been knitted? Because it can be recreated by crossed-stitch knitting.

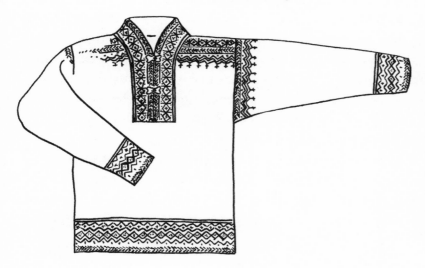

The interlooping technique, which today may be referred to as the Eastern form of *nålbinding,* looks like crossed-stitch knitting but is created with a single needle that has an eye threaded with the working strand. As the work proceeds and more yarn is needed, short strands of loosely twisted yarn are spliced together in sequence. This spliced yarn is one key to identifying pieces worked in this technique that is

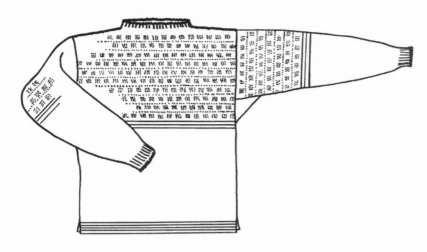

↑

Early gansey with simple knit/purl patterns (page 243).

←

Sami-inspired tunic sweater, made with designs and techniques derived from mittens (page 181).

much older than knitting—however, the splices of highly skilled workers are nearly invisible.

The definitive key to telling which technique was used comes from determining the direction in which the work proceeded from the cast-on. This form of interlooping is worked *down* from the cast-on, so when the loops are free to move, they ladder up. In knitting, which is worked *up* from the cast-on, loops that are free to move will ladder down.

Knitting as it is understood today, and as I will use the term in this book, is a technique in which a nearly continuous strand of yarn is worked into rows of interlocking loops on a set of two or more needles that are pointed at one or both ends. The earliest example of this kind of knitting (patterned cotton socks found in Egypt) dates back to only 1100 A.D.

Many people believe that knitting originated among Arabian nomads, who in turn carried the craft into Egypt. Was it a craft of the Mamluks, descendants of the Mongols? Did it originate in Central Asia? We may never answer these questions. That the craft has its roots in Islamic art is doubtless, and that it spread across North Africa and into Spain along with Islam is questioned by few. From Spain, knitting most likely moved into the rest of Europe under the auspices of the Roman Catholic Church, because the nuns created exquisite liturgical pieces. Knowledge of the craft probably diffused into the populace via the convents. Meanwhile, Spanish and Portuguese sailors carried the skills of knitting to South America, where the natives absorbed the craft into their cultures, where it eventually replaced the interlooping technique to which I referred earlier, evidence of which appears in pieces that predate the earliest possible European introduction.

Obviously, there is room for more research into the history of our craft. However, because knitting can so easily be recycled and has frequently been used to produce items that were ultimately disposable, we are unlikely to find answers to all our questions.

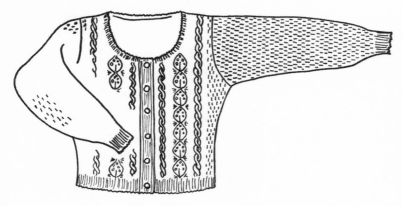

Regardless of where or when it started, knitting swept across the European continent relatively quickly. During medieval times knitted garments became highly prized. Professional guilds soon controlled the market, and the craft belonged in the domain of men. Knitted garments became the fashion of the wealthy class—silk gloves and stockings were a prerogative of the rich. Demand became so great that knitting turned into a cottage industry, with the peasantry subsidizing their meager livelihoods by knitting woolen caps and socks for the gentry. Thus the craft passed into the hands of women, who also began to knit garments for their own families, possibly as early as the fifteenth century.

By the early eighteenth century, knitting was practiced throughout the civilized world by entire populations, young and old, male and female, in widely diverse cultures. But, at the very peak of its popularity, the decline of handknitting as a means of livelihood was foretold by the start of the Industrial Revolution. By 1589, a knitting frame was invented by William Lee of Cambridge, England. As is often the case, the new and old technologies lived side by side in the economy through many generations: some people knitted by hand and others operated the frames. Eventually, however, handknitting as a significant cottage industry all but vanished. Knitting continued in the home, and during Victorian times it became elevated to a feminine parlor art. This ushered in the era of written instructions for elegant young ladies who didn't have the benefit of passed-down samplers and charts, the technical resources that had served the common folk so well for so long. Fashion garments, rather than the craft itself, became the focal point. By the 1930s, flat knitting replaced the natural and efficient circular construction techniques used for generations.

At the same time, however, people in some rural areas kept to the old ways. For them, handknits were a part of everyday wear and knitting remained a minor cottage industry. In these more isolated areas with cultures less affected by external influences, knitters perfected distinctive designs and techniques. Even when new ideas were introduced, the old, proven ways were not discarded.

↑

Tyrolean jacket, embellished with embroidery (page 275).

→

Contemporary sweater constructed with Eastern European intarsia technique (invisible join 2, page 214).

During this period, it was discovered that knitted fabrics made excellent woolen shirts. The oldest fragment known to have been part of such a garment is a sleeve found in Denmark, dating from the seventeenth century. Although records indicate that vests and shirt-like garments were knitted as early as the fourteenth century, probably for use as undergarments, this fragment is the first indication of a knitted woolen garment designed for use as outerwear. Yet because knitted garments, particularly those of the peasantry, were used, worn out, and discarded or recycled, little is known of these early predecessors of traditional folk sweaters.

When did the sweater as we know it today first appear? And where? Possibly in the late seventeenth century, but certainly by the beginning of the nineteenth century, the sweater, often called a *jersey* or *jumper* and sometimes referred to as a *knitted frock* in historic records, seems to have spontaneously appeared in many separate cultures and locations in the northern climes: the British Isles, Scandinavia, eastern Europe—but not North America. The oldest example is possibly the *natrøje,* a damask brocade blouse of Denmark. *Natrøje* translates as *night shirt:* apparently this shirt was worn by itself for sleeping, and also during the day with a vest-like bodice layered on top. This undergarment of little distinction seems to have been transformed into a glorious expression of creativity, and a new era in knitted folkwear was born. I find it interesting that sweaters evolved from a woman's garment, yet early sweaters were worn almost exclusively by men.

Despite all the myths and tales surrounding folk sweaters, the craft skills involved in making them have probably developed only over the last two or three centuries! And yet the most charming aspects of knitting have been expressed in these garments: ingenuity, spontaneity and creativity, functionality, and regional style.

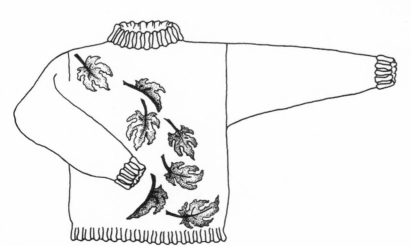

Traditional Yarns

Fiber content:
an overview, and a discussion of wool

Knitting yarns can be spun from wool, silk, flax, ramie, cotton, mohair, down and fur fibers, a legion of synthetic fibers, or combinations of these elements, but yarns for traditional folk sweaters were almost always wool. Sometimes other fibers, such as angora rabbit or silk, were blended in, but wool was the major component of the yarn. Silk was much too expensive for common folk (though in early times it was used in knitted garments for the nobility). Cotton thrives in warm climates with long growing seasons, so it was relatively unavailable, or expensive to acquire, in many regions where knitters worked. Despite these problems, cotton was coveted for its "whiteness" and was used in limited quantities as an accent in accessory items. Linen is inelastic, that is, inflexible and reluctant to spring back into its original shape when stretched. It has thus never lent itself well to most knitting, with the notable exception of stockings; only recently has it begun to play a minor role in the knitting of sweaters. Last, and most obviously, synthetic fibers were developed in the mid-twentieth century. Historically, the synthetics are inappropriate and should have no role in contemporary interpretations because of their adverse properties.

The intrinsic properties of wool should class it as a miracle fiber, possibly the most functional of all fibers available to humanity. Wool can absorb up to 30% of its weight in moisture without feeling wet. When wet, the fiber generates a tiny amount of heat that offsets any clamminess that might result from excess dampness. These properties made wool invaluable for garments used by fishermen and farm workers, who were often out in cold, wet weather. Wool is highly elastic, a characteristic that can be enhanced in the spinning, allowing a garment to flex with movement and yet return to its original shape time and time again. It is soil-resistant and, if properly finished, washable. Almost all wool

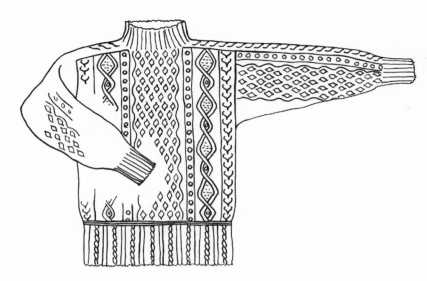

knitting yarns available today are hand-washable, and many can even be machine-washed (although there is a trade-off in quality I am not willing to make—the resulting yarn feels much like a synthetic), making the handknitted garment easy-care with only minimal precautions. Wool is an excellent insulator, used by desert nomads to keep the heat out and by arctic dwellers to keep the heat in. It is a renewable resource, available throughout the world, and not overly expensive, especially when its durability is factored in. If the yarn and fabric are properly constructed, a well-made wool garment will retain its good looks for many years.

Wool does have some negative properties, although with proper handling these can be minimized or even turned to advantages. Take felting, for example. In the presence of any three of four conditions—heat, moisture, pressure, and agitation—wool fibers will mat together, interlocking to form a solid mass. This is how felt fabric is made, and early woolen knitwear was often felted deliberately to make it more wind- and water-resistant. Felting can be disastrous if the process is triggered accidentally (as anyone who has inadvertently put a wool sweater through the washer and dryer on the hot settings will attest), but care in handling virtually eliminates the danger.

When washing, don't agitate the wool. Instead, allow it to soak clean.

Don't place wool directly into hot water. The heat isn't the problem. What must be avoided is shocking the wool with either extremely hot or cold temperatures. Wool can actually be boiled without matting or shrinking *if* the process begins in warm water and the temperature is raised to the boiling point very gradually, and then gradually allowed to cool.

Don't wring out the moisture; gently squeeze it out. After you've squeezed the excess moisture out, the fibers, yarn, fabric, or garment can be placed in a laundry bag and spun in a washing machine to extract more moisture and speed the drying process. The centrifugal force alone *will not* result in felting.

Aran fishing shirt, heavily cabled (page 261). Textured designs often benefit from being worked in smoothly spun, plied yarns.

Pilling is another problem that arises with some wool yarns, but again there are ways to deal with this. Pilling is simply the balling-up of short, loose fibers on the surface of the fabric. The more loose fibers that are available, the more likely it is that pills will develop. In most cases, the pills break off as they form; simply picking off any excess will usually control the problem. Pilling is seldom extreme or unsightly—except in the presence of a synthetic within the yarn. Your choice of yarn can minimize the problem, for pilling relates directly to the number of short, loose surface fibers and noils (very short fibers clumped together) that are free to form the pill. A yarn with a smooth surface, free from excess fuzz, will resist pilling. Also, the more firmly spun the yarn and the more uniform the fiber length, the fewer pills will develop. You can check a yarn for its pilling potential by drawing it between your fingers repeatedly to see if it tends to fuzz up. Pull out several individual fibers from the end of the yarn to check their length—the longer the fibers, the fewer the pills.

One of the most common complaints about wool garments is scratchiness. Many people claim an allergy to wool. Yes, wool fibers can be irritating to the skin *if* a harsh and scratchy wool fleece is used in the yarn. But a number of sheep breeds—Merino is the best-known but not the only type—produce a soft, fine, non-irritating fiber. Actually, much of the skin irritation attributed to wool during the last half-century may have been caused not by the wool itself but by changes in the fiber during processing, because of dyes, added chemicals, and harsh physical treatment. Careful selection of yarn can eliminate this problem. For example, many find that today's machine-washable wools eliminate scratchiness. To be sure, always test the yarn against a tender spot— neck, cheek, or forehead—and not just with your fingertips. Of course, if you ask me, handspinning is the best option! A yarn made from a carefully selected fleece, lovingly processed, and washed with a gentle detergent (not soap), will result in a non-irritating yarn—only those with a rare *true* allergy will find wool of this type to be a problem.

Yarn construction, color, and selection

Two basic spinning systems are used in commercial yarn construction: woolen and worsted. Woolen yarn is made from shorter wool fibers (ranging in length from about 1 inch to 4 inches) that have been spun into a light, fluffy, somewhat fuzzy yarn of randomly arranged fibers.

Worsted yarn, on the other hand, is made of longer fibers (typically at least 4 inches long), all of the same length, prepared so that they lie parallel to each other, and spun into a strong, smooth, dense yarn.

The mass production of commercial knitting yarns begins with fibers that are processed in large quantities to remove the oils and extraneous vegetable matter. Throughout manufacturing, the fibers are subjected to acid baths, mechanical picking, and other chemical and physical processes, any or all of which may damage the fiber, making it harsher-feeling and reducing its durability.

For woolen yarns, the fibers are then carded by being passed through a system of rollers with wire teeth that produces a thin web. The web is then divided into long narrow strips called *slivers* (pronounced to rhyme with *divers*), which are drafted, doubled and redoubled, condensed to form a roving, then spun into the final yarn.

Worsted yarns are treated in the same way through the sliver stage. At this point, the sliver is drawn through a combing system that straightens and aligns the long fibers while removing the shorter ones. The remaining long fibers are then drawn out into a continuous, long, smooth form called *top*.

In the spinning process itself, the woolen roving or the worsted top is drawn through rollers that stretch the fiber mass and reduce it to a specified diameter. Then it is wound onto revolving bobbins that insert twist, thus creating *singles* yarn. Singles may be used without further spinning, but singles are most often combined in varying numbers to create *plied* yarns. (Some people erroneously call a single-strand yarn a "one-ply." You can have *two-ply* or *three-ply* or *twelve-ply* yarn, but "one-ply" is a misnomer.)

The commercial spinning process is a mechanized, standardized extension of hand methods that have been done for centuries. But in handspinning, the processing techniques are adapted to suit the fiber. In mechanized spinning, the fibers—whether long or short, coarse or fine—are subjected to the requirements of the machine. Yet we have recently begun to see a move away from total homogenization, even in millspun yarns. Some fibers are sorted by breed as well as grade, then spun to enhance their natural character; the lovely Icelandic and Shetland yarns are good examples. With the recent resurgence of interest in textile crafts and especially in handknitting, many of today's commercial yarns

Contemporary vest with American folk art motifs, adapted for color-stranding (page 197).

Bavarian cardigan, front and back views (pages 272–73). Patterns of this type require a well-spun yarn that will produce clear stitch definition.

are less rigorously processed than in the past, thus retaining their naturally soft, non-irritating *hand* or feel.

Any yarn may be lightly or more firmly spun. Few handknitting yarns are tightly spun today, while older traditional knitting yarns, including those spun commercially, were almost always firmly twisted. The more lightly spun yarns are softer and more lofty than, but not as durable as, more firmly spun yarns—today, we tend to emphasize comfort more than durability, although these qualities can, of course, coexist beautifully under the right conditions.

You must consider sweater design in order to choose an appropriately spun yarn. For example, firmly spun yarn produces a clear definition of stitches that's appropriate for most designs, whether the patterning comes from texture or from color. A softly spun yarn fluffs up and closes the interstices between stitches, resulting in a uniform, matte-finish surface; this can be especially nice in stockinette. Another factor to consider is that a softly spun, slightly fuzzy yarn incorporates a lot of air and will be much warmer than a smooth, compact yarn. However, the smooth, compact yarn will have less tendency to pill.

Most commercial knitting yarns are plied—that is, they are made of two or more fine strands twisted together. There is usually little twist in the individual strands or in the plying, thus the yarn is both elastic and lofty. Although plying can increase a yarn's strength, selecting between a yarn with two plies and one with three or more plies is largely a matter of design preference. Although there are exceptions, the structure of a two-ply yarn will usually be more visible on the knitted surface, making the fabric more robust in nature than a similar textile made of a multi-ply yarn. In the two-ply version, the individual plies must be larger and therefore remain more visible. The multi-ply yarn will be more smoothly rounded, with the individual plies less obvious, and the resulting knitted surface will be smoother to both hand and eye, and the fabric in the finished sweater will have an enhanced capacity to drape elegantly. Those who have "a thing" about pilling should choose the multi-ply yarn.

If the yarn is a singles, choose one with a smooth surface, relatively low twist, and moderately long fibers with good crimp (to provide loft). Short fibers have more crimp than long fibers, but they reduce the yarn's strength while increasing its tendency to mat and pill. The truly long fibers will have minimal crimp, making for a very dense and heavy yarn. Be wary of too much twist in singles, because singles that have not been properly steam-finished can produce a decided bias slant in the finished garment. This is seldom a problem with commercially spun singles and it need not be a concern with handspun singles if they are properly spun and finished. I am personally very fond of singles for knitting—not because they require less time to spin but because I like the hand and visual appeal of the yarn and the resulting fabric. However, you should be aware that singles are more prone to pilling than plied yarns. Many commercial yarns are now wet-spun, creating a slightly felted surface that resists pilling and permits more durable singles to be spun from fine wools.

Highly textured yarns, often called *novelty* or *designer* yarns, are a relatively recent development. Yarns with unique visual and tactile qualities can be produced by plying together dissimilar strands; by spinning or plying under variable tension; or by creating thick-and-thin, slubby, or snarled effects. Novelty yarns have opened new avenues for contemporary garment design, but have no place in the construction of traditional folk sweaters because their variability doesn't enhance complex color or texture patterns.

You must also consider the impact of color on sweater design. Solid, evenly dyed colors show off patterned knitting best, although the subtle color shifts of a heathered yarn can enhance visual appeal. Yarns that are highly variegated in color can be distracting in both color-stranded and textured designs; these modern yarns have little use in traditional garments. The greater the contrast between colors, the more commanding the patterning. Likewise, a soft woolen yarn will mute the sense of contrast between colors while a smooth worsted yarn increases the sense of contrast.

As you can see, any yarn selection will involve compromise. You'll simply have to think about each project individually and satisfy its most important needs while compromising on the less important qualities.

More about fiber content

Natural fibers other than wool

The "other" natural fibers include silk, cotton, flax, hemp, and rayon (which is a regenerated fiber, not a synthetic). They have become increasingly popular for handknitters working with traditional patterns because they are appropriate for the construction of sweaters that can be worn in warm weather or climates.

Because these fibers have little to no crimp, they have little to no elasticity. You *cannot* expect yarns spun from any of these fibers to return to their original shape after being stretched—they simply will not do this. You must provide for this characteristic in the design of the garment. The neckline and cuffs cannot be of the same dimensions as those in a wool sweater; they must be larger, or must have placket openings and some means of closure. When worked in inelastic yarns, ribbings will appear "flat" while garter stitch or seed stitch will retain a degree of depth. This means that edge treatments worked in garter stitch or seed stitch will be more pleasing visually than ribbing. As an alternative, you can carry textured patterning into the edgings to eliminate the need for distinctive cuffs, hems, and so on.

Wearers of handknitted silk discover that their garments tend to "grow" as the day progresses, in reaction to body temperature and moisture. This effect can be mitigated if you avoid sweater shapes that are tailored to fit the contours of the body. This is especially important for the shoulders unless they are stabilized by other means! If you simply must fit the shoulder contours, I have found that it helps either to bind off the stitches together or to sew the shoulder seams with a cotton yarn that is finer than the silk yarn. Myself, I prefer to use silk in a sweater that accommodates the nature of the fiber—one with dropped shoulders or raglan sleeves.

Cotton, flax, and hemp—all vegetable fibers—can be quite heavy in a sweater. The yarns are dense in comparison to wool, and finishing techniques in particular must take this into account. Turned facings tend to be overly bulky; for this reason, I avoid designs that require a hem or cutting.

When washed, sweaters made from cotton yarns tend to grow in width as the yarn tries to straighten out horizontally in the knit stitches. I call this the "up and out" characteristic, and my first defense against it involves knitting at a firm gauge that does not give the yarn room to move around. After washing, I tumble the sweater in the dryer with low heat for a few minutes to increase loft, then hang it on a padded hanger to finish drying. This helps to pull the stitches back into the vertical conformation.

Linen and hemp have a different problem: they tend to grow in length if hung to dry. They must lie flat while drying, even though they take much longer to dry this way. Beware of lace patterns in all but the finest yarns, because the garment may stretch in length even when dry.

This may sound like a lot of bother; ah, but the extra effort is worthwhile! Cotton is so comfy in summer, while linen and hemp have incomparable capacities to drape.

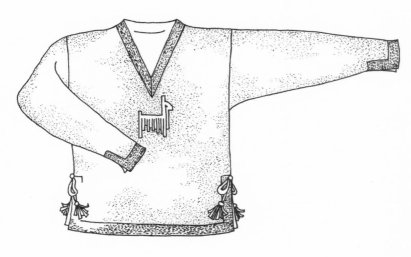

Contemporary design worked in fine llama or alpaca yarn (two-step intarsia, page 209).

Rayon is a regenerated cellulose fiber. It can be made of cotton linters, wood fibers, and other cellulosic bits. These are chemically treated to form a solution that is forced through spinnerets to create filaments, which are then allowed to harden. Pure rayon yarns are always dense, so the knit stitches "hang" under the weight of the yarn. If rayon plies are used as supplemental elements in a mixed yarn, their distinctive sheen adds visual interest without significantly increasing the difficulty of handling the yarn.

Luxury fibers

Today, it is not unusual to find knitting yarns made entirely or partially of alpaca, llama, cashmere, angora, camel, or qiviut—all fibers once limited to use by the wealthy but now available in greater supply. Knitters today, many of whom are more affluent than knitters in the past, have ready access to these fibers, especially in blends with wool. The appeal of these fibers has also increased because of a change in attitude among avid knitters: there is an ever greater sense of the hand-knitted garment as a luxury item in itself, and the use of luxury fibers

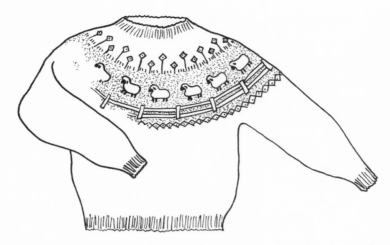

has become a means of expressing pride in the craft.

Luxury fibers have more in common than simply cost. They share a special silkiness of hand that makes us want to caress the yarn. This property we so love comes at a price we pay in design: any attempt to secure the stitches for cutting is doomed to failure, and any design that requires this type of construction is a recipe for disaster! Some people find it much slower to work flat, but in this case it is essential. All of the openings in the garment must be formed on the needles: armholes, front bands, everything.

Synthetics

When used alone for the construction of knitting yarns, synthetic fibers can produce inexpensive yarns that are easily cared for with machine washing and drying. Acrylic, a synthetic that can be made to look like wool, often shows up in knitting yarns. However, synthetic yarns offer little value to the serious handknitter. They lack the ability to absorb moisture, which makes them unpleasant to wear, and they have a marked propensity to pill and to retain said pills.

Blends and mixtures

In *blended yarns,* the fibers are combined before they are spun into singles. The blending of the "other natural fibers" with a small percentage of wool (as little as 20%) can be advantageous. The yarn will retain the characteristics of the dominant fiber and will acquire loft and elasticity from the wool.

Although blends that combine cotton and wool are not new, they have only recently become popular in knitting yarns. I am particularly fond of this blend because all too often pure cotton yarn looks and feels like string. The addition of wool does not reduce the appeal of the mostly cotton yarn for summertime wear—in fact, the wool enhances the absorbency of cotton, one of an ideal hot-weather yarn's primary functions!

Again, combining flax and wool is nothing new in the spinning world: the linsey-woolsey of historic times was a woven fabric with a linen warp and a wool weft. For knitting yarns, the fibers are blended before they

Contemporary sheep-motif sweater, worked in a South American intarsia technique (yarn-over join, page 210). A design like this makes good use of small amounts of luxury or blended yarns.

are spun—an advantageous process through which the small amount of wool rounds out the yarn without altering the characteristics of the flax, especially its unique "linen" drape.

When wool and silk are blended in a yarn, the wool is usually the dominant fiber. The silk adds luster and sparkle plus a high degree of the "silkiness" that we all love. In addition, silk/wool blends are much less expensive than pure silk yarns.

Synthetic fibers are blended with natural fibers to enhance the performance of the final yarn, primarily its durability. A small percentage of nylon or polyester added to a "traditional" knitting yarn will improve durability without appreciably increasing the incidence or retention of pills. I personally cannot abide the use of any acrylic, in part because of the abuse of this fiber in all-acrylic knitting yarns.

In *mixture yarns,* singles are spun from individual fibers and then a yarn is made with strands of different types plied together. The characteristics of the finished yarn depend on the number and kinds of singles it contains.

Yarn into fabric

Gauge

After selecting a yarn appropriate for your sweater design, you need to determine your gauge and how much yarn you'll need. The gauge is the number of stitches in a given measure of fabric, commonly expressed as *stitches per inch.* A 4-inch (10-cm) measure will give you a more accurate gauge than a 1-inch (2.5-cm) section of fabric, especially if you're working with very bulky yarns or with handspun yarns that may vary in diameter.

The initial consideration in determining gauge is fairly obvious: the larger the yarn diameter, the larger the needle, and the fewer the stitches per inch. But the degree of twist and loft of the yarn must also be taken into account. A softly spun yarn is usually knitted more loosely to allow the yarn to fill the interstices of the stitches. A more firmly spun yarn is knitted in a finer gauge, because the yarn contains less loft to fill in the spaces. Bulky to very bulky yarns are knitted somewhat loosely; if worked tightly, they compress into stiff, heavy fabrics.

Experience and personal preference are the best guides for making decisions about yarn and needle size. What we usually look for today is a knitted fabric that is slightly firm, smooth, and elastic, neither board-like nor loose and loopy. Historically, though, many of the earliest sweaters were *very* firmly knitted of hard-spun yarns. There are records of sweaters made from such tightly spun, harsh yarn that people needed to wear neck scarves and wrist-wrappings to protect their skin from abrasion. The first Aran fishing shirt to come to public attention was almost board-like in its density and stiffness—able to stand without support! Some ganseys of fine handspun yarn were so firmly knitted that an average man's snugly fitted sweater weighed more than two pounds. In the northern European countries, sweaters were often deliberately felted to make them more wind- and water-resistant. Preferences varied, however; both the Færoe Islands and Iceland have longstanding traditions of using softly spun woolen yarns. These early garments were, more often than not, fulled (subjected to some shrinking and felting) to make them more comfortable and durable under harsh conditions. Today we have the same wide latitude of choice, although there are generally accepted standards of durability, comfort, and fashion.

Wraps per inch and approximate yardage requirements

Estimating gauge, needle size, and amount of yarn for a plain sweater, adult medium, 36–38-inch chest with 4–6 inches of ease.

	Yarn size	Wraps per inch	Typical gauge in stockinette stitch		Approximate needle size		Approximate yardage
			stitches per inch	*stitches per 10 cm*	*US sizing*	*metric sizing*	
Ultra-fine *	baby to lace weight	18	8+	32+	00, 0, 1, 2	2–3mm	1800–2200
Fine *	fingering weight	16	6–8	24–32	2, 3, 4	3–3.75mm	1600–1800
Medium **	sport weight	14	5–6	20–24	4, 5, 6	3.75–4.5mm	1400–1600
Heavy **	worsted weight	12	4½–5	18–20	7, 8, 9	5–6mm	1200–1400
Bulky ***		10	3½–4	14–16	10, 10½, 11	6.5–7.5mm	1000–1200
Very bulky ***		8 or less	2–3	8–12	13, 15	9–10mm	800–1000

* Measure over 1 inch to determine wraps per inch.

** Measure over 2 inches and divide by 2 to determine wraps per inch.

*** Measure over 3 inches and divide by 3 to determine wraps per inch.

Wraps per inch

How does one go about coordinating all the variables of yarn size, needle size, gauge, and yardage requirements? The simplest way to start is by wrapping your yarn around a pencil, dowel, or other round device and counting the number of wraps per inch. This number can be used to determine a tentative needle size and gauge and to estimate yardage.

A ruler is convenient for counting wraps per inch, but it's difficult to maintain consistent tension while wrapping around a flat, sharp-edged shape. I prefer to wind the yarn onto a narrow, cylindrical form. Wrapping around a pencil or knitting needle will work, but is inconvenient because it's hard to hold the yarn in place while you measure it.

Because of the usefulness of the wraps-per-inch count and the drawbacks involved in wrapping normal rulers and pencils, I've made my own ruler for measuring wraps per inch. All you need is a piece of doweling between 6 and 8 inches long, some time, and a little patience.

Cut a notch about ¼ to ⅜ inch deep and ⅛ inch wide into the center of one end of your dowel. Sand the dowel and the notch until they are very smooth, so that your yarn can wrap easily without snagging. Mark the dowel at 1-inch intervals, beginning at the base of the notch; be sure to make the marks in a way that will not accidentally discolor the yarn. Methods that work nicely include wood burning or cutting small, V-shaped notches. The ruler should be of a size comfortable for you to turn in your hand; I like ⅜-inch doweling for finer yarns and ½-inch doweling (with a correspondingly wider notch at the top) for heavier yarns.

To measure wraps per inch, catch the end of your yarn in the notch. Tying a knot in the end of finer yarn or fraying out the end of bulky yarn helps secure it in the notch. Rest the notched tip lightly between your thumb and first two fingers, and turn the dowel with the other hand so the yarn winds evenly around it. Wind the yarn smoothly, with each pass of yarn just touching the one before it, but *not tightly;* the object is not to pack the yarn onto the tool. Measure fine

---

Quick! How much yarn do I need?

1. Measure wraps per inch (see main text at right).
2. Multiply by 100.
For a plain-vanilla, adult, medium sweater (think "hand-knitted sweatshirt"), you're done. That's approximately how many yards you need.

Guiding principle: Always buy or spin extra yarn. Use any leftovers to make a scarf, hat, socks, mittens . . . or for color work on another garment.

3. For a *size* other than adult medium, increase or decrease the number in step 2 by the percentages in the top chart on page 38.

4. For a *different type of design*—more ease or length, no sleeves, texture patterns or color work—increase or decrease your basic number (from step 2 or step 3) by the percentages in the bottom chart on page 38.

Point of advice 1: A heavily cabled sweater uses lots more yarn than a plain sweater: all that dimensional depth is created by extra fiber.

Point of advice 2: A few design elements, like shawl collars, consume yarn very quickly.

Point of advice 3: Weight is the least reliable way to measure yarn. One pound will probably not be enough for a plain-vanilla, adult, medium sweater (except for very fine yarns). Two pounds will almost certainly be too much (except for very bulky yarns). Otherwise, weight depends on the vast array of variables in fiber and in yarn construction.

yarns over 1 inch, medium to heavy yarns over 2 inches, and bulky to chunky yarns over 3 inches. Divide by the number of inches you used as a measuring unit to get the number of wraps per inch. (You'll get a more meaningful number if you wrap several representative sections of yarn and average the results, especially with most handspun yarns.)

Once you have your wraps-per-inch number, the chart on page 36 will help you decide which needle size to use; what your gauge will probably be; and about how much yarn to use to make a plain, average adult, pullover sweater (size 36- to 38-inch chest, with 4 to 6 inches of ease, comparable in size to a unisex size medium sweatshirt).

Calculating yardage: quick rough estimates

Here's a fast way to get from wraps-per-inch to approximate yarn requirements for the adult size medium sweater, as described in the chart on page 36. *The yardage estimate is simply the number of wraps per inch multiplied by 100.* In other words, a plain-vanilla, average sweater will require about 100 yards for each wrap around the ruler. Obviously, *this is only an approximation.* Your actual yardage will vary depending on how tightly you wrap the yarn around the ruler, the gauge at which you actually knit, and the design features of both your yarn and the garment.

Adjustments for other size ranges

To accommodate a range of sizes, designated below by chest measurements, adjust the estimated yardage by the amounts in this table.

Size range	Chest measurement	Adjustment amount
Child	up to 25″	minus 30%
Small	32–34″	minus 10%
Medium	36–38″	use as is
Large	40–42″	plus 10%
Extra large	44–46″	plus 20%

Adjustments for other styles of sweaters

Of course, not all sweaters are plain pullovers! For other styles, adjust the estimated yardage according to the guidelines in this table.

Design characteristic	Adjustment amount	Comments
Greater ease	add up to 10%	
Extra length	add up to 10%	
Sleeveless vest	subtract about 30%	The body requires about 60–70% of the total yardage.
Heavily textured design	add about 10%	The amount of yarn needed depends on the take-in factor of the design elements. It can be significantly greater than this in cabled designs.
Color stranding	add up to 50%	Reduce the amount of yarn required for the main color when adding other colors, although the actual amounts will depend on the design.

Chapter
3

Equipment

Needles

Knitting needles have improved over the years. You can choose from a wide range of materials, including wood, bamboo, metal, and many kinds of synthetic materials. Circular needles have largely replaced double-pointed needles for sweaters, and have gone a long way toward replacing the single-pointed needles common since the beginning of the twentieth century. For knitting in the round, circular needles eliminate the transition from one needle to the next that so often frustrates the beginner. For sweaters, circular needles can be used for everything except small tubular areas, such as the neck edge and the lower sleeves. A 16-inch circular needle can be used for the upper sleeve and often the neck ribbing, but I much prefer to work on a set of five double-pointed needles. Why a set of five double-points instead of a set of four double-points? Having the stitches on four needles with a fifth working needle makes a square with minimal tension at the corners. Having the stitches on three needles with a fourth working needle makes a triangle that puts the yarn under greater tension at each angle. A 24-inch circular needle will handle the body of many sweaters, but large garments will require a 29-inch to 32-inch needle.

Magnetic row-marker
& your internal rhythm

A welcome modern tool is the magnetic row-marker. This is a metallic board with flexible magnetic strips that mark your place in a pattern. Place your knitting instructions or chart on the board and position the strips directly *above* the place where you are working; this way you can compare the completed rows on the chart with those on the sweater. But let me caution you that using a row-marker can become a detriment to your work if you discover that you cannot make a move without reading every stitch on the chart. If you depend on the chart too heavily, you will be like someone who uses training wheels to learn to ride a bike but never attains enough speed to quit leaning on them. Instead, I encourage you to learn your pattern and only to use the chart or instructions as a reference point. On all but the most difficult patterns, you will find a rhythm in the designs if you notice how the pattern is constructed and then trust yourself. Your knitting will become more joyful from the investment of a little time in the beginning.

Another invaluable tool is the handy pocket calculator. "Knitting in the old way" means working each sweater from a basic plan derived from experience with proportions, instead of from a line-by-line pattern. A calculator simplifies the mathematical calculations necessary (and I'm sure our folk knitters of the past would have used this tool, if it had been available). As modern knitters, we work with many different yarns to make a variety of styles from many cultures. Memorizing all the necessary variants is impossible. But knowing some basic formulas and working out the calculations for each sweater will guarantee a good fit.

In addition to these basics, you will need standard cable needles for some embossed designs; blunt tapestry needles and sharp, large-eyed crewel needles; a tape measure; and some markers. Markers can be yarn loops or the little rings sold especially for knitting, but I've found that an assortment of the split rings used by fishermen work extremely well. They're inexpensive, available in a wide range of sizes, and thin but durable. They slip easily from needle to needle, and won't snag the yarn.

One item often missing from today's knitting bag is a pad of graph paper. Before line-by-line patterns became common, graph paper was standard equipment for knitters, and before that knitters made, and

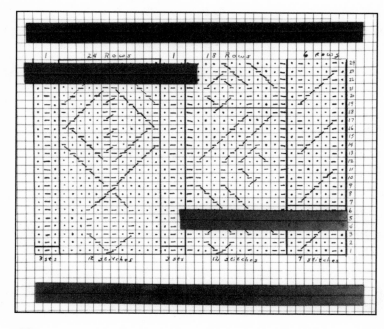

Magnetic row-marker

A charted design with magnetic strips placed above the rows in progress. Because the two sections have different repeats, the strips have been placed at different locations.

referred to, samplers. Paper with four squares to the inch (standard quad paper) is a good choice for charting textured and lace designs. Knitter's graph paper is better for working color-stranded designs. It is divided into rectangles instead of squares, to give a better representation of the finished pattern, because almost all knit stitches are wider than they are tall (see page 133). The paper I use for all my work has 5 stitches and 7 rows to the inch. Finally, you'll need colored pencils, highlighters, or the neat-colored gel pens now available (don't get the ink on your yarn!). Correction fluid is also useful, both for fixing errors and in case you want to change the design on the chart without redoing the entire piece.

Yes, I know many of you can work out your patterns on the computer—but since I cannot pack my computer in my knitting bag, I have opted out on this choice.

Colored pencils or pens & correction fluid

. . . and a computer, if it fits your style

Chapter

4

Knitting Methods

Folk knitters around the world developed a level of skill that permitted them to create extremely elaborate designs through simple, efficient means. Because they often knitted to subsidize meager incomes from other sources, speed was important. As textiles produced by industrial knitting frames began to supplant handknitted garments, individual knitters embellished their work with intricately constructed texture and color patterns that could not be duplicated on the frame. Even in areas where the need for profit did not influence ethnic designs, the competitive spirit did: many beautiful patterns were perfected in response to the intricate work of a fellow knitter.

The wisdom of these knitters comes to us in ways that craftworkers who depend on patterns have not been encouraged to discover. To understand how folk knitters produced intricate, sophisticated garments by looking at the fabric as it grew in their hands, we need to go back to basics. This chapter will explain three concepts on which their skills rest. It also looks at three approaches to constructing knitted fabric that were developed in different parts of the world: although there is a single path, individuals have discovered many ways of walking it. When you understand the alternatives, you can choose those that best fit your own strengths and vision.

The three basic concepts are (1) knitting in the round, (2) the idea of stitch mount, and (3) open or twisted stitches. The first concept—knitting in the round—is essential to developing the skills of a folk knitter. Therefore it is basic to the use of this book.

You can knit happily for years without understanding the other topics in this chapter—stitch mount, open or twisted stitches, and the three fundamentally different approaches to making knitted fabric. Most of

Three basic concepts

1   Knitting in the round
2   Stitch mount
3   Open and twisted stitches

Three approaches to making fabric

1   Eastern
2   Western
3   Combined

the comprehensive guides to knitting either don't mention these ideas or treat them as something you may rarely encounter.

Yet you may want to acquaint yourself with these ideas and techniques over time. They represent subtly but profoundly efficient ways of going about the job of knitting. Each will give you a slightly different perspective on our craft. Familiarity with all of them will deepen your understanding, will increase your proficiency (along with your ability to quickly identify and fix problems), and will ultimately lead to mastery.

Why bother with mastery? Because it opens doors in knitting that you otherwise wouldn't imagine existed.

And because it's *fun!*

Three basic concepts

Knitting in the round

This piece of information is essential: the simplest way to increase speed and simplify intricate stitches is to knit in the round whenever possible. Garments with complicated shaping that are knitted in flat sections, later sewn to make body-fitting tubes, are the work of the yarn companies and professional designers. Two-dimensional plans fit well on paper, as written patterns. But for many reasons, the knitters of old used other construction techniques.

Knitting in the round is essential to the skills of a folk knitter. You can knit happily for years without understanding the other topics in this chapter.

Working in the round keeps the face of the fabric toward the knitter—even when, as in some cultures, the preferred working method is purling! This makes it much easier to work complex patterns and reduces the amount of time spent on finishing tasks, especially the sewing of unnecessary (and often unsightly) seams. In addition, shaping is simpler for most knitters to work on the fabric's face side than on its reverse.

When construction requires a flat, rectangular surface—for instance, on the yoke sections between armholes—knitters who work primarily in the round can select one of three alternatives: knit across and purl back; knit across and knit in reverse on the return; or, for some projects, knit in the round and slash the work during finishing to make the openings.

There are only two possible stitch mounts: with the leading side in front of the needle or behind it.

Leading side in front of needle and trailing side behind it, called *Western style.*

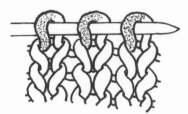

Leading side behind needle and trailing side in front of it, called *Eastern style.*

Stitch mount

Knitting is a simple craft that consists of only one—or maybe two—stitches. Some say there is one stitch, the knit stitch, and argue that the purl is only its reverse. Some say there are two stitches, the knit and the purl. The end of this debate does not matter to the knitter.

What does matter is that knitting consists of a series of loops held on pointed needles, and that each new stitch is a loop drawn in turn through a loop from the previous row of stitches. For simplicity, we'll call the stitch from the previous row the *foundation stitch* and the loop that is drawn through it the *new stitch.*

The appearance of the new stitch depends on two things: *stitch mount,* or how the foundation stitch is positioned on the needle, and *working method,* or the way the working needle enters the foundation stitch and how the yarn is wrapped around that needle to form the new loop. (This in turn determines the new stitch's *stitch mount;* the working method also affects the appearance of the foundation stitch, a subject that will be covered on the next several pages.)

Because of the way the needles hold the stitches, each loop on a needle must angle across that needle. One side, or leg, of each loop lies in front of the needle and one lies behind it. I'll refer to the two parts of each loop as the *leading side* and the *trailing side.*

Open stitches and twisted stitches

The three approaches to knitting that will be discussed in the next section are known as *Western, Eastern,* and *combined.* Before we consider them, we need to introduce *open* and *twisted* stitches.

The *working method* does two things.

First, it determines the way the new loop is mounted on the needle. While this has implications for the way stitches in the next row will be worked, it is a temporary condition: the stitch mount of the new loop can be changed before the stitch is worked.

Second, however, the working method controls the way the foundation stitch becomes fixed in the fabric. This is permanent and contributes to the appearance of the cloth.

Some working methods do not twist the foundation stitch (they produce an open stitch) and some do (they produce a twisted stitch).

To twist a stitch, you work into the *trailing* side of the foundation stitch. The resulting twist can lean to the left (right over left, characteristic of Western knitting) or to the right (left over right, characteristic of Eastern and combined knitting).

Most knitting today is worked with open loops. To knit open-stitch fabric, you work into the *leading* side of the foundation stitch. When a fabric has been worked with open stitches, the construction method—Eastern, Western, or combined—cannot be determined after the fact.

And this is important to us. It means we may use different stitch mounts freely, choosing at any time the method that produces the highest degree of excellence. The method used to reach excellence will not be the same for all of us.

Three fundamental approaches

Around the world, three fundamental approaches to creating knitted fabric (to forming the stitches) have evolved. The differences between them involve both *stitch mount* and *working method.* These approaches can be called *Western, Eastern,* and *combined.*

In Western knitting, the leading side of the loop is on the *front* of the needle for both knit and purl stitches, and the stitches are worked on pointed needles.

In Eastern knitting, the leading side of the loop is on the *back* of the needle for both knit and purl stitches, and the stitches are worked on needles that are pointed on one end and hooked on the other.

In combined knitting, the leading side of the loop for *knit* stitches is on the *front* and for *purl* stitches is on the *back,* and either type of needle may be used.

Western knitting

The Western method is the standard in North America and in western and northern Europe. The leading side of the loop is on the front of the needle and the trailing side is on the back of the needle. To create a new stitch (either knit or purl), the right needle tip enters the front (leading side) of the stitch and the yarn is wrapped from front to back over the needle tip. The resulting fabric is made of open stitches.

The yarn can be held in and tensioned by the right hand (English–American style) or the left hand (Continental–German style), but the stitch formation and the results are identical. The right-hand carry prevails in some regions, the left-hand carry in others. Until the latter

There are two final results for a worked stitch: open or twisted.

The stitches in this fabric are open. They have been worked through the leading side of the foundation stitch.

The stitches in this fabric are twisted. They have been worked through the trailing side of the foundation stitch. A stitch can twist either to the right or to the left, depending on how it is worked.

Quick summary of stitch mounts and working methods

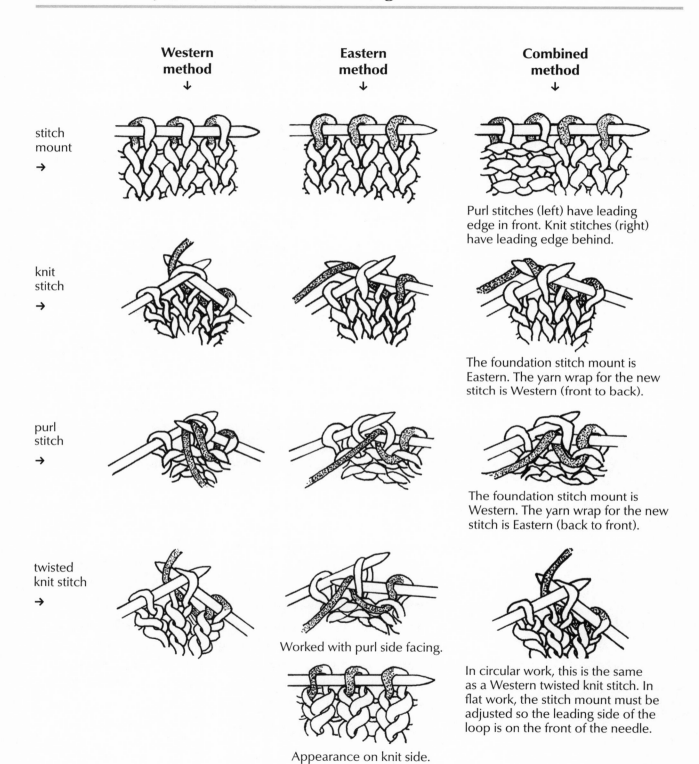

	Western method ↓	**Eastern method** ↓	**Combined method** ↓

stitch mount →

Purl stitches (left) have leading edge in front. Knit stitches (right) have leading edge behind.

knit stitch →

The foundation stitch mount is Eastern. The yarn wrap for the new stitch is Western (front to back).

purl stitch →

The foundation stitch mount is Western. The yarn wrap for the new stitch is Eastern (back to front).

twisted knit stitch →

Worked with purl side facing.

Appearance on knit side.

In circular work, this is the same as a Western twisted knit stitch. In flat work, the stitch mount must be adjusted so the leading side of the loop is on the front of the needle.

half of the twentieth century, the right-hand carry dominated in the United States; today we have a relatively even mix of the two styles.

Choose between right-hand carry and left-hand carry on the basis of which you find most comfortable. Incidentally, speed is not related to a specific technique. Speed depends on an individual's mastery of a preferred technique. For either carry, there are many variations in how to tension the yarn and manipulate the hands. I will detail techniques that I have personally found to be most successful.

Right-hand carry

When you hold the yarn in the right hand, that hand moves forward with the yarn to wrap the stitch, and the needle is pushed out of the loop with the tip of the left forefinger (for the knit stitch) or with the left thumb (for the purl stitch). This can become painful for arthritic joints if you use an exaggerated finger motion to wrap the yarn and bend your wrist to pull the new loop through. The method can be very comfortable if you keep your hand in a relaxed, neutral position and use the whole arm to move the right hand forward.

Left-hand carry

When you hold the yarn in the left hand, the working strand remains in a steady position while the right hand manipulates the needle to pick up the yarn and pull the new loop through the old one. This approach makes the knit stitch very easy; however, I have seen knitters use all kinds of contortions to get the yarn around the needle for the purl stitch—this is why some Continental-style knitters avoid purling as much as possible. The resulting extreme wrist motions of purling can be painful for people who have repetitive stress injuries (including carpal tunnel problems), and they are not necessary if you lean the tip of the left forefinger forward to bring the yarn into position. Some find they can ease the stress involved in making a purl stitch by working very close to the tip of the left forefinger and the tips of both needles; with the yarn firmly tensioned, the right needle moves the yarn forward into purl position (if coming off a knit stitch) and slides into the stitch in a continuous movement. A slight turn of the left hand brings the yarn into position so you can draw it through the loop.

Eastern knitting

This is considered the oldest method of knitting. It was practiced primarily in regions that fell under Islamic influence, including South

America—the Moors carried it to Spain and Portugal, and from those countries it traveled to the Americas.

The leading side of the loop is on the back of the needle; the trailing side is on the front. The knitter tensions the yarn by taking it around the back of his or her neck and the yarn falls into the natural purl position. All the work is purled. The needle enters from the back; the left thumb brings the yarn forward to be scooped through the existing loop to form a new stitch. This is very efficient when the knitter is using the traditional hooked needle, especially when there are multiple colors within a row!

Following the pattern from the purl side is not as hard as it may sound. Why? Because the knit side is on the outside of the circular tube; the tube faces away from the knitter and the work continues on its far side—the pattern is visible even though the knitter is purling. Those who work on the knit side are knitting on the near side of the tube.

Combined knitting

Combined knitting incorporates aspects of both Western and Eastern techniques. This type of knitting is typical of the various Eastern European cultures and of their descendants in North America. Why bother putting the two types together? Because the completed fabric can sometimes be more consistent than work produced by using all-Western or all-Eastern techniques.

When knitting in the round with the knit side facing, the leading side of the stitch lies on the front of the holding needle. The stitch is worked like a Western knit stitch: the working needle scoops the yarn through the foundation stitch to form a new loop. When the purl stitch is scooped through, the leading side of the new loop lies behind the needle (Eastern). When working flat, the knit stitch must be worked through the leading side (back of the needle) of the foundation stitch; the leading side of the resulting loop is then on the back (Western). The resultant fabric is stockinette. The yarn is traditionally tensioned in the left hand, but it can be worked just as easily with the yarn tensioned in the right hand.

One advantage of combined knitting may be seen in the ball of yarn waiting to be used. The twist in the waiting yarn remains balanced because in the combined method the knit stitch is scooped counterclockwise and the purl stitch is scooped clockwise. In the Eastern way, both are clockwise motions. In the Western way, they are both counterclockwise. With combined knitting, there are no more snarls in high-twist plied yarn and low-twist singles don't drift apart.

And, all other things being equal, the stitches made by this method are incredibly even. Why? When you wrap a Western *knit* stitch, the yarn comes in a straight line from the last stitch made; when you wrap a Western *purl* stitch, the yarn must cross the needle at an angle. Thus the amount of yarn wrapped for a purl stitch is slightly longer than that for a knit stitch. The opposite is true in Eastern knitting. The yarn crosses at an angle for the knit stitch and goes in a straight line for the purl stitch.

These amounts of difference sound insignificant. And they usually are, when you are knitting with an elastic yarn like wool—until you change from working circularly (for the body) to working flat (when you divide for the armholes). Then you may find that your gauge has changed, becoming looser. Or, when you fancy a summer sweater that requires an inelastic yarn, you may notice a radical change. With the knit side facing, every other row will appear just a tad looser. But if you turn to the purl side, you will see a major difference—this is called *rowing out,* and it is not a mark of excellence.

Perhaps you see no difference in your work. Many knitters unknowingly make adjustments without adapting the stitch wrap. What kind of needles do you use? On slick needles, the yarn can slide around to adjust the difference. How do you hold the needles? Knitters who hold their needles parallel are more likely to have this problem than knitters who hold them at 60- to 90-degree angles. Yes, Continental–German knitters are more likely to experience rowing out than English–American knitters—and it is much easier for a Continental–German knitter to make the shift to combined knitting than it is for a knitter who carries the working yarn in the right hand. Finally, how do you tension your yarn? Some knitters automatically increase the tension when purling, unaware that they are fixing a problem before it occurs. Knowledge is empowering!

When you work a gauge swatch, it is imperative that you understand the difference in the amounts of yarn used to work the knit stitch and the purl stitch in the standard Western method. Standard wisdom says if you are going to work flat, work your gauge swatch flat. And if you are going to work circularly, work your gauge circular—*or,* let me add, work a flat swatch but wrap your yarn with the leading side on the back when purling, that is, with combined knitting.

Rowing out

This fabric irregularity is caused by a difference in tension between rows worked with knit stitches and those worked with purls. The effect is more pronounced with inelastic yarns, and can be minimized through a shift in tools and working methods.

Toward more versatile knitters

Knitting skills have advanced tremendously during the past decade. Ten years ago, English-style knitting was the standard in the United States, except for a few very vocal Continental-style knitters. Most knitters who used the combined method maintained an apologetic silence as they stoically continued to knit. The occasional Eastern-style knitter quickly adapted to "the right way" in order to conform to a new environment. For those who depend upon published material, English-style was, and all too often still is, *the* way to knit. But in studying old pieces from many corners of the world, I (and many others) have learned that we have other options.

A savvy knitter must become increasingly process-oriented, rather than project-oriented. Patterns are still important as both guide and inspiration—and yes, I "use" a pattern if I find a specific sweater that I *have* to make. But I know patterns usually give a bare-bones approach to the instructions and that achieving the best results requires a lot of additional knitting knowledge. Patterns don't give detailed information; they give us a design. *We* have to know the best way to execute that design.

> A savvy knitter must become increasingly process-oriented.

And to improve the process, understanding the stitch mount and its effect is one part of the puzzle. Clearly, there is no *one best way* to knit. We need to embrace all ways, with each of us finding the right combination for each situation, personalizing the craft.

We have the whole world of knitting at our doorstep. All we have to do is take that first step. We owe it to ourselves to pursue knitting as fine craft, instead of working by rote.

With the reality of space limitations and the awareness that, for most of you, working in the Eastern and combined methods is unfamiliar, throughout this book I have illustrated the common techniques that you will need in the Western style. Those of you who understand the differences will find it easy to convert the information to your preferred style. Those of you who are just learning the differences: take one technique at a time. Learn to make fabric and patterning thoroughly from one approach. When you are fully comfortable, experiment with producing the same results using a different approach.

Knitting is very forgiving. But your experiments will lead you toward levels of mastery where your skills will be refined and this bonus quality of the craft will no longer be necessary.

Chapter

5

Techniques

Most folk sweaters use only a few of the most basic knitting techniques, which I will discuss here. If you need more in-depth knitting instruction, my perennial favorite resources are three classics, still in print: *Mary Thomas's Knitting Book, Mary Thomas's Book of Knitting Patterns,* and Barbara Abbey's *The Complete Book of Knitting.*

Casting on

The first step is to select the right cast-on. Cast-ons can be divided into two basic types: elastic cast-ons (long-tailed) and inelastic cast-ons (short-tailed). An elastic cast-on makes an edge with give, as for a standard ribbing. An inelastic cast-on is appropriate when the edge needs to be smooth, as for a divided welt in garter stitch or for corrugated ribbing (where the knit stitches are in one color and the purls in another). There are many, many ways to accomplish both types. This section includes only the techniques that I've found most useful.

Stitches cast onto a circular needle

The stitches lie neatly within the circle. When joining, make sure the stitches are not twisted.

Cast-on with double-pointed needles

Be sure that the stitches are not twisted between the needles before you join the round.

51

Because folk sweaters are usually worked in the round, you will form your cast-on stitches on a circular needle for the body and, in some cases, double-pointed needles for the sleeves. In both situations, you must be very careful not to twist the cast-on edge when you join the two ends. Check carefully to be sure that the cast-on edge lies neatly within the circle of the needles, as shown in the illustrations. If you allow the cast-on row to twist, you'll end knitting a Möbius strip, not a circular tube! There's no way to fix this problem except to go back to the cast-on row and make the join correctly. If you've used a cabled cast-on, reverse your needles before you join the circle, because the working strand will come off the left needle when the cast-on is complete. Or knit the first row and join the circle at the end of this row rather than at the cast-on edge; with two rows in place, it can be easier to see whether the join is twisted or straight.

Twisted-loop cast-on

When I learned this cast-on, it was called "the old Norwegian sock cast-on"—at the time, I was living in a region heavily populated by Norwegian descendants! A *twisted-loop cast-on* is highly elastic and durable, thanks to the extra twist between edge and loop. It's also called an *elastic cast-on,* in part because it's very difficult to draw the stitch too tightly. With some cast-ons, it's helpful to cast on over doubled needles or onto a needle of a larger size than you intend to knit with, in order to keep the stitches even. With this technique, you don't need to.

To start this long-tailed technique, draw an initial strand of yarn from the ball—in a medium-weight yarn, about 1 inch for each stitch (slightly less for a lightweight yarn and slightly more for a heavyweight one). There are two sets of instructions for performing this cast-on: right-hand carry (page 53) and left-hand carry (page 54).

The principles that yield beauty in crafts are unchanging and timeless. We do not admire work because of the past but because of its enduring present.

Soetsu Yanagi (1889–1961)
from *The Unknown Craftsman*

52

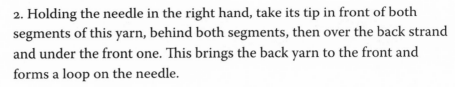

Twisted-loop cast-on, right-hand carry (English style)

1. Place a slip knot on the needle for the first stitch, with the long tail of yarn coming from the needle around the back and to the front of the left index finger (or thumb).

2. Holding the needle in the right hand, take its tip in front of both segments of this yarn, behind both segments, then over the back strand and under the front one. This brings the back yarn to the front and forms a loop on the needle.

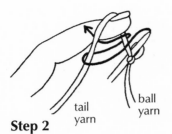

Step 2 tail yarn ball yarn

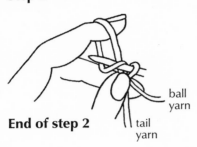

End of step 2 ball yarn tail yarn

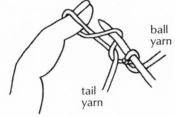

Step 3 ball yarn tail yarn

3. Continuing to hold the loop under tension on the left index finger, twist the needle slightly up and to the right so the loop is drawn into knit position.

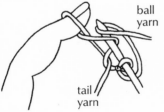

Step 4 ball yarn tail yarn

4. Take the ball yarn in the right hand and wrap it around the right needle tip. This is the normal action for forming a knit stitch in right-hand–carry knitting technique.

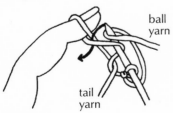
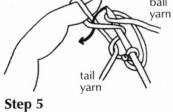

Step 5 ball yarn tail yarn

5. Draw the yarn just wrapped through the loop pulled up from the fingertip. This forms a stitch on the needle.

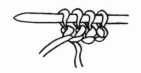

Here is how a series of stitches looks on the needle.

Twisted-loop cast-on, left-hand carry

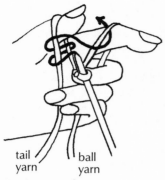

tail
yarn   ball
yarn

Steps 2 and 3

1. Place a slip knot for the first stitch on the needle, with the long tail of yarn around the thumb and the ball yarn around the index finger of the left hand, with this first stitch in between.

2. First you will pay attention to the two sections of yarn that are on your thumb. Twist the needle tip in front of the strand closest to you, then under both strands, pulling the yarn up on the needle tip to form a loop.

3. Next you will pay attention to the yarn on your index finger. Swing the needle over the top of the section closest to you and draw up a loop on the tip of the needle.

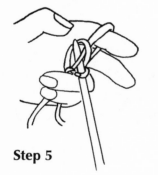

Step 4

4. Take the tip of the needle down and out to the front to make a stitch on the needle. You many need to turn your thumb slightly to make room for the needle to pass through to the front. It doesn't matter where within this loop you pass the needle; the yarn will make a loop after it comes through the figure-8. This loop tightens up in the next step, and the twist you see drops below the needle and forms the edge of the cast-on.

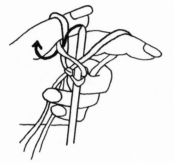

Step 5

5. Drop the yarn from the thumb.

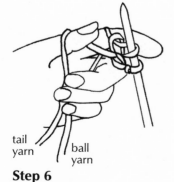

tail
yarn   ball
yarn

Step 6

6. Pull on the tail yarn with the thumb to gently tighten the loop on the needle.

54

Cabled cast-on

A *cabled cast-on* forms a very firm, inelastic edge. It is made with two needles and a single strand of yarn.

Make a slip knot near the end of the yarn and place it on the left needle (preparation). Then:

Step 1a

Step 1b

1. Knit a stitch through the slip knot (step 1a), but instead of dropping the old stitch from the left needle, leave it there and transfer the new stitch to the left needle also (step 1b).

Step 2

2. Pass the right needle *between* the two loops on the left needle and knit a stitch, again slipping the new stitch off the right needle onto the left. Repeat step 2 for each cast-on stitch required.

Continuing the cabled cast-on. Bring each new stitch up from between the two preceding stitches.

❈

Backward-loop cast-on

A third method of casting on, which is used when the work is already in progress, is the simplest of all. It involves placing a series of backward loops on the needle. This is the first cast-on many new knitters conquer when they are learning.

Increases

Make-one raised (M1R)

I like the make-one raised increase (M1R), represented by the symbol shown above. As the name implies, the new stitch is raised from the row directly beneath the working row. Slip the tip of the left needle down *between* the stitches of the preceding row, lift the connecting yarn, twist it to form a loop, and knit this loop as shown. This increase is only slightly directional; even so, in a symmetrically shaped piece it is best to work these increases in pairs, one leaning left and one leaning right. There must always be at least one stitch between paired increases.

Make-one raised (M1R) leaning left

Step 1

1. Slip the tip of the left needle between the stitches of the preceding row and lift the connecting yarn; note the direction in which the needle tip catches the yarn.

Step 2

2. To work this increase so that it leans *left,* twist the raised yarn to form a loop that crosses as shown. Then knit through the loop.

Make-one raised (M1R) leaning right

Step 1

1. Slip the tip of the left needle between the stitches of the preceding row and lift the connecting yarn; note the direction in which the needle tip catches the yarn.

Step 2

2. To work this increase so that it leans *right,* twist the raised yarn to form a loop that crosses as shown. Then knit through the loop.

☞ **Paired increase**

To produce a symmetrical double increase, work an M1R leaning right on the right and an M1R leaning left on the left.

Decreases

There are three basic decreases: right, left, and balanced, represented in charts by the symbols shown with their descriptions. The first two are single decreases (one stitch is eliminated). The balanced decrease is a double decrease (two stitches are eliminated).

While decreases are usually worked on knit stitches, you will occasionally need to decrease while working purl stitches.

Decreases that lean right

Knit two together (K2tog)

The simplest decrease, knit two together (K2tog), leans to the right and is worked just as its name implies, by knitting two stitches as one.

Purl two together (P2tog)

The P2tog is the reverse of the K2tog: slip the right needle tip through two stitches as if they were one and purl them together. I use two symbols to represent this decrease, depending on my needs.

Decreases that lean left

Slip, slip, knit (SSK)

For the sake of symmetry, a decrease that leans to the left is necessary to balance a K2tog. I use the popular technique known as *slip, slip, knit,* abbreviated as SSK:

1. Slip two stitches separately knitwise.

2. Pass the left needle tip back through the two reversed loops.

3. Knit the two stitches off together.

Slip one, knit one, pass slipped stitch over (S1, K1, PSSO)

An alternative to the SSK is the older version, S1, K1, PSSO: *slip one, knit one, pass slipped stitch over.* Remember to slip one *knitwise* in this combination, or this decrease will not balance the K2tog.

Slip, slip, purl (SSP)

The SSP is the reverse of the SSK. Although this technique may sound complicated, it is not:

Step 1

1. Slip two stitches separately knitwise, then pass the left needle tip through on the front to move the stitches back to the left needle.

2. Take the right needle tip around the back so that it enters the second stitch first and continues through the first, moving from left to right. Then purl the two stitches off together.

Step 2

Balanced (double) decrease

Slip two together, knit one, pass two slipped stitches over (S2tog, K1, P2SSO)

Step 1a

1. Slip two stitches together knitwise (step 1a). They will sit in an overlapping position on the right needle (step 1b).

Step 1b

Step 2

2. Knit the next stitch.

Step 3

3. Pass the two slipped stitches together over the knit stitch.

Balanced double decrease, completed.

Finishing edges

The philosophy of the folk knitter is to avoid any unnecessary binding off, because the inflexibility of bound-off edges on knitted garments makes them vulnerable to wear. When binding off is essential, there are several techniques that can be used.

Standard bind-off

The standard binding-off technique is to knit the first two stitches, then slip the first stitch over the second stitch; knit the third stitch, then slip the second stitch over; and so on until all the stitches have been removed. (When binding off ribbing or a pattern stitch, maintain the pattern as you work, instead of knitting each stitch.) The bind-off should always be worked loosely so it will be as flexible as possible. To maximize flexibility, you can work this edge with larger needles.

Alternate bind-off

For a slightly more elastic bind-off, knit two together, slip the new stitch back onto the left needle, K2tog, slip the stitch to the left needle, and so on, until all stitches have been bound off.

Grafting off as an edge finish for ribbing

A relatively new, more flexible way to close off the stitches of a ribbing is one that I refer to as *grafting off,* because the technique involves grafting the knit stitches to the adjacent purl stitches. This technique is excellent for use with K1, P1 ribbing and works very well with K2, P2 ribbing, although in this case the second knit stitch is slightly distorted.

The detailed instructions on the next page involve K2, P2 ribbing, because that is the more elastic ribbing and the one I recommend. You will want to break off a sufficient length of the working yarn to complete a full round of ribbing, plus some extra for insurance. Thread this strand of yarn into a blunt tapestry needle. If you break the yarn, run out, or prefer not to work with a long strand, add a new length of yarn whenever you need one and work the tails in after you are done.

**Grafting off
on ribbing**

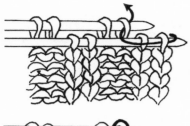

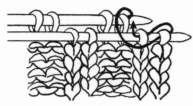

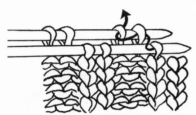

1. Begin work with the first half of the stitches to be grafted off. Prepare by sliding the knit stitches onto one needle (to lie in the front) and the purl stitches onto another needle (to lie in the back).

2. With the yarn coming from the back, enter the first knit stitch on the front as if to purl, but do not remove it from the needle. Enter the first purl stitch on the back as if to knit, but do not remove it from the needle.

3. On the front, enter the first knit stitch as if to knit and remove it; enter the next knit stitch as if to purl, but do not remove it.

4. On the back, enter the first purl stitch as if to purl and remove it; enter the next purl stitch as if to knit, but do not remove it.

Repeat steps 3 and 4 until most of the stitches in the first half have been removed. Slide the remainder of the stitches onto the two needles as before, with the knit stitches on the front needle and the purl stitches on the back needle, and continue grafting off. When one stitch remains on the front needle and one on the back needle, knit off the front stitch and purl off the back stitch. End by entering the first knit stitch removed as if to purl, then take the yarn to the back to work its tail down a rib.

With practice, you may not find it necessary to realign the stitches onto two needles, one for the front stitches and one for the back stitches. I continue to work in this manner because I can lay my work down when necessary without losing track of where I am in the procedure.

Selvedges

Many knitters prefer to slip the first stitch of each row, because this firms up the edge and minimizes its tendency to curl. This is desirable when working an edge that will later be picked up and worked in ribbing, such as along a cardigan front. I am not fond of the effect on edges that are to be seamed, because this edge is less elastic than the main fabric areas. When I am going to be picking up in stockinette stitch, I do not use a slipped selvedge stitch, because it's necessary to move in one row from this chained edge to have the correct number of stitches from which to pick up the new stitches, and this makes extra bulk.

Joining edges

Binding off two sets of stitches together

Binding off two sets of stitches together is a useful technique for eliminating a sewn seam, for instance at the shoulders. Do this on the wrong side for a smooth finish, or bind off on the right side to create a decorative ridge.

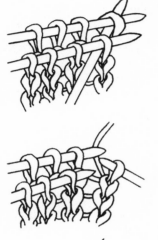

1. Arrange the stitches on two needles held parallel. Put the tip of the right needle through the first front stitch and then the first back stitch.

2. Knit the two stitches off together. Repeat with a second pair of stitches, one from each needle.

3. When two new stitches have been made, slip the first one over the second to bind it off in the standard manner. Knit together another pair of stitches (one from each needle), pass the second new stitch over this new third stitch, and so on.

Grafting edges together

Grafting, sometimes called *Kitchener stitch,* is a technique for joining the stitches of two edges together invisibly; the two edges must contain equal numbers of stitches. Note that when you join pieces worked in different directions (as at the shoulders, where the technique is most often used) the joining points will not match perfectly. They will be off by one-half stitch.

Thread a strand of yarn in a tapestry needle; the strand should be about three times as long as the distance to be joined. Hold the two pieces of fabric with their wrong sides together. The joining yarn follows the path that a row of knitting would follow on the right side.

Work according to the sequence at the top of the next page, beginning with the first stitch on the front needle.

61

Grafting two sets of stitches together

The needle passes through each stitch twice, following the path that a new row of stitches would take between the two existing rows.

1. Bring the tapestry needle through the first stitch on the front needle as if to purl, leaving it on the knitting needle.

2. Bring the tapestry needle through the first stitch on the back needle as if to knit.

3. Bring the tapestry needle through the first stitch on the front needle as if to knit, and slip this stitch off the needle. Bring the tapestry needle through the next stitch on the front needle as if to purl, again leaving it on the needle.

4. Bring the tapestry needle through the first stitch on the back needle as if to purl, and slip this stitch off the needle. Then bring the tapestry needle through the next back stitch as if to knit, leaving it on the needle.

Repeat steps 3 and 4 until all stitches have been worked. Remember that the tapestry needle must enter each stitch twice. You may need to tighten or loosen the loops of this grafted row with the tip of your tapestry needle so that the tension matches that of the rest of the knitting.

Perpendicular join

This is a valuable technique that eliminates bound-off edges and seams. You can use it in any situation where there is a perpendicular juncture, such as on some neck edges and on saddle shoulders, but not for an extended distance because of the difference between row gauge and stitch gauge. You can join two pieces together (one knitted and one joined along one of its edges) or three (one knitted and two joined, one on each of its edges).

At the end of each row of the fabric piece that you are knitting, work the final stitch of that piece together with an open stitch from the fabric that you are joining to it. Use a slip, slip, knit decrease (SSK) at the end of a knit row. Use a purl two together (P2tog) at the end of a purl row.

In particular, see the application described with Plan 8, Sweater with Gussets and Saddle Shoulders (page 96).

A narrow band being joined to the open stitches of a separate piece of fabric: the final stitch in the band is worked with one open stitch in an SSK.

Short rows

Knitting short rows shapes a knitted garment invisibly. Short rows can be used to make the neck higher in the back than in the front (so it fits the body more accurately) and to shape the shoulders. This shaping process is suggested for, and described with relation to, the yoke patterns of Plans 12 and 13 (pages 103–09) and one of the shaped sleeve cap options in Plan 15 (page 115). I recommend a different way of working short rows for each of these applications. Once you are comfortable working short rows, you will discover many ways to apply them.

My favorite short-row technique

I deciphered the technique that I prefer from a Japanese machine-knitting book. Unlike most short-row techniques, it does not require that you wrap the turning stitch. This is the method I use when shaping yoke sweaters to produce a more anatomically adapted front yoke and neckline. Diagrams on pages 106 and 109 indicate the positions of the turning points, with one sample reproduced here for ease in visualizing the process.

To set up each short row, work up to the turning point. Turn and slip the first stitch; at every turn, the row begins with a slip stitch. Do not stack the turns so that they are on top of each other. In order to have a smooth angle on the joining row, the individual short-row turns must be spread apart by a few stitches.

Here are step-by-step instructions for short-row shaping to increase the number of rows on the sides and back of sweater:

1. Short rows begin immediately below the yoke pattern.

2. Knit across to the point where you will reverse for the start of the short row. Turn.

3. Purl side facing, slip the first stitch as if to purl. Purl across to the point where you will reverse for the end of the short row. Turn.

4. Knit side facing, slip the first stitch as if to purl. Do not pull the working yarn in tightly when crossing behind the slip stitch to work the following knit stitch. Knit across to next turning point.

5. Repeat steps 3 and 4 until there are 3 to 5 turns on each side of the front, evenly spaced 5 stitches apart.

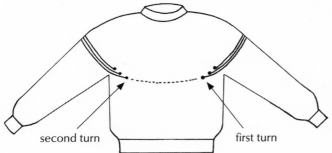

Example of short-row shaping on a yoke, with three turns on each side of the front.

second turn   first turn

63

Work as many short rows as necessary to bring the back of the garment to the right height relative to the front (three short rows for heavy to bulky yarns or five short rows for fine to medium yarns). Before beginning the yoke design, work one round to bring all the short rows into a smooth, continuous round. As you work this round, pay attention to the slip stitches at the turning points and incorporate them in the round with the short-row joins described below. First use the short-row join, knit side facing, for the right side of the short rows. When you have worked across all the turns on the right side, knit across center front to left side. Work the short-row join, right side facing, for the left side of the short rows.

Short-row join, right side of short rows (knit side facing)

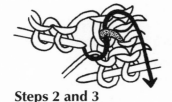

Steps 2 and 3

1. Work up to and including the first slip stitch.

2. Fold the work forward to expose its back side, and with the left needle tip lift the bar that connects the slip stitch to the next stitch on the left needle. This bar, when lifted, tightens the slip stitch just worked.

Step 4

3. Lift the bar from the top of the stitch to its bottom with the left needle tip, with the leading side of the bar loop on front of the needle.

4. K2tog to join the slip stitch and the bar loop of the previous row.

Short-row join, left side of short rows (knit side facing)

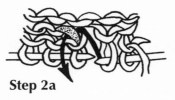

Step 2a

1. Knit across the front stitches to one stitch *before* the slip stitch. Slip this stitch to the right needle as if to knit.

2. Fold the work forward to expose its back side, and with the right needle tip lift the bar that connects the slip stitch to the next stitch on the left needle (step 2a). This bar comes directly out of the bottom of the slip stitch on the left needle: the slip stitch on the left needle and the bar loop on the right needle form a straight line when the needles are held parallel (see step 2b). The two loops will be tight. The bar loop must be lifted from bottom to top, with the leading side of the bar loop on the back of the needle.

Step 2b

3. Wrap the yarn around the right needle tip, then draw the yarn through the bar loop to create a new stitch on the right needle.

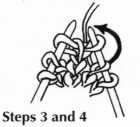

Steps 3 and 4

4. With the left needle tip, pass the stitch that you slipped to the right needle a moment ago over the new stitch to complete the join (PSSO decrease).

64

Wrapped-turn short-row technique

The most common short-row method involves wrapping and slipping the stitch where the reversal occurs. While I do not routinely use this technique any more, it is useful now and then. See in particular Plan 15, the alternative described toward the bottom of page 115.

To work a wrapped turn on the knit side

1. Work up to the turning stitch, slip that stitch knitwise to the right needle, and turn the work.

2. To wrap the turning stitch: take the yarn to the back, slip the turning stitch purlwise to what is now the right needle, then bring the yarn to the front.

3. Purl across to the position of the next turning stitch.

To work a wrapped turn on the purl side

1. Work up to the turning stitch, slip that stitch purlwise to the right needle, and turn the work.

2. To wrap the turning stitch: take the yarn to the front, slip the turning stitch knitwise to what is now the right needle, then bring the yarn to the back.

3. Knit across to the position of the next turning stitch.

Completion round

In each case above, the slipped turning stitch has been encircled by the working yarn. When you have completed all of the short rows, work one smooth, continuous round to blend the turning stitches with the main fabric.

A series of wrapped turns worked on the knit side.

A series of wrapped turns worked on the purl side.

Every time you reach a wrapped turn that slants to the left, knit the wrap and the turning stitch together.

Wrapped turn slanting to left.

Every time you reach a wrapped turn that slants to the right, slip the turning stitch knitwise to the right needle, place this stitch on the left needle (the loop is now reversed), and knit off together the wrap and the reversed loop of the turning stitch.

Wrapped turn slanting to right.

Details

Picking up stitches

Early folk knitters avoided seams, picking up stitches along an edge whenever possible. The process of picking up stitches is simply that of knitting through the fabric edge. With the right side of the work facing you and starting from the right edge, pass the needle through the first stitch of the edge. Knit this "stitch" as usual, and proceed across.

Stitches are wider than they are high, so when you are picking up along a vertical edge (composed of rows), you will pick up fewer stitches than the number of rows. The number of stitches you need for a given length can be calculated based on gauge. I don't bother with figuring the actual number; instead, I use a "standard" for stockinette stitch that works regardless of gauge. The standard is to pick up one stitch at the end of each of four rows, skip one row, and repeat. Your stitches will be grouped in fours on your needle, which makes counting them easy.

Because ribbing is elastic, I use a slightly different formula to pick up stitches for ribbing: pick up one stitch at the end of each of two rows, skip one row, and repeat. Working two out of three rows produces handy groupings for K1, P1 or K2, P2 ribbing. If a selvedge has been worked by slipping the first stitch of each row (for example, for a cardigan), the number of stitches at the edge is half the number of rows. In this case, working one stitch in each of the selvedge stitches is satisfactory.

Splicing strands and securing ends

Splicing is a technique for joining a new ball of yarn without a knot. This technique is especially good for handspun or softly spun yarn, because it makes an invisible join and eliminates the need to work in loose ends. Untwist the plies at the end of the old ball and the beginning of the new one. Break off the plies at different lengths, overlap the old and new yarns about 3 to 4 inches, twist the ends together, and rub vigorously to enhance cling. To splice bulky singles, taper about 4 to 6 inches of the ends of the old and new strands by pulling out fibers. Overlap and twist the two together and rub vigorously.

The splicing technique can also be used for millspun yarns, although if your yarns are very smooth and regular the join may show. In this case, end the old ball at the side seam and pick up a new ball there, leaving the tails to be worked in later.

Not everyone can be an artist, writer or composer. But if you can take yarn and fashion from it an article that is good to look at, you have created a masterpiece of practical art.

*Barbara Abbey
from 101 Ways to Improve Your Knitting.*

To work in yarn ends, use a sharp-pointed needle, piercing through the backs of the stitches, rather than tucking the yarn ends under them. That way the ends won't work loose. Divide the plies of heavy yarns and work each in separately, to keep the ends from adding bulk.

Buttonholes

Horizontal buttonholes

It's been my experience that buttons rest more securely in horizontal buttonholes, a must when knitting for children.

Horizontal buttonholes should *not* be centered on the placket. The outside end of the buttonhole should extend just slightly beyond the center of the placket. When the button is sewn at the center of the opposing placket, the button will come to rest at the outside end of the buttonhole. The buttonhole side of the placket will cover the button side neatly, eliminating the gaping placket between buttons!

I am a convert to the one-row buttonhole, finding it tidier than the old two-row version. Work as follows:

1. When you reach the point where the buttonhole will start, bring the yarn forward. Slip the next stitch to the right-hand needle. Take the yarn to the back and drop it. This yarn is not used on the first half of the buttonhole.

2. Slip the next stitch to the right-hand needle. Pass the first slipped stitch over the second slipped stitch to bind it off. Slip the next stitch to the right-hand needle, passing the loop from the first bind-off over. There are now two bound-off stitches. Continue slipping and passing over until you have bound off the necessary number of stitches.

3. Slip the last loop from the bind-off process back to the left-hand needle. Turn the work.

4. Using the yarn dropped earlier and the cabled cast-on, cast on the number of stitches bound off *plus* one stitch. Resist the temptation to pull the yarn firmly on the first stitch!

5. Turn the work. With the yarn forward, slip the first stitch from the left-hand needle to the right-hand needle. Pass the "plus one" cast-on stitch over the stitch slipped from the left-hand needle. Take the yarn to the back to continue work on the remainder of the row.

Vertical buttonholes

Vertical buttonholes *must* be centered on the placket, with the top of the buttonhole corresponding to the button position on the opposing placket. You will make a vertical slit in the center of the placket by working the two sides of the buttonhole separately.

1. Work the first side to the necessary length, ending on the buttonhole edge. Place these stitches on a holder and break off the yarn.

2. Return to the beginning of the buttonhole and rejoin the yarn. Work a corresponding number of rows on the second side.

3. On the following row, work across the stitches of the first side of the buttonhole. The buttonhole is now complete.

When you finish the sweater, there will be a tail at each end of every buttonhole. Use these tails to reinforce the ends of the buttonholes.

Tools for Planning Sweaters

Freedom in knitting comes from learning to think of a knitted project in organic terms, rather than as a series of linear instructions. Attention to gauge means that a garment can be planned so that it will fit. Charts of color and texture patterns give you the ability to hold whole sequences of stitches in your head, easily seeing how they fit together as you work the stitches. Structural sketches help you combine shaping options, again eliminating the need to knit with your eyes on a piece of paper. You can learn to watch the growing fabric and *know* what to do next for both pattern and structure.

Our intention is to reclaim the technical confidence and design pleasure enjoyed by knitters of earlier times.

Gauge

Gauge is the number of stitches and rows in a given measure. It is usually expressed as stitches and rounds (or rows) per inch, but it's best measured over at least 4 inches (10 cm). An accurate determination of your gauge is *the* single most important measurement in knitting, as all subsequent work is based on this figure. Therefore, this measurement must be accurate, even to the half-stitch.

The vital figure is the number of stitches per inch, because that's a measurement of width; it determines fit. In addition, once you have cast on and begun to work, you are committed to the number of stitches within a design repeat. The number of rows per inch is less important, because the length can be adjusted by measuring your work as you go, although it's helpful to know the number of rows when positioning design elements.

To determine gauge, first knit a sample. Always knit the sample in the pattern that you'll use in the garment, whether textured or color-stranded. A good swatch size for ultra-fine to fine yarns is 5 inches square; for medium to heavy yarns make your swatch 7 inches square; and for bulky to chunky yarns cast on for a swatch that's 9 inches square. After knitting the sample, remove the swatch from the needle (bind off, or leave the stitches unbound and handle the swatch gently) and lightly steam the fabric. Lay a ruler over the surface, placing a pin at each end of the area to be measured. Count the number of stitches between the pins and divide by the number of inches between the pins. Repeat this in several places on the swatch, using the average of all the measurements. This is *your* gauge for *this* yarn on *these* needles.

Remember that your gauge in flat knitting may differ from that of circular knitting! As most of the knitting for an ethnic-style sweater is circular, it's a good idea to knit a circular swatch. If you do not want to do that much knitting, work your swatch in combined knitting, for which the gauge is the same, circular or flat (see pages 48–49, plus 46).

Your swatch should have the hand and the visual appeal that you want. If it doesn't, try again. For a firmer hand, use smaller needles; for a softer hand and a more elastic fabric, use larger ones. Remember that firm yarns work up best into firm fabrics, while softer yarns are more suitable for soft fabrics. You wouldn't, for instance, want to knit a fluffy angora yarn into a tight, stiff fabric. Tentative gauges for various yarn weights and needle sizes are given on page 36.

The percentage system

A simplified method of pattern drafting uses percentages to express proportions. This method is based on the premise that each part of the garment is proportional to the other parts, just as one part of the body is proportional to another. With a pocket calculator, it is easy to convert proportions to inches, and then to numbers of stitches or rows, or vice versa.

proportion = percentage = fit

All the calculations for a basic sweater are based on one measurement: the chest measurement plus ease. This becomes the circumference of the sweater, and can be stated as follows:

circumference = chest + ease = 100%

The amount of ease can vary according to preference: 4 inches for a snug fit, 6 inches for a comfy fit, or 8 inches or more for a loose fit.

70

Unless loosely fitted, many sweaters have snug ribbings at the hips, so the hip area often requires fewer stitches than the full circumference. You'll need about 90% of the circumference for a hip band worked in ribbing or garter stitch (otherwise the hip band will tend to fold upward). Seed stitch needs no adjustment.

Your head is smaller than your chest, and so the neck opening is proportionately smaller than the sweater circumference. For an adult crewneck sweater, the head opening is typically 40 to 45% of the circumference. Use 50 to 55% for the neck opening of a child's sweater.

A typical upper sleeve is 50% and the cuff is 20% of the circumference.

All of the above measurements are of circumference. These relationships between the parts, and therefore the percentages, will also vary according to your desired style and fit. Other necessary dimensions have to do with length, and can be determined with a tape measure.

Remember that the percentage system is a guide, not a set of rules. Your best resources are careful measurements of the person who will wear the sweater and of the gauge for your yarn. Watch with particular care when you are working a raglan or yoke sweater for someone who is not "average." The tall or thin may need greater depth in the upper body. On a raglan, you may work one or two extra rounds between sets of decreases. On a yoke sweater, you may work several additional plain rounds between decrease rounds. For a short or heavy person, you may need to reduce the upper-body depth, placing raglan decreases closer together (on every round as necessary) or reducing the number of plain rounds between decrease rounds on a yoke.

Even for those who fall into the average category, you may customize for a perfect fit. To adjust length, change the number of rounds. To adjust width, change the stitch count.

Charts and diagrams

I use two types of symbols, derived from a variety of sources, to plan and document sweaters. Pages 72 and 73 contain reference copies of the symbols I use to chart patterns and to diagram structures. Groups of symbols are also duplicated in the sections of the book where they are discussed.

Until the mid-1800s, knitters recorded their ideas on samplers or in charts, or they passed them along verbally. Knitted patterns have a rhythmic repetition, with each row related to the previous one. For this reason, patterns can be more easily learned and followed when they're presented visually. Almost any pattern can be put on a graph-paper chart, including intricate textured and lace designs. Likewise, knitted structures fit together according to a logic that lends itself to visual presentation.

Charting symbols for patterning and shaping

Basics

knit stitch (K1)

purl stitch (P1)

twisted stitch, knit through the back loop

twisted stitch, purl through the back loop

slip one stitch (left) or two stitches (right) knitwise (S1 or S2; see chart for knitwise style)

slip one stitch (left) or two stitches (right) purlwise (S1 or S2; see chart for purlwise style)

yarn forward

yarn back

wrap yarn around

pass stitch over (or bind off)

selvedge stitch (knit last stitch of row; slip first stitch of row)

not a complete row (dark squares are not stitches)

Decreases

knit two or three stitches together (K2tog or K3tog)

slip, slip, knit (SSK)

double: slip two stitches together, knit one, pass slipped stitches over (S2tog, K1, P2SSO)

purl two stitches together (P2tog)

purl three stitches together (P3tog)

Increases

yarn over (yo)

make-one raised (M1R)

Miscellaneous patterning processes

work bobble: instructions given separately

pass three stitches over (bobble sequence)

work in the row below

twisted purl stitch, right

twisted purl stitch, left

bind off in purl

purl chain

work all stitches in one

Charting symbols for cables and traveling stitches

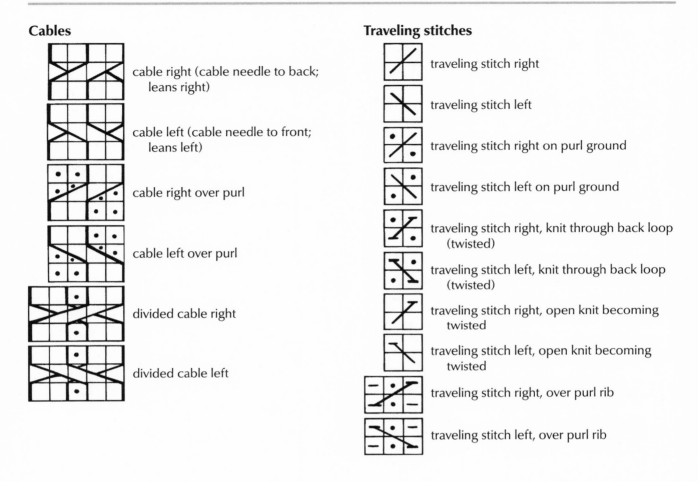

Cables

cable right (cable needle to back; leans right)

cable left (cable needle to front; leans left)

cable right over purl

cable left over purl

divided cable right

divided cable left

Traveling stitches

traveling stitch right

traveling stitch left

traveling stitch right on purl ground

traveling stitch left on purl ground

traveling stitch right, knit through back loop (twisted)

traveling stitch left, knit through back loop (twisted)

traveling stitch right, open knit becoming twisted

traveling stitch left, open knit becoming twisted

traveling stitch right, over purl rib

traveling stitch left, over purl rib

Diagramming symbols for structure

∨ knit

∩ purl

I stitch

— row or round

◢ knit two together (K2tog) decrease

◣ slip, slip, knit (SSK) decrease

▲ double decrease (balanced)

Ω make-one raised increase (M1R)

⧚ selvedge or edge of steek

ℓℓℓℓℓ pick up stitches

∧∧∧∧ graft or bind off

•—• linear measure

⌷ circular measure

← ↑ direction of work

⊣⊢ place stitches on holder

Growing a Sweater: A Sample Plan

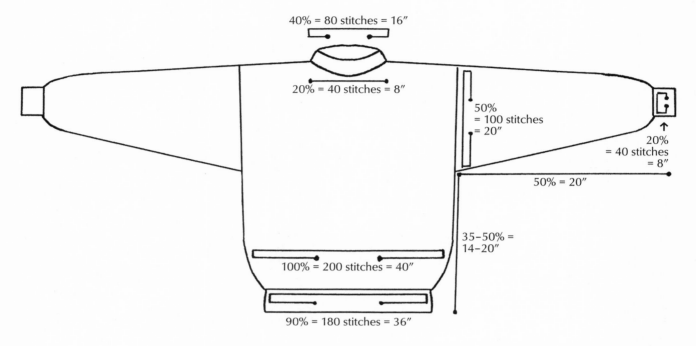

40% = 80 stitches = 16"

20% = 40 stitches = 8"

50% = 100 stitches = 20"

20% = 40 stitches = 8"

50% = 20"

35–50% = 14–20"

100% = 200 stitches = 40"

90% = 180 stitches = 36"

A simple sweater that shows how to design using both percentages and a construction diagram will help you understand this easy method of drafting. Here's an example of how to figure the numbers and the construction approach you need to make a sweater for an adult with an actual chest measurement of 36 inches who wants 4 inches of ease (a snug but reasonable fit). The gauge in this sample is 5 stitches and 7 rows per inch.

chest + ease = circumference × stitches/inch = 100% of stitches

36" + 4" = 40"

40" × 5 stitches/inch = 200 stitches

circumference = 40" = 200 sts = 100% of stitches

All other width measurements can be determined by taking a percentage of the circumference. Using the hip band as an example:

hip band (HB) = 90% of C

HB = .90 × 40" = 36"

HB = .90 × 200 stitches = 180 stitches

Here is the summary of all the basic calculations:

gauge = 5 stitches and 7 rows per inch

circumference = 100% = 40″ = 200 stitches

hip band = 90% = 36″ = 180 stitches

neck = 40% = 16″ = 80 stitches

upper sleeve = 50% = 20″ = 100 stitches

wristband = 20% = 8″ = 40 stitches

Above the hip band, you must increase from 90% to 100%, in this example a 20-stitch increase from 180 stitches to 200 stitches. This requires an increase after every ninth stitch (180 ÷ 20 = 9). Going from a 90% to a 100% circumference *always* involves an increase after every ninth stitch, no matter what the total number of stitches is. For a snugger hip band, you would use 80% of the circumference for your ribbing. In the example, you would cast on 160 stitches for the ribbing and increase to 200 stitches for the body, an increase of 40 stitches, or one increase after every fourth stitch (160 ÷ 40 = 4).

The neck in the example is 40% of the circumference, so it includes 80 stitches, half for the front neck and half for the back. Therefore the center 40 stitches on both front and back must be set aside for the neck opening.

The sleeves, if knitted from the wrist to the underarm, require an increase of 60 stitches between cuff and upper edge. The increases, one on each side of a center underarm "seam"-line stitch, will need 30 rows.

You'll notice that when knitters depend on charts and diagrams, written abbreviations for stitch processes are not required—except as a convenience in the explanatory text about these techniques.

Shaping sleeves

How often to work an increase row depends on how long the sleeve is. Assuming you want the increases to occur smoothly along the whole length of the sleeve, you can determine how often to increase by converting the length of the sleeve from wrist to underarm into the equivalent number of rows. For example, if the sleeve length is to be 20 inches total, minus 2 inches for the wristband, an increase of 60 stitches must be made over a distance of 18 inches, or 126 rows (18″ × 7 rows per inch = 126 rows). An increase must be made every .6 inch or every 4.2 rows (126 rows ÷ 30 increase rows = 4.2 rows). The practical way to accomplish this is with an increase after every fourth row, or every ½ inch.

An increase on every fourth row will usually result in a 30% increase from the wrist to the underarm, yielding the standard upper-sleeve measurement of 50% of the body's circumference. Following this pattern, average row figures for the increases can be used to produce sleeve variations: every fourth row for the 50% sleeve, every fifth row for the 40% sleeve, and every sixth row for the 35% sleeve. If the sleeve is worked from shoulder (or cap) to wrist, reversing the direction of the work, start counting at the underarm and decrease at the same intervals.

If you choose to work this *average* number of rows between increases (for example, 4), rather than the *actual* number (for example, 4.2), the sleeve won't always work out perfectly. You may have to make adjustments; because knitted fabric is very accommodating, they won't affect the final appearance of the garment. These minor adjustments are fairly simple.

How to adjust the rate of sleeve shaping

Sleeves worked from wrist to upper arm

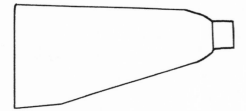

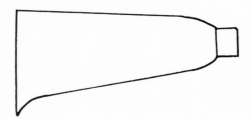

If the sleeve is being shaped too rapidly, stop increasing when you reach the correct number of stitches and then work even to the desired length. The finished sleeve will have a longer area of full width.

If the sleeve is being shaped too slowly, increase more frequently in the last section. The upper sleeve will have a shorter area of full width. The effect resembles a half-gusset worked on the sleeve instead of the body.

Sleeves worked from upper arm to wrist

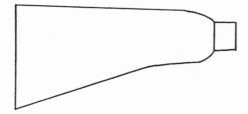

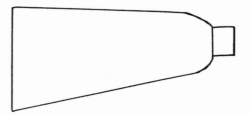

If the sleeve is being shaped too rapidly, stop decreasing when you reach the correct number of stitches and then work even to the desired length. The sleeve will have a longer area that fits the arm closely.

If the sleeve is being shaped too slowly, decrease out all the extra stitches in the last row before the wristband. The sleeve will be slightly bloused. This is used as a design element in some sweaters (for example, the Berchtesgaden Sweater on page 276).

Notes on the sleeve-to-body connection

On many traditional sweaters, stitches for the sleeves are picked up along the armhole and worked down to the cuffs.

For those who prefer to work sleeves from cuffs to shoulders, I suggest binding off into the armhole or grafting the stitches in place (as indicated in the sample diagram on the next page). In most knitting reference works, *grafting* and *binding off together* are worked with two sets of live, or open, stitches. Variations of these techniques can join one set of live stitches to an edge. For sleeves that are worked separately, these techniques make the best-looking joins possible. They are flexible and sleek, without any extra bulk. They are also easy to work.

Binding off through an edge

There are two ways to accomplish the bind-off.

In the first, you work the live stitches of the sleeve through the row ends of the armhole edge. Sometimes knitting instructions call this "slip-stitch crocheting" or "crocheting" the sleeve stitches to the armhole, but the process can be worked with knitting needles. Draw each stitch through the edge of the fabric in sequence and bind off as you go.

In the second, you pick up a set of stitches around the armhole equal in number to the stitches at the top of the sleeve. Then bind off together to join the stitches around the armhole with the stitches on the sleeve (see page 61). This is often called a *three-needle bind-off*.

Grafting live stitches to an edge

My favorite technique involves grafting the live stitches of the sleeve to the armhole. Grafting, worked with a single-eye needle, can be worked on one set of live stitches and an edge (or, for that matter, on the ribbing at the top of a sock). I sometimes call the edge-to-live-stitch variant a *half-graft*.

Fit the sleeve into the armhole. Then form the join as you would any other graft, using an eyed needle to carry a strand of yarn through the ends of the rows on the solid edge of the armhole and the live stitches of the sleeve. Don't try to work with sufficient yarn to go around the entire sleeve; join new lengths as you need them.

Try this technique when you sew down the band of a crew neckline: the method eliminates the bind-off that some knitters work too tightly, making the sweater hard to pull over the head, and others make so loose that it is sloppy.

A Sweater Diagram Showing Construction Techniques

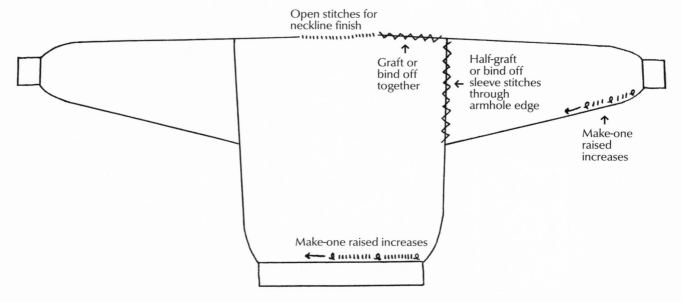

Open stitches for neckline finish

Graft or bind off together

Half-graft or bind off sleeve stitches through armhole edge

Make-one raised increases

Make-one raised increases

Schematic diagrams are helpful tools. I use a set of symbols for various structural elements and construction details to develop plans for sweaters in any size and style. Diagramming lets you think through how the pieces fit together, and symbols indicate where structural changes take place. Some symbols that I use are indicated and explained on the diagram above, and a full set appears both at the bottom of this page and in the general reference set on page 73.

The sample diagram on this page indicates an increase after every ninth stitch above the hip band (from 90 to 100%), with the neck-opening stitches set aside and the shoulder seams grafted or bound off

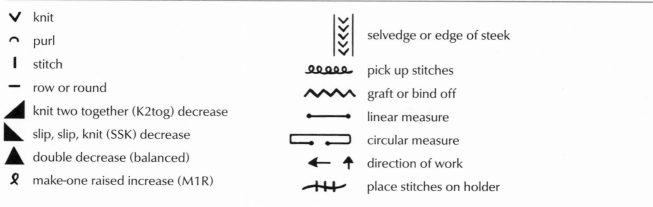

V knit	**selvedge or edge of steek**
⌒ purl	
I stitch	**pick up stitches**
— row or round	**graft or bind off**
◢ knit two together (K2tog) decrease	• linear measure
◤ slip, slip, knit (SSK) decrease	circular measure
▲ double decrease (balanced)	← ↑ direction of work
ℛ make-one raised increase (M1R)	place stitches on holder

together. It also shows the sleeve worked from wrist to upper sleeve, with an increase on every fourth row (from 20 to 50%), and then bound off into the armhole. This simple example shows how you can use construction symbols to take the place of line-by-line instructions.

When you learn to think this way, you will be able to imagine your knitting in three dimensions, instead of as flat pieces that need to be assembled. You will also become free to knit the sweaters you see in your imagination with a minimum amount of delay between vision and cast-on. This is "knitting in the old way."

For efficiency, incorporate all figures, symbols, and dimensions into a single diagram. Plan the entire sweater, showing all measurements in both inches and stitches or rows. Make the diagram as complete as possible, positioning design motifs to best advantage. Planning ahead doesn't mean that adaptations and adjustments won't be necessary or possible. Should the need for adjustments arise, you'll be able to handle it with little or no frustration.

When you learn to imagine your knitting in three dimensions, you will be free to knit the sweaters you see in your imagination. This is "knitting in the old way."

Chapter

7

An Evolution of Shapes

When you've taken the time to knit a sweater by hand, you want a garment that is unique and distinctive, yet in a style that you can wear year in and year out. Traditional designs and patterns that have been handed down from generation to generation generally fit these criteria—seldom "in style" but never "out of style" best describes the genre. The simple, classic shapes of folk sweaters also are the basis for many handknitted fashion sweater variations today. Thus understanding and using traditional sweater styles opens the door to both ethnic and high-fashion knitting.

Like the work of the knitters of old, these 15 basic plans are based on gauge and proportion. Yet today a pocket calculator provides the key to freedom. Same system, new language!

We've covered the percentage system and diagramming in general terms, without getting into the wide variety of possible sweater styles. We can now consider plans for bodies, sleeve shapings, and neck openings, beginning with the earliest shapes and carrying through to modern garments. Each sweater shape requires its own plan, and some plans represent only minor variations on previous ones. Yet if you look at the shapes and techniques in sequence, they show how knitted sweater structures seem to have evolved through the years.

Fifteen basic sweater plans appear in this chapter, moving from the simplest to the most complex. Boxes highlight construction techniques that suggest the idea of evolutionary stages. Chapter 8 covers styling alternatives that can be combined with the basic plans. It includes several methods for making cardigans, followed by extensive information on neckline variations.

The plans and variations are based on gauge and proportion, just like the work of the knitters of old. But those proportions have been refined and converted to percentages, so the number of stitches in each section can be determined through simple math. Many knitters have become familiar and comfortable with the modern applications of this time-proven approach through Elizabeth Zimmermann's invaluable work. Today, a pocket calculator provides the key to design freedom. Same system, new language!

Presented in a wide range of shapes from boxy to yoked to raglan and more, the plans will help you become an interpreter of design or an independent designer, liberated forever from that mass-produced look. All the diagrams are drawn to the same scale, so you can trace different features and combine them into one garment. Special techniques necessary to knit each style are emphasized.

The sweater plans have been adapted for modern fit. They aren't necessarily reproductions of the original ethnic sweaters, but they are firmly founded on traditional shapes and construction techniques. To adhere to every detail of a style from a hundred years ago would be of little practical use today, unless we limited our interest strictly to the historical. While that's useful, our intention is to reclaim the technical confidence and design pleasure that knitters from those times enjoyed.

The percentages in the plans are based on an "average" fit for an "average" person. Of course, we are not all "average." The percentages can and should be adjusted to reflect individual shapes and preferences. Keep records of your work and you will discover the percentages you need to get a perfect fit in every sweater, for yourself and for your loved ones.

Create and preserve the image of your choice.

*Mohandas K. Gandhi
(1869–1948)*

Plan 1: Basic Blouse

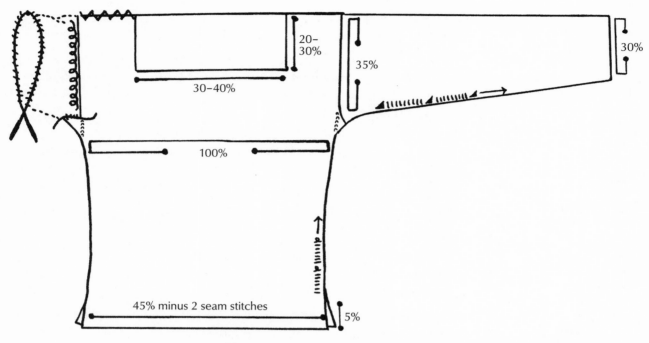

20–30%

30–40%

35%

30%

100%

45% minus 2 seam stitches

5%

The earliest sweater shapes were based on rectangular woven garments: boxy, with gussets that provided underarm shaping and a split welt for the hem treatment. Possibly the earliest of these garments was the Danish *natrøje*, a night shirt or undergarment that evolved into the brocade blouse of Danish folkwear. The *natrøje* was short in length and snugly fitted, taking advantage of the fact that knitted fabric has greater elasticity than woven cloth.

To make a basic blouse, begin knitting two welt hem sections. The diagram suggests using 90% of the total stitch count for the waist area, with 45% each on front and back. Your actual stitch count will depend on an individual waist measurement, plus the desired amount of ease.

Work the two welt hem sections separately, using a non-rolling stitch, like seed stitch. When they reach the desired depth, join them to form a circular tube by overlapping two stitches. The overlapping stitches reinforce the join and establish a "seam" marker at each side, separating the front and back sections. To overlap the stitches, lay the front section over the back and purl together the

Construction detail: The split-welt hem

Overlap welt by two stitches to form side seam.

82

last two stitches of the one piece and the first two stitches of the second piece. These purled, overlapping sets of stitches will make a visible line that looks like a seam. Continue this two-stitch purled column up to the underarm, where it will facilitate the neat insertion of a half-gusset.

As you knit the body of the garment, you will need to work regular increases so that the garment will fit well at the chest. In the sample, the chest measurement of 100% is based on an individual's actual measurement, plus the desired amount of ease. For a form-fitting garment like the original, ease might be as little as 2 inches or as great as 4 inches. Make the necessary increases on each side of the purled side stitches at regular intervals. How many increases you work and how often they occur will depend on (1) the additional ease necessary for the bust compared to the waist and (2) the length from waist to underarm.

When you reach the underarm, insert a half-gusset. To do this, begin with a purl increase on each side of the two purled side stitches. These new purl stitches will become dividing-mark stitches between the armhole and the sleeve. The gusset must increase in size rapidly. While continuing the P2 column of stitches, make two K1 increases on every round, one immediately after the first P1 marker stitch and one just before the second P1 marker stitch. Continue increasing until the depth of the half-gusset is about half its width.

At this point, place the half-gusset stitches on a strand of yarn, leaving the P1 stitch at each edge of the half-gusset on the needle with the body stitches. Then divide the front and back bodices and work them separately, continuing to purl the P1 stitch at the edge of each armhole.

After you've worked enough depth for the armhole, join the shoulder seams by grafting or by binding the stitches off together.

Pick up the sleeve stitches around the armhole; include the half-gusset stitches, which simply become part of the sleeve. Continue to purl the two stitches that mark the side and underarm, as established. Work each sleeve down to the wrist, tapering the sleeve to reduce its width with paired decreases placed on each side of the purled column. Because the lower sleeve is not snugly fitted, these decreases do not occur as often as is typical on modern sweaters.

Finish the sleeve hem with a welt to match or coordinate with the bodice hem.

Construction detail: The half-gusset

The half-gusset is a squat triangle formed only on the body section.

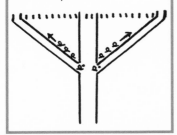

Plan 2: Basic Gansey

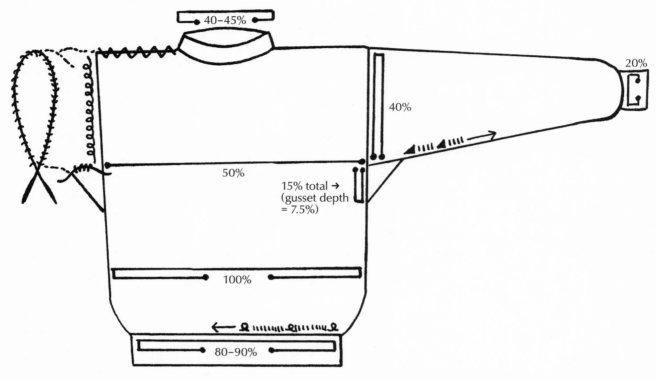

The gansey represents a modification of the Basic Blouse (Plan 1). The early gansey was a fairly long garment with a split-welt hem treatment, as on the Basic Blouse, although many knitters have replaced this type of waist finish with a band of ribbing.

The work begins at the hip band. Knit a ribbing band about 2 inches wide. (A K2, P2 ribbing holds its shape better than a K1, P1 ribbing.) After completing the band, use evenly spaced increases to reach the 100% circumference stitch count. As in Plan 1, work a two-stitch purled marker column at each side seam. If you used a K2, P2 ribbing, produce this marker by continuing a P2 rib from the band up each side.

Work even on the body stitches until you are about 7.5% (usually about 2 or 3 inches) below the underarm, at which point you begin forming the gusset. Start the underarm gusset by working a raised increase between the two purl stitches. The style of gusset used on this garment is a long, diamond-shaped piece. Work it by making paired increases on every *other* row to the desired depth, perhaps 2 to 2½ inches. Put the

Construction detail: The underarm gusset

The gusset is an elongated diamond shape. Its first half is formed with the body, and its second half with the sleeve.

Increase to shape the first half along with the body.

Decrease to shape the second half along with the sleeve.

gusset stitches on a strand of yarn, leaving the purl marker stitches with the active body stitches. Then work the front and back separately, maintaining one purl stitch at each edge of the armhole. Bind the shoulders off together; some early knitters bound these stitches off on the right side of the gansey, where the join served as a decorative element.

Pick up the sleeve stitches along the edge of the armhole, including the gusset stitches. As you begin to work the sleeve down toward the wristband, purl one sleeve stitch on each side of the gusset stitches and work paired decreases at the edges of the gusset on every other row until one stitch remains. The final stitch is decreased with one of the purl stitches. You will now have a two-stitch purl column extending from the tip of the gusset. Continue working these purl stitches right into the wristband, which is worked in the same ribbing as the hip band.

Plan 3: Steeked Jersey

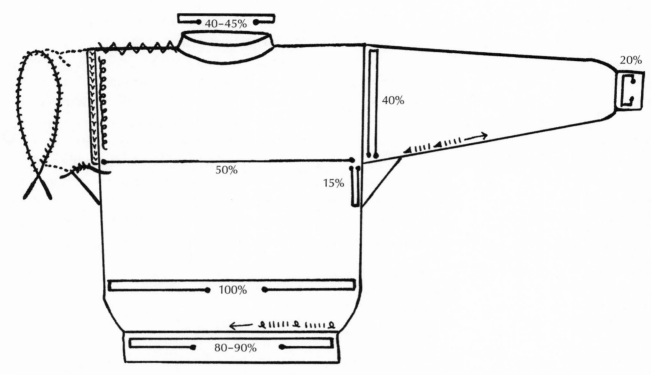

The earliest folk sweaters were knitted in one color, enriched with textured patterns. At some point, knitters began to use color-stranding techniques. These double the fabric thickness, creating a warmer garment with patterns in contrasting colors. These sweaters were knitted in the round, and the body tube extended all the way to the shoulders. Various treatments of the armhole area allowed this tube to be slashed to make room for the insertion of the sleeves.

On Fair Isle, in northern Scotland, early color-stranded sweaters followed the gansey shape and contained gussets. For sweaters of this type, start at the hip band and work up to the gusset, omitting the purled side-marker stitches. Knit the gusset in the main color or work it with two colors alternately, to produce a speckled effect. Changing colors every other stitch gives an interesting pattern, yet does not leave long strands carried across the back of the gusset.

When you have completed the first half of the gusset, transfer the gusset stitches to a holder. Join the back and front with a steek and continue in the round to the shoulder. *To steek* loosely translates as *to close,*

When you are knitting a color-stranded pattern and you pick up and knit sleeves down from the armholes to the cuffs, the Vs of the knit stitches will be inverted on the sleeves. See the additional information on this topic in the text for Plan 4.

and that is what the steek does: it closes a gap so you can continue circular knitting. This means you can work all of the intricate color-stranded rows with the right side (and the design) facing you. As wonderful as steeks are, they have some technical limitations. Don't try steeking with anything but wool; luxury fibers are too slick and vegetable fibers are too dense. Also, the technique is recommended for use with medium to fine yarns. With heavy yarns, it produces bulky seams.

After removing the gusset stitches to the yarn holder, bridge the gap by adding stitches with a backward-loop cast-on (page 55). For medium to medium-heavy yarns, a 5-stitch steek is about right. For fine to medium yarns, use about 7 stitches. Cast on in alternate colors. Continue to work in the round. When you knit the steek stitches, alternate the colors in each row and from one row to the next. When you've worked the armhole to its full depth and it's time to insert the sleeve, cut the steek. Yes, *cut* the steek! In early days, this area was simply slashed down through the middle stitch; with fuzzy Shetland-wool yarn, it wasn't necessary to secure the stitches before cutting. Today, most knitters machine-stitch twice on each side of the center stitch before slashing. Don't worry about the edges. They will be finished neatly after you make the sleeves.

If the yarn is lightweight, graft the shoulder stitches, including the top of the steek; heavier yarns should be bound off together, to keep the seam from stretching. Pick up the sleeve stitches along the armhole, including the gusset, and work each sleeve down to the wristband. The body of the sweater is worked from the hip band *up* and the sleeve is worked from the shoulder *down,* so remember to reverse the placement of the color-stranded pattern bands when you work the sleeves. In order to have the sleeve patterns align with the body patterns when the sweater is worn, begin the sleeve with the part of the pattern that appears at the midpoint of the armhole or slightly below that level. Because this type of sweater has a dropped shoulder line, forgetting to make this adjustment in the sleeve patterning often produces an unpleasant jog in the design when the garment is worn.

After you've completed the sleeves, you'll see that the edges of the steeks fold neatly back against the body of the sweater, where they can be secured with closely spaced herringbone stitches. To make the herringbone stitching neater, separate the plies of your yarn until you have single strands to work with. Thread one strand into a sharp needle and make small stitches, catching only the backs of the sweater stitches.

Construction detail: The steek

The steek, also known as a Scot's steek, covers the gap that results when you hold the gusset stitches on a strand of waste yarn while you work the upper part of the body in the round.

Machine-stitch twice on each side of the steek, as shown with the dark lines, and then cut through the middle column of stitches to make the armhole opening. This is only unnerving the first time. Then you'll love the technique.

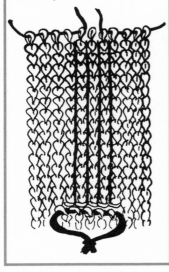

Plan 4: Shaped-Steek Jersey

As garment shaping received greater emphasis, the dropped shoulders of the color-stranded gansey shapes gave way to moderately fitted shoulders. While the steek was still used on sweaters from Shetland Island, this different sort of construction replaced the gusset.

Work even from the hip band to the underarm. Then remove a number of underarm stitches (about 5% of the circumference at each side) and place them on strands of holding yarn. Close the gap with a steek, as described for Plan 3, worked in alternating colors. Continue to work in the round, decreasing on each side of the steek on every row or every other row until enough stitches have been removed to bring the armhole in line with the edge of the shoulder—about 5% of the circumference will be decreased at each edge of each armhole opening. When you slash this type of steek, it will open at an angle because of the decreases along its edges. Slash the steek and join the shoulders.

The more traditional method of making the sleeves involves picking up stitches at the armhole and working the sleeves from the shoulders down to the wristbands. When you are working a color-stranded pattern, the Vs of the knit stitches in the sleeves will be inverted in relation to the Vs in the body stitches. Depending on your design, this difference in stitch direction, and therefore the orientation of the patterning, may be negligible or obvious. It's most noticeable when the pattern involves isolated stitches in a color that contrasts with the background.

If the inverted V of the stitches on the sleeves is bothersome to you, work the sleeves from the wristbands up to the shoulders and join the sleeves, stitch by stitch, to the body (see page 77 for ideal joining techniques).

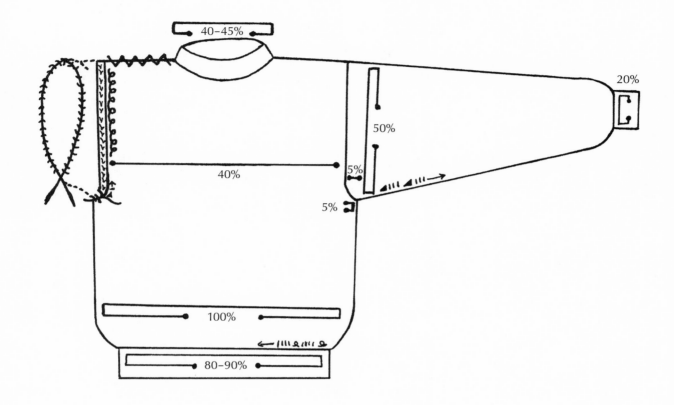

We must take a fresh look at real folkcraft of the past, for it is there that we may find healthy and genuine beauty expressed.

Soetsu Yanagi (1889–1961)
from *The Unknown Craftsman*

Plan 5: Sweater with Locked Turning Stitches at Edges

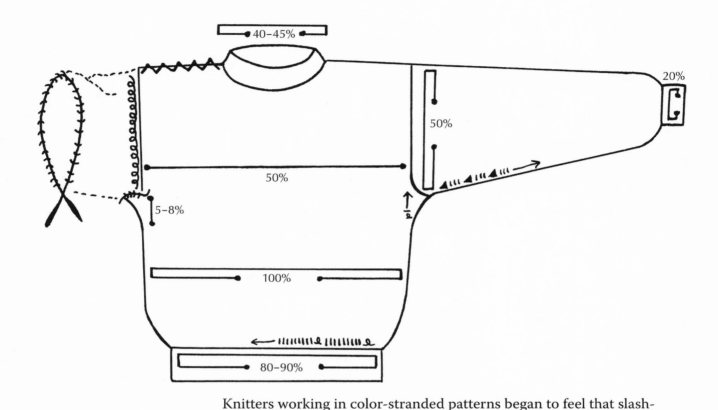

Tips on working with heavy yarns

Knitters working in color-stranded patterns began to feel that slashing techniques were inferior. Working back and forth across the yoke area is slower than working in the round, and the natural rhythm of the repetition of design is broken when you have to turn the work. Yet many knitters began to work back and forth across the yoke area. This technique does eliminate the need to finish cut edges and the resulting seam bulk. It also produces good results when the knitter uses heavy yarns.

Bulky yarns require different approaches than fine- or medium-weight yarns. Bulky-weight yarns are best worked back and forth, because a slashing technique produces thick and intrusive seams. Sweaters worked in heavy yarns contain fewer stitches than those worked in more moderate yarns, so working back and forth does not become tedious. In bulky sweaters, a true gusset was seldom used. Rather, ease at the underarm can be provided by incorporating a half-gusset, formed through a short series of paired increases. Begin the increases about 3 inches below the

90

armhole and repeat them about every third round. When you reach the underarm depth, remove these half-gusset stitches to a holder.

Locked turning stitches at the armhole improve the finished product when the front and back are worked flat. Locking all the colors within the final stitch of each row insures that the stitches in the next row will be smooth and even. There are no gaps or holes in the work, since all the yarns go from one side to the other.

Locked turning stitch

Divide the work into front and back, designating the last stitch of each as a locked stitch. When you come to the last stitch, twist the supplementary colors with the main color to secure them to the back of the last stitch. Then turn and work the first stitch of the following row in the main color.

If you choose not to steek because of the fiber type or your personal objection to cutting, consider working the knit rows in the standard manner and the purl rows without turning, working the knit stitches in reverse (page 200). If your gauge is noticeably looser on the reverse-knit (normally purl) row, wrap the yarn with its leading side on the back of the needle; in this case, the knit-row stitches will need to be entered through the back and wrapped in the standard manner (see page 46, righthand column, second drawing from top: combined-method knit stitch).

Plan 6: Sweater with Laddered Openings for Sleeves

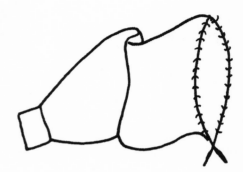

Construction detail: Platform stitches, and the laddered opening

When you plan to ladder an opening, thread scrap yarn through a set of platform stitches on the row where you want the laddering to stop.

Knit to the top (shoulder, for an armhole), then release the stitches above the platform set.

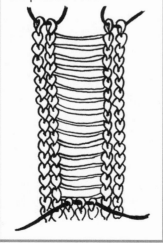

In Northern Europe, the slashing technique often involved laddering the stitches (freeing the loops to run down several rows of stitches), cutting these open strands, and tying them off in pairs. Today's knitter can machine-stitch along the edges of the stitches to be laddered, using a zipper foot to get close to the stitches. For a neat appearance, all the ends should be tucked in.

To prepare for laddering the stitches, designate about three "platform" stitches at the base of the armhole. Run a yarn through the platform stitches, but *do not remove* them from the needle. Continue to work in the round, maintaining your pattern, and knitting all yarns of each row in every stitch of the ladder: you must knit *every* color of yarn in *every* stitch designated for laddering. When you've reached the full depth of the armhole, remove the designated stitches from the needle and ladder them down to the platform stitches.

Today, stitching around the armhole with a double row of machine stitching is more common than laddering. After stitching, the armhole is slashed (shown opposite). This doesn't work as well as laddering, because it doesn't provide a set of platform stitches. Without them, the underarm stitches at the turn are awkward, bulky, and less durable. If you feel that the old laddering technique is too time-consuming, use a Scot's steek instead (page 87).

However you choose to create your armholes, begin at the hip band, work the sweater to the underarm, close the armhole either with a

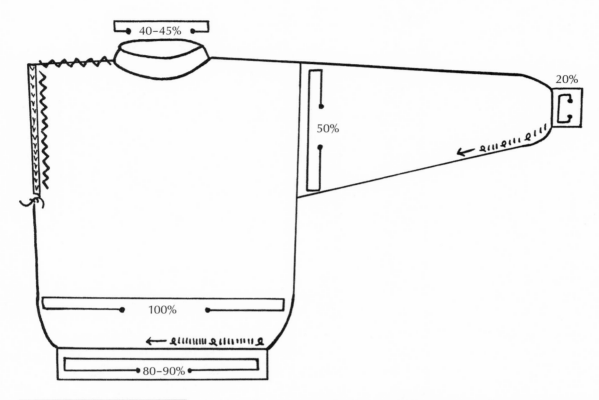

**Construction detail:
Modern Nordic
stitching and slashing**

Machine-stitching the
opening without a set of
platform stitches is fast,
but the results are inferior.

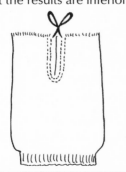

ladder above 3 to 5 platform stitches or a steek across 3 to 5 stitches. Continue to work in the round for the upper body, including the stitches of the platform area or steek.

Work the sleeves from the wristband to the shoulder. Then lace all the stitches of each sleeve on a string and divide them evenly into the armhole before you attach the sleeves to the body. The sleeve stitches can be bound off into the armholes (incorporate the platform stitches as you go) or you can join them stitch by stitch to the body of the sweater (in this case, graft the platform stitches). The latter method is somewhat less bulky and more flexible.

If you are using lightweight yarns, you can graft the shoulder seams. Heavier yarns should be bound off together instead, to add stability to the shoulder. In some old sweaters, a small gusset was inserted in the shoulder seam just next to the neck opening.

Plan 7: Sweater with Square Armholes

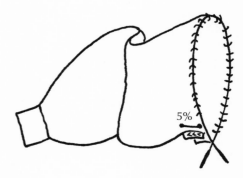

When the shaping of shoulders became more common, the Northern European laddering technique was modified. Enough stitches were included in the platform to create a square armhole that went straight to the point of the shoulder.

The upper sleeve needs to be modified to fit into the resulting square armhole. At the underarm, it requires an opening half as deep as the platform is wide (if the platform consists of 10% of the stitches, the opening in the sleeve underarm goes to a depth of 5%). Instead of laddering this short distance, mark the underarm point at which the opening needs to occur. While continuing to work the sleeve in the round, each time you reach the marked point wrap the yarn around the working needle several times. On the following row, drop the established wraps and wrap the needle again. Repeat this dropping and wrapping process until the sleeve and its short opening have reached the desired length. Slash the wraps and open the underarm out flat; the slashed area on the sleeve will equal the total underarm width on the body. The sleeve can be bound off into the armhole or joined to it stitch by stitch (see page 77 for techniques).

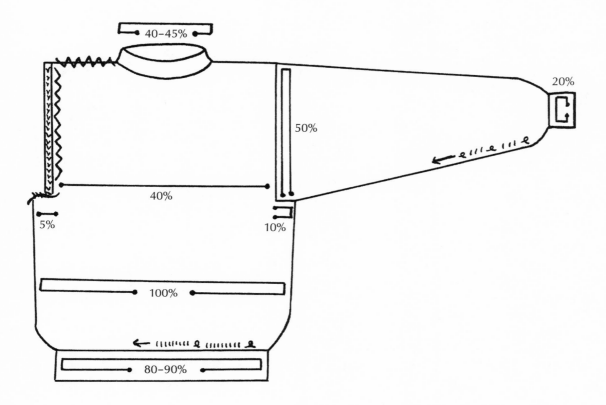

Hand knitting was taken for granted until "progress" did away with the need for its regular practice. But the cost to humanity in the loss of these skills and the ability to employ them has exceeded the value of the theoretically higher standard of living. We need to work with our hands, creating objects that are unique and also enduring. We need things natural, not synthetic. We can secure more reliable satisfaction by having a few possessions that satisfy our souls, instead of many disposable items that briefly assuage fleeting desires.

Plan 8: Sweater with Gussets and Saddle Shoulders

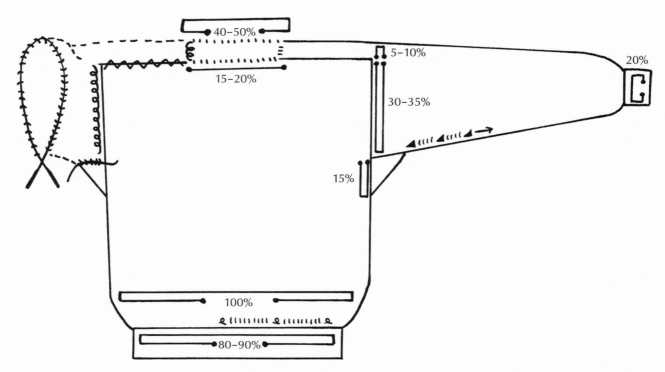

A style common to parts of Great Britain is the saddle shoulder, also called a shoulder strap. This style was often used in Scottish ganseys. The body of the sweater is knitted like the Basic Gansey (Plan 2, pages 84–85), beginning at the hip band, until the half of the gusset that is worked with the body has been completed. Place the gusset stitches on a holder, and work the front and back pieces separately, back and forth, until those sections reach the base of the neckline. On both front and back pieces, divide the stitches into three parts: a center section for the neck (15–20%) and two side sections for the shoulders.

Work one shoulder at a time. Place the front stitches of one shoulder on one needle, and the corresponding back shoulder stitches on another. These sections will be joined with a shoulder strap that is worked between the two pieces, at right angles to the stitches of the front and back. At the neck edge, cast the number of stitches required for the shoulder strap (5–10%) onto the righthand needle. Knit the first stitch on the left needle, and pass the last cast-on stitch over this stitch. Turn and purl back across to the last shoulder-strap stitch, purling it and the first shoulder stitch off together (purl two together, or P2tog). Turn and knit back to the last shoulder-strap stitch, working these two stitches together with the slip, slip, knit decrease (SSK). One shoulder stitch at the end of each shoulder-strap row (not at both ends of each row) is combined with and removed by the strap stitch. In a textured pattern, work the pattern across all but the first and last stitches; these two stitches must be reserved to join the three sections, ending each knit row with an SSK and each purl row with a P2tog.

To make the shoulder-strap cast-on invisible at the neck edge, cast on and work one row in a waste yarn, preferably a slick cotton or nylon ravel cord, before continuing with the sweater yarn. When you are ready to knit the neck band, remove the waste yarn and pick up the loops, incorporating them into the neck band.

When all of the shoulder stitches have been worked into the edge of the shoulder strap, the sleeve can be worked down to the wristband. The sleeve stitches include the open stitches of the shoulder strap, stitches picked up along the edges of the armhole, and the gusset stitches from the holder.

Plan 9: Sweater with Straight Saddle Shoulders

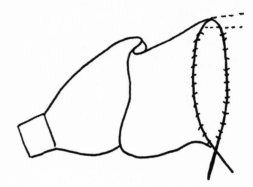

The straight saddle shoulder was used in the earliest Aran fishing shirts (see pages 261–62). Most sources suggest the old garments were seamed, although circular knitting was long established in that part of the world. I prefer to work sweaters of this type in the round, eliminating unnecessary seams. The process is similar to that for Plan 8.

Begin at the hip band and work to the armhole. Divide the work evenly, front and back, with 3 to 5 platform stitches at the underarms to make the turning a bit smoother and more durable. Work the front and back flat to the neck. Then divide each piece into three sections, for the neck and two shoulders.

Knit the sleeves from the wrist up. When you reach the shoulder, work across the stitches designated for the shoulder strap. Then set them aside on a yarn holder.

There are two ways to set the sleeves into the armhole. One involves starting at one shoulder edge, with the right sides of the sleeve and armhole together, and simultaneously binding off the sleeve stitches and

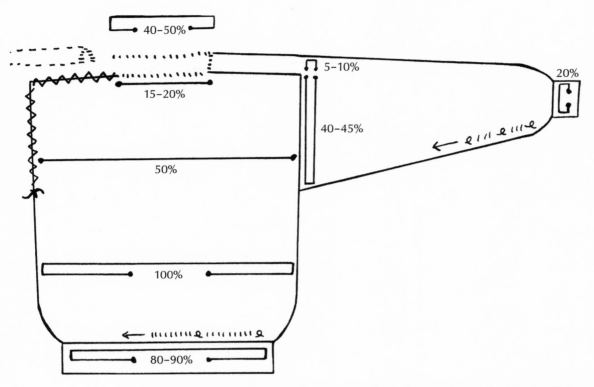

joining them to the sweater body by working the bind-off through the ends of the rows along the armhole edge. I prefer a process that is less bulky, although it is slower: join the sleeve to the armhole stitch by stitch as though grafting. To complete the shoulder strap, put the shoulder-strap stitches and one set of shoulder stitches on one needle, and the other set of shoulder stitches on the other needle. Work back and forth, doing a perpendicular join—with a P2tog or an SSK—at the end of each row, as described for Plan 8. Continue until all of the shoulder stitches have been secured.

Plan 10: Sweater with Shaped Saddle Shoulders

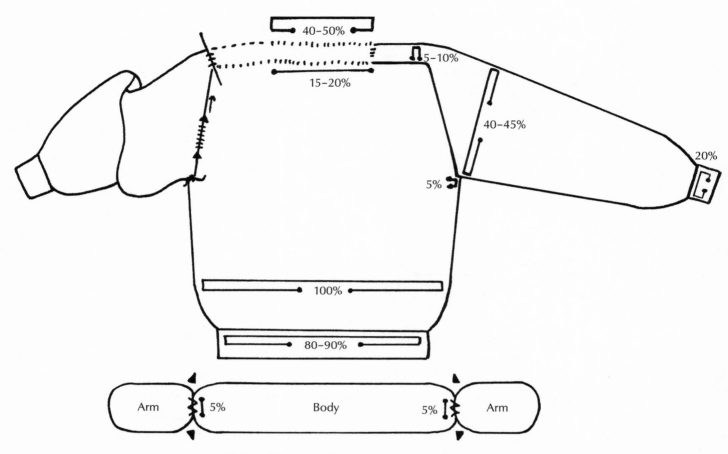

The saddle shoulder can be shaped, to reduce some of the boxiness of the style. This can be especially effective when using heavy or bulky yarns.

Work the sweater from the hip band to the underarm as before (Plans 8 and 9), and remove the underarm stitches to a holder; they will be grafted later. Set aside the sweater body and work the two sleeves from the wrists to the underarms. At each sleeve underarm, reserve stitches on yarn holders for grafting to the body; set aside the same number of stitches on each sleeve as you did on the corresponding body underarm. Now join all three pieces on one large circular needle in this order (as shown in the diagram): first sleeve; body front stitches; second sleeve; body back stitches.

When you knit the first round, knit the edge stitches of the body and sleeve pieces together to reinforce the join. Keep track of the four stitches where this occurs with markers, in the following way. Knit across first set of sleeve stitches to the last stitch; knit that stitch together with the first stitch of the body front and place a marker. Knit across the body front stitches to last stitch; slip a marker onto the needle before that last stitch, and then knit it together with the first stitch of the second sleeve. Knit across the second set of sleeve stitches to the last stitch; knit that stitch together with the first stitch of the body back and place a marker. Knit across the body back stitches to the last stitch; slip a marker onto the needle before that last stitch, and then knit it together with the first stitch of the sleeve that you started with—this becomes the first stitch of the second round. The seam stitches will be at the edges of the sleeve segments, next to the markers.

Work about six or eight rounds even. Begin to work decreases at each seam marker on every sixth to eighth round (the wider spacing between decreases results in a more pronounced shoulder strap). When using light- to medium-weight yarns, I like to use a balanced double decrease: the stitch just before the seam stitch and the seam stitch are slipped together knitwise, the next stitch is knitted, and the two slipped stitches are passed over the knit stitch together. (Also described as *S2tog, K1, P2SSO*.) For bulkier yarns, I suggest pairing a K2tog with an SSK, working one of these single decreases on each side of the seam stitch.

When you've reached the desired armhole depth, place the remaining sleeve stitches on a double-pointed needle, leaving the rest of the stitches on the circular needle. Work a perpendicular join, forming the saddle while joining one loop from the body on each side; see page 97 for an illustration of this technique. Continue to work in this way until you've reached the neck; then repeat the process with the other shoulder.

Plan 11: Sweater with Raglan Sleeves

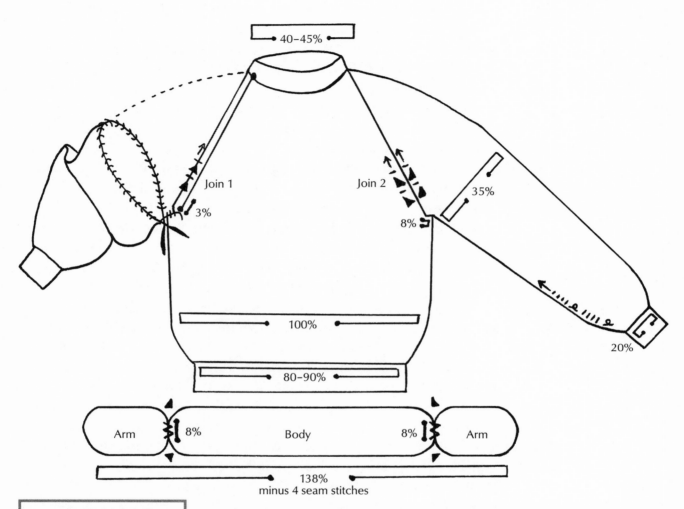

40–45%

Join 1

Join 2

3%

8%

35%

100%

20%

80–90%

Arm 8% Body 8% Arm

138%
minus 4 seam stitches

Construction detail: Raglan joins

Join 1: Single-stitch

Shown on left sleeve/ body join: slip 2 together knitwise, knit 1, pass 2 slipped stitches over.

Join 2: Three-stitch

Shown on right sleeve/ body join: knit 2 together; knit 1 (seam stitch); slip, slip, knit.

The raglan shape, of fairly recent origin, rapidly replaced the saddle-shoulder; this is particularly evident in modern Arans (page 264). To the underarm, the sweater is worked like the shaped saddle shoulder, including the removal of underarm stitches to be grafted and the placement of body and sleeve stitches on a circular needle (pages 100–01).

Work between 1 and 1½ inches even. Then begin to work a paired decrease at each seam on every other round. If the person who will wear the sweater is not "average," see the notes on page 71 about modifying the decrease rate. I prefer the decorative three-stitch join, listed as join 2. Continue decreasing until the sleeve stitches are used up, shaping the neckline as you go (neckline treatments are covered on pages 122–30).

Plan 12: Sweater with Full Yoke

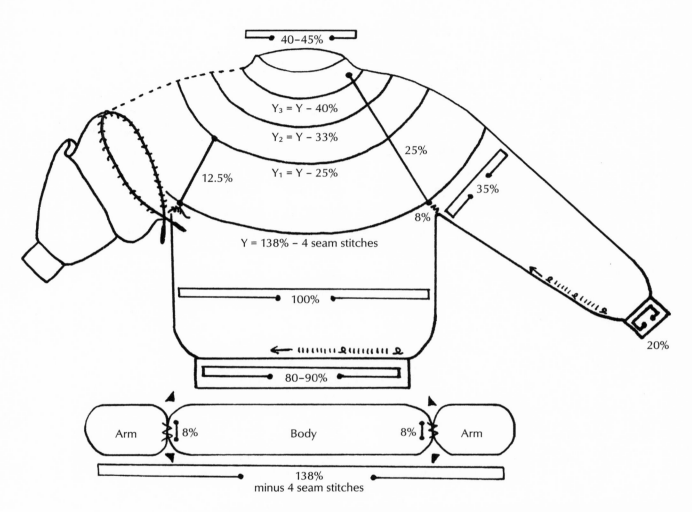

40–45%

$Y_3 = Y - 40\%$

$Y_2 = Y - 33\%$

25%

$Y_1 = Y - 25\%$

12.5%

35%

8%

$Y = 138\% - 4$ seam stitches

100%

20%

80–90%

Arm   8%   Body   8%   Arm

138%
minus 4 seam stitches

Many people believe that the circular yoke sweater, the final traditional shape in this sequence, was developed in the Bohus knitting cooperative in Sweden, circa 1940. In the mid-1950s, circular-yoked sweaters became the rage around the world, when Icelandic knitters utilized roving-type yarns in the natural colors of their native sheep to create bold yoke patterns, reminiscent of the beaded-yoke neckwear of Greenland.

Although the yoke sweater looks complicated, it is easy to work. As with the raglan, the body and sleeves are worked separately to the underarm. Then they are joined on a large circular needle, as described in Plan 10 (pages 100–01): knit together the first and last stitches of adjacent sleeve and body sections and place a marker at each join.

Basic full-yoke construction

To form the upper body and shoulders, you will establish regularly spaced rounds of decreases within the yoke pattern area. Regardless of how you do the decreases, the neck opening should end up at 40–45% of the circumference.

The simplest way to work a shaping sequence is to place three rounds of decreases within the yoke pattern area. For a person of average build, the depth of the yoke (from underarm to neck front) equals about 25% of the body circumference. See page 71 for a discussion of constructing yokes for people who are taller, thinner, shorter, or heavier than "average."

Divide the yoke depth into three sections. The first decrease round (labeled Y1 in the diagram on page 103) occurs halfway to the neck. On this round, you will remove 25% of the stitches by working (K2, K2tog) all the way around. The second decrease round (labeled Y2) occurs when you have worked ⅔ to ¾ of the yoke depth. On this round, eliminate 33% of the remaining stitches with a round of (K1, K2tog). Just before you reach the base of the neck, work the final decrease round (labeled Y3), reducing the stitches by 40% with a round of (K1, K2tog, K2tog). Here's a summary of the three-round decrease sequence:

1. **Decrease by 25%—(K2, K2tog) around**

2. **Decrease by 33%—(K1, K2tog) around**

3. **Decrease by 40%—(K1, K2tog, K2tog) around**

Decreasing this way in concentric circles works for any design that can be divided into three bands. If you're working a continuous pattern, you'll have to adapt the decreases to fit the pattern, although the general locations and rates of decrease remain the same. As one alternative, you could work five decrease rounds, following this sequence:

1. **Decrease by 10%—(K8, K2tog) around**

2. **Decrease by 15%—(K5, K2tog) around**

3. **Decrease by 20%—(K3, K2tog) around**

4. **Decrease by 25%—(K2, K2 tog) around**

5. **Decrease by 33%—(K1, K2tog) around**

To work the decreases into a design, first determine the number of rows required for the entire depth of your yoke pattern. Next, think of the yoke as a cone and divide it into 14 to 20 equal parts around the base. Choose a number that works well with your total number of stitches. As a general rule, there will be fewer sections if you are working with bulky yarn and more sections for fine yarn. For any sweater, there will be a given number of stitches at the base of the cone, and a given number that you're aiming for at the top or neck; the difference between these two numbers indicates the total number of stitches you need to decrease while working the yoke.

Figure out how many stitches per segment you need at the base of the cone and how many you need at the top. As an example, assume that 100% for your sweater is 200 stitches. At the base of the yoke, you will have 138%, or 276 stitches. Subtract 4 seam stitches (276 − 4 = 272). Sixteen equal sections at the base will contain 17 stitches each (272 ÷ 16 = 17). If you plan to have a neckline equal to 40%, or 80 stitches, each of the 16 sections will contain 5 stitches at its top.

On graph paper, mark out the number of stitches at the base of each cone segment, count the number of rows in the yoke, and mark off the number of stitches at the center top of the cone segment. (Any leftover stitches can be removed at the base of the neck ribbing.) Remember that the decreases should occur in the upper half of the yoke. Look at the examples below of how a cone segment might look,

---

Construction detail: Basic full-yoke shaping

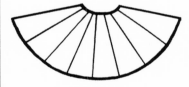

Think of the yoke as a cone, and divide it into 14 to 20 equal parts around the base. This shows a 16-section division, with 8 on the front and 8 on the back.

Figure out how many stitches per segment you need at the base of the cone and how many you need at the top. In these examples, there are 17 stitches at the bottom of each segment and 5 at the top.

✱

Experiment with placing decreases evenly within the upper half of the yoke.

✱

The option at near right uses double decreases. The option at far right uses single decreases, more closely spaced. Match your solution to your pattern.

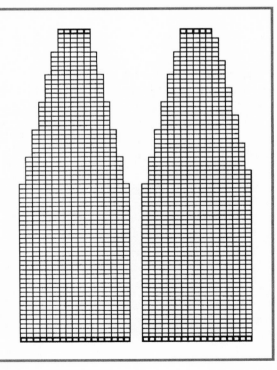

and experiment with placing decreases in the cone segment of your pattern.

Full yoke shaped with short rows

The result of the basic procedure just described is a round yoke, with identical front and back body and neck areas. For better fit, shape the sweater with short rows so that there are more rows around the arms and back of the sweater than in the center front. This lowers the front neckline slightly and produces a more anatomically shaped front yoke and neckline. Your pattern stays the same.

Short rows are worked back and forth in a specific area of a garment. In order to make the short-row insertions inconspicuous, the end points at which you turn and work in the other direction are placed a few stitches apart. The short rows begin and end on the garment front immediately before the start of the yoke patterning. The turns of the short rows are spaced about 5 stitches apart. For heavy or bulky yarns, you will work three sets of turns, and for fine or medium yarns you will work five sets of turns.

To begin, knit across the front, the first sleeve, the back, and the second sleeve. This returns you to the edge of the sweater front. When you intend to use three sets of short rows (for a heavy or bulky yarn), work into the front by 10 stitches. Turn; purl across the second sleeve,

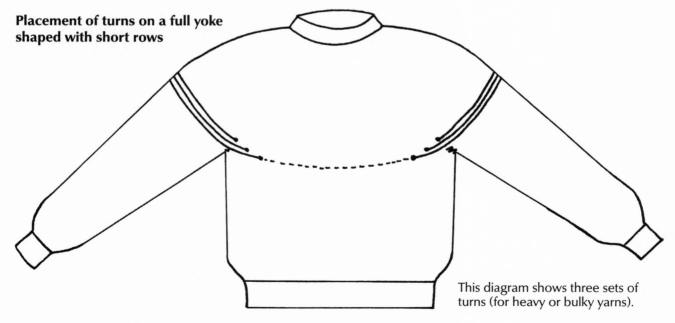

Placement of turns on a full yoke shaped with short rows

This diagram shows three sets of turns (for heavy or bulky yarns).

the back, and the first sleeve to return to the far side of the front. Work into the front at this side by 10 stitches. Reverse again. On the next row, you will work into the front by 5 stitches on each side and on the following row you will reverse at the outside edges of the front section (no stitches).

There are several ways to work short rows. The most common way involves wrapping and slipping the stitch where the reversal occurs, although I prefer an alternate technique I discovered by exploring techniques used by machine-knitters in Japan. A description of working short rows in this way and then returning to work in the round appears on pages 63–64.

Space the turns of your short rows evenly, 5 stitches apart, as shown in the diagram on the opposite page. Work short rows until you have between three and five turns on each side of the front. You will use three short rows for heavy to bulky yarns and five short rows for fine to medium yarns.

Once you have completed as many short rows as necessary to bring the back of the garment to the right height relative to the front, work one round to bring all the short rows into a smooth, continuous round before you begin the yoke design. As you work this round, pay attention to the slip stitches at the turning points and incorporate them in the round with the short-row joins described on page 64. First use the short-row join, knit side facing, for the right side of the short rows. When you have worked across all the turns on the right side, knit across the center front to the left side. Work the short-row join, right side facing, for the left side of the short rows.

Then start the yoke design, beginning at the back edge of one of the sleeves. There will be a jog in the pattern at this point when you complete each round and start the next. Work the sweater yoke design, following the decreasing sequence that you've chosen.

Some people's bodies can be fitted better if more short-row shaping is done in the vicinity of the neckline. These people are more comfortable if the front neckline is deeper and the back neckline is higher than usual. You can do this shaping by eye, or you can calculate the amount. Measure from the top of the shoulder to the desired front neckline depth, adjusting for the width of the neckline band. Convert this measurement to a number of rounds by multiplying the depth by the number of rounds per inch in your gauge. Divide by two for the number of turns at each side.

Short rows will shape your sweater so there are a few more rows on its back. It will fit the body better.

When you have finished the short rows and are ready to return to working in the round, work short-row joins (illustrated on page 64) to obscure the turning points.

Plan 13: Sweater with Shoulder Yoke

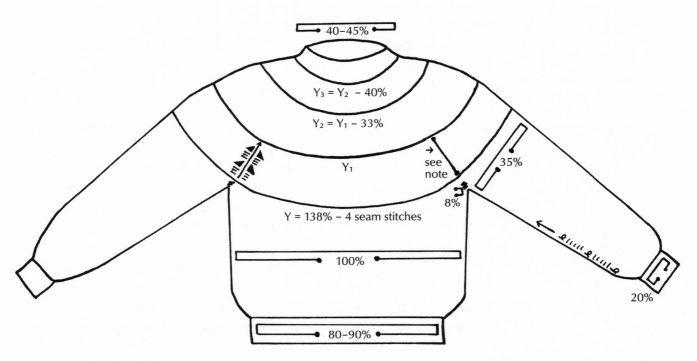

40–45%

$Y_3 = Y_2 - 40\%$

$Y_2 = Y_1 - 33\%$

Y_1

→ see note

35%

8%

$Y = 138\% - 4$ seam stitches

100%

20%

80–90%

Note: Some of the underarm fullness is decreased out during the construction of the first section of the yoke. Work these decreases as described at right until you have completed slightly less than half of the yoke depth. Full yoke depth is 25% of the base circumference measurement, so the half-depth is 12.5%.

To make the decreases unobtrusive, work them as SSK, K1, K2tog.

A shoulder-yoke sweater is shaped the same as a full-yoke sweater, but the patterning doesn't start until halfway up the yoke.

For a smooth fit, you will need to remove some of the underarm fullness. After joining the sleeves and body with K2tog stitches, which are designated as seam stitches, knit three rounds even. Decrease one stitch on each side of the seam stitch. To make this as inconspicuous as possible, work an SSK decrease, knit the seam stitch, then work a K2tog decrease. Paired decreases leaning in toward a center stitch make a relatively subtle seam, because the decreases produce "full-fashion" marks instead of a straight line. Repeat these paired decreases at each seam stitch on every fourth round until you've reached the base of the pattern section or have completed slightly less than half of the yoke depth.

At this point, start working short rows as described in Plan 12, Sweater with Full Yoke (pages 106–07, plus 63–64), using the placement shown on the next page. With the fine yarns typically used to make sweaters with shoulder patterning, you'll need to repeat the short rows five times to bring the back up to the desired height. At the same time, continue decreasing at the seams. When you've finished the short rows, discontinue decreasing at the seams; at this point, you will have reduced the number of stitches by approximately 25%, so only two additional decrease rounds should be necessary.

Using short-row joins (page 64), work one round to bring all the short rows into a smooth, continuous round. Work the yoke design, beginning at the back edge of one of the sleeves. Then work even until you've completed ⅔ to ¾ of the total depth. On the next round, decrease the stitches by 33% with a round of (K1, K2tog). Continue to work even to the base of the neck, then reduce the stitches by 40% with a round of (K1, K2tog, K2tog). The neck is now 40–45% of the base circumference measurement.

The decrease rounds can be worked in any number of ways; don't be afraid to experiment. For a discussion of fitting bodies that are taller, thinner, shorter, or heavier than "average," see page 71. Just remember that the goal is the orderly decreasing of stitches in the upper half of the yoke, with a greater rate of decreasing as you get closer to the neck. You may want to work additional short-row shaping around the neckline (see the discussion with Plan 12, at the bottom of page 107). Regardless of how you work the decreases, the resulting neck opening should be 40–45% of the original 100% circumference.

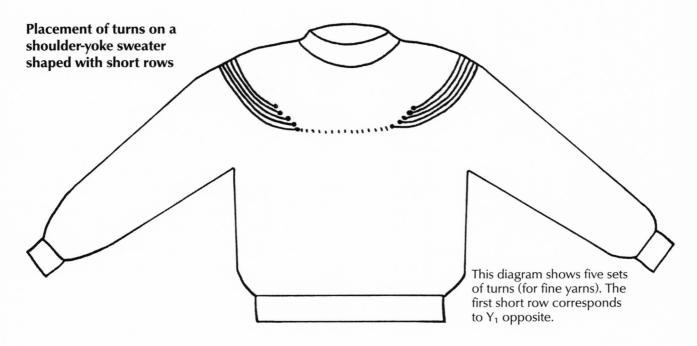

Placement of turns on a shoulder-yoke sweater shaped with short rows

This diagram shows five sets of turns (for fine yarns). The first short row corresponds to Y_1 opposite.

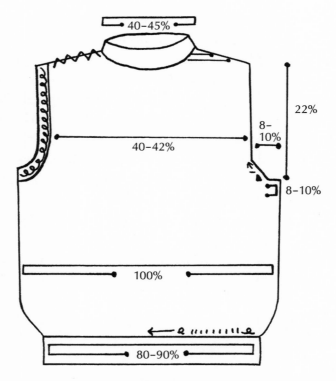

Early in the twentieth century, shaping knitwear more closely to the contours of the body became important. Shoulder seams were slanted, and sleeve caps were shaped to fit. Flat knitting began to replace circular knitting.

Having shaped shoulders and sleeve caps doesn't require that you work each segment separately and then seam all the pieces together. After all, seams are less durable and often more unsightly than the smoothly shaped, continuous surfaces that you can achieve by knitting in the round. The body and sleeves of almost any sweater can be worked in the round up to the underarm. The garment can then be divided into front and back and worked back and forth, with the armhole openings shaped as you go. Or, when a color-stranded design is involved, the openings can be steeked and the garment can be shaped on each side of the steek. The knitter simply adapts the old way of constructing fabric to accommodate shaping.

To make a shaped vest, only minimal adaptation of the old way is necessary. The depth of the armhole and the underarm width are increased slightly, to accommodate a finish for the armhole—ribbing or another type of edge treatment.

Work from the hip band to the underarm, and then bind off the underarm stitches. Continue to work the front and back separately. To form the curve at the base of the armhole, decrease at both ends of every other row. When the curve has been completed, work straight to the shoulder. Slope each shoulder in increments of three to five steps, depending on the weight of the yarn (the heavier the yarn, the fewer the steps). To slope the shoulder, divide the total number of shoulder stitches by the number of steps you need, and work using the following short-row technique.

For this example, assume there are 30 stitches in each shoulder and that you're working the shoulder front and will shape three steps. Beginning at the neck edge, work 20 stitches (⅔ of the stitches), then turn and work back to the neck edge. Turn and work 10 stitches (⅓ of the stitches), then turn and work back to the neck edge. This shoulder shaping is now complete; the first step includes the 10 unworked stitches from the first pass, the second step includes the 10 unworked stitches from the second pass, and the third step includes the final 10 stitches. However, to bring all the stitches into a straight and even line, you'll work an additional row from neck to armhole, joining the yarn behind the turning stitch to the first stitch in the step below.

Place the 30 stitches of the shoulder front on a holder while you work the corresponding shoulder back. Then graft or bind off together the two sets of stitches (shoulder front and back), forming the shoulder seam.

Plan 15: Shaped Sweater

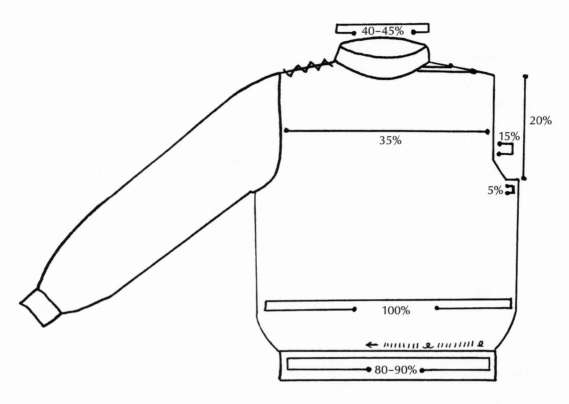

Instructions for figuring decrease rates for sleeves appear on pages 75–76. If you lean each decrease toward the edge of the sleeve, you will produce "full-fashion" marks. If you lean each decrease toward the center of the sleeve, you will have a decrease line.

Adding sleeves to the basic shaped vest requires minor modifications: the depth and width of the armhole need to be reduced, because the sleeve cap provides part of the girth necessary for the upper arm. Except for these adjustments to the armhole, the procedure is the same as for Plan 14, the Shaped Vest.

The sleeves can be worked either from wrist to shoulder or from shoulder to wrist. Both methods are described here, with two variations for the shoulder-to-wrist option.

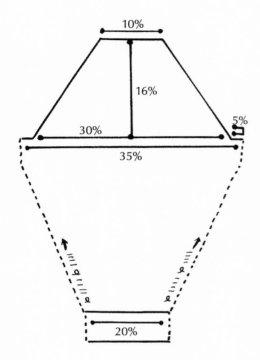

Shaped-cap sleeves

Sleeves worked from wrist to shoulder

Begin at the wrist and knit the sleeves in the round until you reach the underarm. Then bind off the underarm stitches. Work the sleeve cap flat, decreasing as necessary to reach the 10% measurement at the top of the cap, as shown on the diagram at left. Decreases usually occur every other row; make any necessary final adjustments in the rows just before the top of the cap. Bind off the cap, and the only finishing you'll find necessary is to fit the sleeve into the armhole and sew it in place with a back stitch. If there is any excess fullness in the sleeve cap, ease it around the armhole for a smooth fit.

But see also the ideas on the next few pages. Because I will do just about anything to avoid sewing seams, I use the concepts described for the shoulder-to-wrist progression even when I am working from the wrist to the shoulder! (Knitting tricks that work *down* also work *up*.)

Sleeves worked from shoulder to wrist

There are at least two ways in which you can knit the sleeves from the shoulders down. The first, described on the next page, is my favorite. It was devised by Cowichan knitters.

If you are planning to work your sleeves from the shoulder to the wrist, place the underarm stitches on holders instead of binding them off. Complete the body and join the shoulders. Divide the armhole into five sections, beginning from the bottom and marking the sections with pins or other markers. One of these five sections will span, and be divided in half by, the end of the shoulder seam (section 1).

Shaping the cap while picking up stitches

1. Along section 1, pick up stitches to begin the sleeve cap. The number will be about 10% of your master (100%) number, that is, about 20% of the total necessary for the sleeve. Turn.

2. Slip the first stitch and then purl back across these stitches. End the row by picking up 3 or 4 stitches purlwise along the edge of the armhole in the next section; the first of these added stitches must be picked up in the next armhole stitch, immediately at the end of the sleeve cap stitches. If you pass over that very first stitch, a hole will appear at that point as your work continues. Turn.

3. Slip the first stitch and knit across the sleeve-cap stitches, then pick up 3 or 4 stitches knitwise in the next section on the opposite side, again taking care to pick up in the very first stitch of the armhole. Turn.

Alternate steps 2 and 3 until you have picked up stitches along one section on each side of the armhole opening (sections 2 and 3).

4. Count the stitches that you have picked up. Add the number of stitches that are on holders at the underarm. Subtract this total from the total necessary for the sleeve (50% of the master number) and divide by 2. This is the number of stitches you will pick up along the two remaining shaped edges of the armhole (parts of sections 4 and 5).

Shaping the cap while picking up stitches

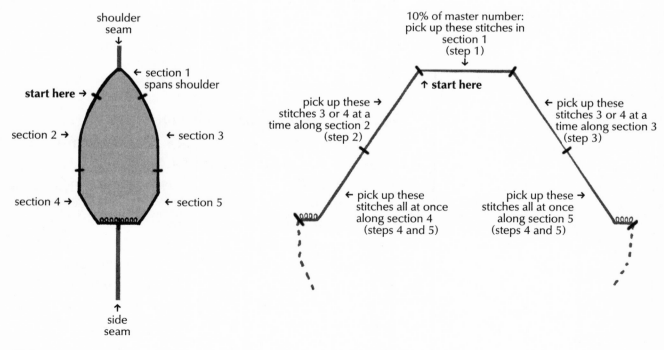

shoulder seam ↓

← section 1 spans shoulder

start here →

section 2 →

← section 3

section 4 →

← section 5

↑ side seam

10% of master number: pick up these stitches in section 1 (step 1) ↓

↑ **start here**

pick up these → stitches 3 or 4 at a time along section 2 (step 2)

← pick up these stitches 3 or 4 at a time along section 3 (step 3)

← pick up these stitches all at once along section 4 (steps 4 and 5)

pick up these → stitches all at once along section 5 (steps 4 and 5)

5. With the knit side facing, pick up the calculated number of stitches in sections 4 and 5, plus the underarm stitches included in those sections. Then begin to work the sleeve in the round.

Shaping the cap with short rows

For the second method, you immediately pick up and knit stitches around the entire armhole. Note that, because of the sequence of operations, sections 2, 3, 4, and 5 are in different positions than in the previous method.

1. With the right side facing, start picking up stitches to the right of the shoulder seam (at the arrow). Pick up about 10% of the master number in each of the five sections. Include the underarm stitches that have been reserved on holders.

2. When you reach the place where you started to pick up, knit to the end of section 1, plus 3 or 4 stitches of section 2. Turn and begin the short-row process, using the technique described on pages 63–64.

3. Purl back across the 3 to 4 stitches of section 2, all of section 1, and 3 to 4 stitches of section 3. Turn for a short row.

4. Continue working back and forth with the short rows, adding 3 to 4 stitches from either section 2 or section 3 each time. When you reach the turning stitch near the end of each pass, work a short-row join (half of these joins will need to be worked from the purl side).

Alternative: If you would like the "designer" look of full-fashioned marks along the upper part of the sleeve cap, work the short rows with wrapped turns, as described on page 65, instead of using the technique on pages 63–64. However, skip the instructions for the completion round. Just knit each stitch as you come to it, without joining the wrap. The unjoined wrap produces the effect of full-fashioned marks.

5. When you reach the ends of sections 2 and 3, begin to work the sleeve in the round.

Completing both shoulder-to-wrist methods

Knit the sleeves in the round, decreasing as usual to shape the sleeve (pages 75–76), until you reach the wrist.

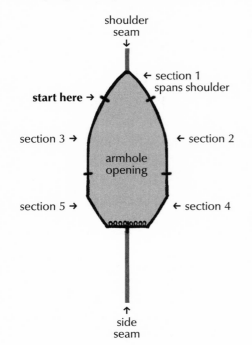

Shaping the cap with short rows

shoulder
seam
↓

← section 1
spans shoulder

start here →

section 3 →

← section 2

armhole
opening

section 5 →

← section 4

↑
side
seam

Chapter

8

Style Alternatives

Any of the preceding plans can be worked as a pullover, as shown in the drawings, or with a buttoned front opening, as a cardigan or buttoned vest. Aspects of different plans can be combined, and you can choose from any number of necklines and collar variations.

Cardigan variations

Here's the basic plan for a cardigan. The armhole measurements are adjusted to accommodate a sleeve. At the hip band (80–90% as usual), the underlap is added only on one side.

A cardigan, or knitted jacket, is a sweater with an opening down the front. This styling alternative can be combined with any of the construction plans described in Chapter 7, and you can produce cardigan openings and edge finishes in a number of ways.

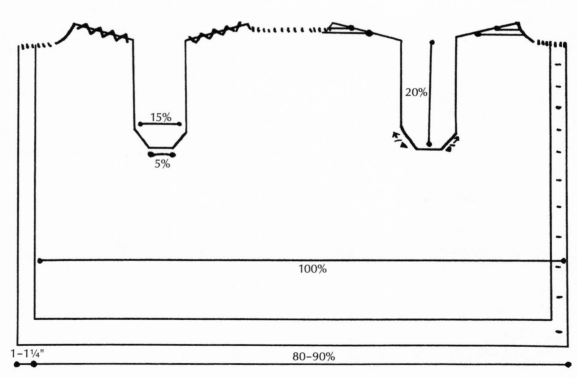

15%

5%

20%

100%

1–1¼"

80–90%

Begin a cardigan of any type by knitting the **hip band** flat; the number of stitches you cast on for the hip band will depend on whether you intend to work the front bands as extensions of the hip band.

You can work the **body** either in the round or flat. To work in the round, knit the hip band and then close the center front with a steek, increase to 100% for the body, and continue in the round. This is the best choice for color-stranded garments; when you finish the body, secure the steek and slash the front opening as preparation for finishing the front edges. If you continue knitting flat and are using a color-stranded pattern, work a locked turning stitch at each edge of the fabric (see page 91).

Option 1: Front bands formed as extensions of the hip band

If the front bands will be formed as extensions of the hip band, begin by casting on enough stitches for the hip band and the overlap/underlap of the front bands (the overlap/underlap equals the width of one band,

Cardigan option 1: Front bands formed as extensions of the hip band

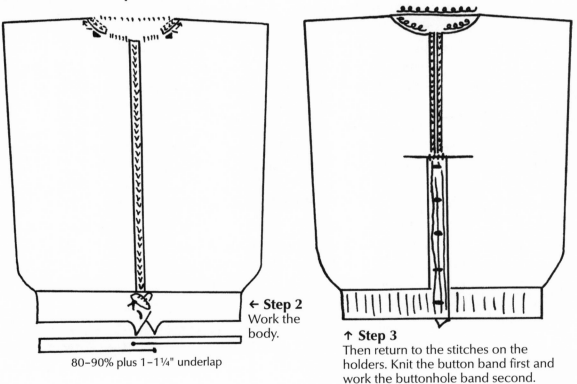

80–90% plus 1–1¼" underlap

← **Step 2**
Work the body.

↑ **Step 3**
Then return to the stitches on the holders. Knit the button band first and work the buttonhole band second.

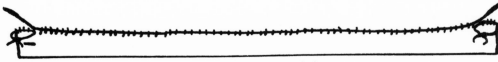

80–90% plus 1–1¼" underlap

← **Step 1**
The front-band stitches go on holders until the body has been completed.

or between 1 and 1¼ inches' worth of stitches for an average adult garment). Knit the hip band to the desired depth and work any necessary buttonholes in the portion of the hip-band stitches allocated for the front band.

When you have completed the hip band, put the front-band stitches on holders; you will complete the front band after the body is finished. You will put stitches at both ends of the hip band on holders: in this example, 1¼ inches' worth of stitches at each end for a finished, overlapped band 1¼ inches wide.

After you have knitted the body, return to the stitches on the holders. From each base set of band stitches, knit a strip up to the neck that is slightly shorter than the garment itself. You can knit these strips as separate pieces and hand-sew them to the edges of the body, stretching each band slightly as you attach it. Or you can attach each strip to the body as you make it, using a perpendicular join (page 97). In this case, knit through the folded edge of the body steek on two out of every three rows and form the join with an SSK on the right side and a P2tog on the left side.

To determine the proper locations for the buttonholes, first work the front band that will hold the buttons. Stitch that band into place, then

measure to divide the space for the buttons. Determine how many rows occur between the buttons and use that number to space the buttonholes on the other front band.

After both sides of the front band are in place, pick up stitches around the neck opening and finish the neck band.

Option 2: Front-edge and neckline finishes worked all at once

Another way to make the front bands is to work them simultaneously with the neckline finish after the body has been completed. To set this up, knit the hip band flat on a number of stitches that has been *reduced* by the number of stitches in one band.

Steek or knit flat for the body. After the body has been finished, use a circular needle to pick up stitches along the edge of the body or through the folded edge of the steek as follows: up one side of the cardigan opening, around the neckline, and down the other side of the cardigan opening. Work back and forth, and form buttonholes on one of the front bands when half the front-band depth has been completed.

Cardigan option 2:
Front-edge and neckline finishes
worked all at once

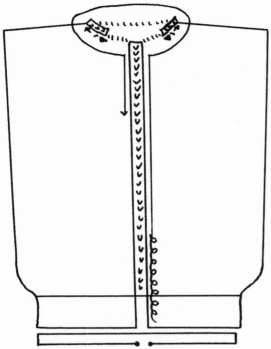

80–90% minus 1–1¼" underlap/overlap

↑ Step 2
Work the body, then pick up stitches along both front edges and around the neckline.

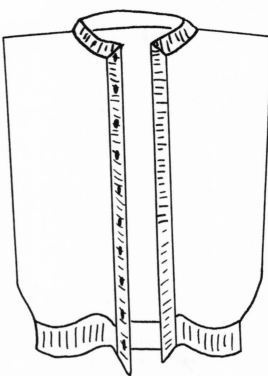

↑ Step 3
Knit around the entire front/neck opening, cornering as shown here if you are working a round neckline (see technique drawing on previous page).

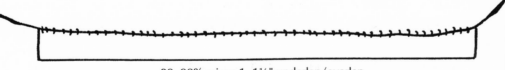

80–90% minus 1–1¼" underlap/overlap

← Step 1
The number of hip-band stitches is decreased by the amount of one underlap/overlap.

On a round-necked cardigan, shape each corner where a front band meets the neck band by working an increase on each side of a center stitch.

This method is ideal for a V-necked cardigan. Yet you can apply it to a round-necked cardigan by shaping each of the two corners where the front bands meet the neck band. To corner, work an increase on each side of a center stitch on every other row while maintaining your pattern.

119

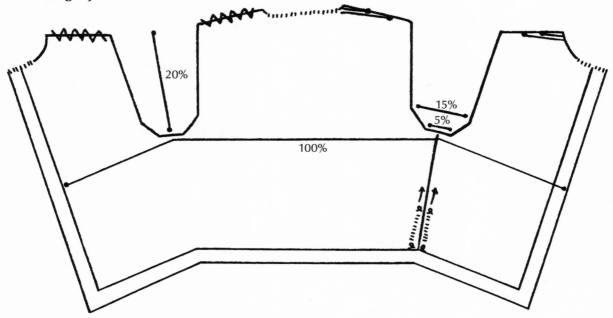

Shaping plan for a fitted, waist-length jacket

20%

15%

5%

100%

Fitted jackets

Textured "jackets" of other nations are often waist-length and snugly fitted. A series of increases, placed on either side of the underarm seamline, produces the increase in garment circumference between waist and bust.

Other edge treatments

Many other edge treatments can be used instead of knitted front bands. The cut edges of a steek can be bound with woven fabric. Or you can crochet an effective finish, working through the edge of the folded steek.

Woven fabric or crochet

Many knitters like a tubular-cord edging (often referred to as "idiot cord" or I-cord), which is easy to work and very attractive. Although not a traditional technique, the tubular cord is a nice finish for folk designs.

Tubular-cord edging (I-cord)

However, I-cord alone will not control the tendency of stockinette fabrics to roll forward at their edges. The tendency to roll forward can be reduced if you place a vertical column of purl stitches at each edge of the steek to serve as the fold line. (Standard steeks, as described on page 87, tend to fold neatly in any case. The addition of a vertical purl column is only advantageous when you plan to finish with I-cord.)

To make the tubular-cord edging, cast 3 stitches onto a double-pointed needle (short needles are good for this). With the right sides of both I-cord and garment fabric facing you, use a second double-pointed needle to pick up a stitch through the garment edge or through the foldline of the steek; pass the third cast-on stitch over this stitch. Do not turn the work—instead, slide the 3 stitches to the other end of the needle, pull the working yarn snugly (but not tightly) behind the 3 stitches, and begin the next row by knitting the first cast-on stitch.

Henceforth, each row is worked in the same way, by sliding the stitches along the holding needle and beginning from the same end: (K2, S1, pick up 1 stitch through the garment edge, PSSO; slide stitches to other end of needle). All the rows are worked without turning, and a knitted tube forms along the edge of the fabric. If you feel the need for a larger cording, you can use 4 stitches, taking care to pull the yarn snugly between the last and first stitches of the tube.

There are a couple of ways to incorporate buttonholes. The easiest of these places the buttonholes between the tubular cord and the body fabric. For each buttonhole of this type, work several rows (enough to accommodate your button) without attaching the cord to the garment: just knit the 3 stitches and slide them to the other end of the needle, without picking up a stitch through the body or slipping a stitch over.

Alternatively, you can work two or three tubular-cord edgings attached to each other. The buttonholes will be formed between the cords. Knit the first cord as usual. To construct each subsequent cord, pick up stitches through the edge of the previous cord. Because you will "cover" 1 stitch of each I-cord while knitting its neighbor, I recommend using 5 stitches for all but the last cord, which can be made of 3 or 4 stitches. Form the buttonholes between two adjacent cords by working series of unattached rows at each button location.

To turn a corner with your edging, work one row unattached on each side of an attached row at the point of the corner.

Including buttonholes and turning corners with tubular-cord edgings

Neckline variations

So far we have not covered neck treatments, though the neckline must be shaped along with the upper garment. The necklines described here can be used with any of the sweater types. After you've decided on a sweater to knit, choose a neckline and superimpose it onto the sweater, working its shaping simultaneously with the upper body. You can divide your work and knit flat when you do the neckline shaping, or you can steek the neckline to maintain your circular progress.

Crewnecks
On a straight neckline

Among the earliest neck finishes was a crewneck banding set on a straight neckline opening. This may not be a particularly comfortable finish—if the banding extends for more than a few rows, the band rubs on the bottom of your chin.

A more comfortable variation involves a rectangular neckline opening, formed when a shoulder strap of some sort is added to give the neckline depth. The neck opening has squared corners; these corners are pulled into a more rounded shape when the ribbing band is added. Although much traditional knitting was worked circularly, this ribbing band was traditionally an exception. By working it flat, the knitter could produce a finished opening that would be closed with a buttoned underlap. When the buttons are released, the opening as a whole becomes larger and fits easily over the head.

On a shaped neckline opening

Today, a crewneck on a shaped opening is usually preferred to a straight neckline. The shaping allows the front of the neckline to be

Crewneck variations on a straight neckline with a rectangular opening

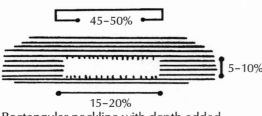

Rectangular neckline with depth added at shoulderline.

Plain circular finish.

Flat-worked finish, with underlap and button closure.

122

lower and more comfortable. This type of neck finish can be worked in many variations. Here are some possibilities:

❧ Pick up stitches around the shaped neckline, work ribbing to the desired depth, and bind off or graft off.

❧ Work ribbing to double the desired depth, fold the band in half to the inside, and work the neck-ribbing stitches off one by one (as when grafting) with the stitches at the base of the neckline. This eliminates bound-off stitches. When the final, joining row is worked loosely, this neck treatment is more durable than the single-layer version.

❧ Extend the length of a crewneck band even more and fold it into a turtleneck; the depth to knit depends on how high you want the turtleneck to extend.

❧ Widen the flat crewneck opening so it can accommodate a shirt collar nicely.

Variations on shaped crewneck openings

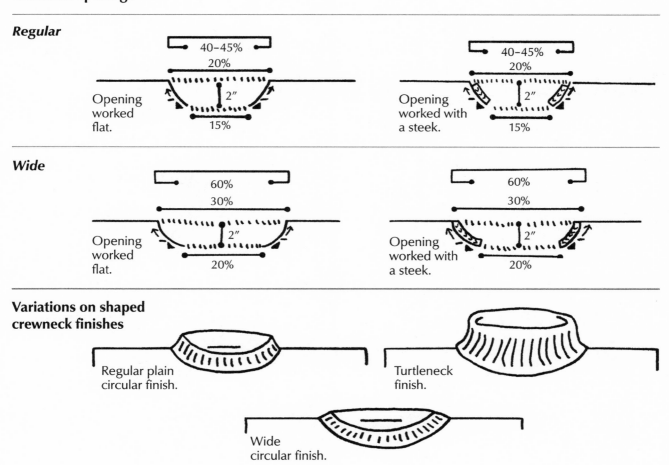

Regular

40–45%
20%
Opening worked flat. 2″
15%

40–45%
20%
Opening worked with a steek. 2″
15%

Wide

60%
30%
Opening worked flat. 2″
20%

60%
30%
Opening worked with a steek. 2″
20%

Variations on shaped crewneck finishes

Regular plain circular finish.

Turtleneck finish.

Wide circular finish.

V-neck finishes

The V-shaped neckline first became popular on early golfing sweaters, then later on vests. When you reach the point of the V, divide the front stitches in half and begin to shape the opening. Either steek the opening or work flat on the two front sections. The width of the front opening equals that of the back neckline, or 20% of C, and the number of stitches in the back and front shoulders will match. I like to reserve the center stitch or stitches at the bottom of the V (center front) on a holder, to retrieve later. If you are working with an odd number of stitches in the front body, set aside 1 stitch. For an even number, set aside 2 stitches.

The angle of the V neckline can vary and is determined by how often you decrease on each side of the opening. The more closely the decreases are spaced, the wider the point of the V will be. The farther apart they are, the narrower the point of the V. The precise sequence will depend on the depth of your neckline and the ratio of stitches to rows in your gauge. For a typical (basic) V neckline that is about as deep as your armholes, decrease 1 stitch on each side of the neck opening on every third or fourth round (or row) until you have removed the same number of stitches as are in the back neckline (this works out to 10% of C on each

Basic V necklines

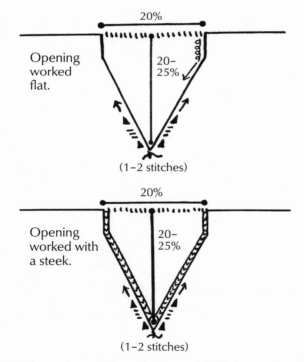

To shape the neckline opening, work decreases on about every third or fourth round: decrease on one round; work two or three rounds even; repeat.

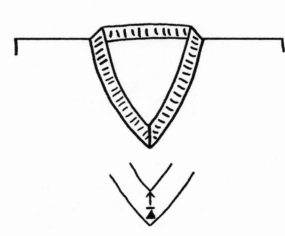

Ribbing

At the point of the V, work a double decrease in the ribbing on every other round.

124

Wide V necklines

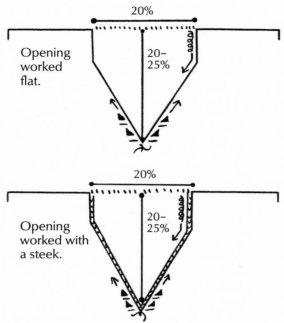

Opening worked flat.

20%

20–25%

Opening worked with a steek.

20%

20–25%

For a wider neckline opening, work decreases on about every second or third round. Reserve 1–2 stitches at point of V, as on the basic V neckline.

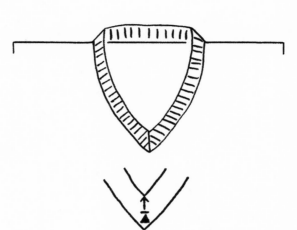

Ribbing

At the point of the V, work a double decrease in the ribbing on every other round (the same as the basic V).

Narrow V necklines

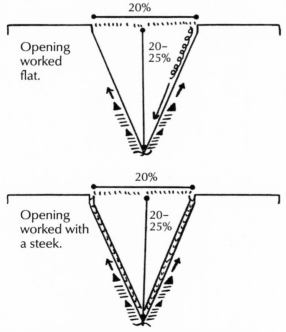

Opening worked flat.

20%

20–25%

Opening worked with a steek.

20%

20–25%

For a steeper neckline opening, work decreases on about every fourth or fifth round. Reserve 1–2 stitches at point of V, as on the basic V neckline.

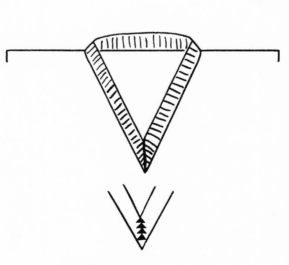

Ribbing

At the point of the V, work a double decrease in the ribbing on every round.

side of the neck opening). Then work the sides of the neckline even until you reach the shoulder. If you want a wider point on your V, decrease at the neck edge on every second or third round (or row). Again, you will work a section straight to the shoulder; it will be a longer section than for the basic V. For a narrow point and a steeply angled neckline, decrease at the neck edge every fourth or fifth round (or row). You will have a very short straight section, or none at all, at the top of the neck opening.

Complete the neck opening and join the shoulders. Then pick up stitches around the neck opening on a circular needle to work the neckband. Begin at a shoulder: cross the back; go down one side of the V (4 stitches for every 5 rows); take the reserved center stitch(es) from the holder; then go along the second side of the V.

Work the ribbing in the round, decreasing at the point of the V. Typically, you will decrease one stitch on each side of the center-front stitch(es) on every other round. For a sharply defined point (as on a narrow V), try a double decrease on every round. You might need to experiment to find the decrease ratio that produces the neatest results.

Shawl collars

A shawl collar can be inserted into a V-shaped neck opening. The collar can be either deep or shallow, and the choice is determined by the way you start and then by the sequence in which you pick up stitches

The Cowichan knitters of Canada have developed ingenious alternative methods of constructing shawl collars. One of these is described on pages 186–87.

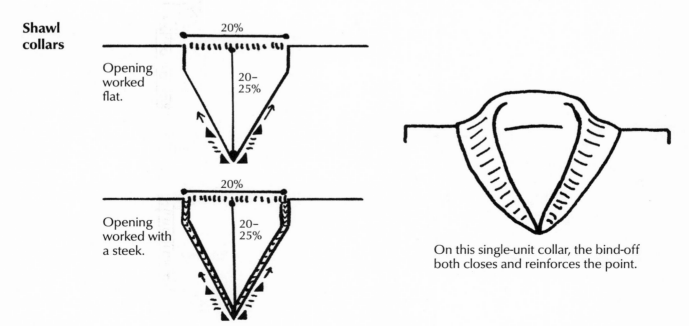

Shawl collars

Opening worked flat.

20%

20–25%

Opening worked with a steek.

20%

20–25%

On this single-unit collar, the bind-off both closes and reinforces the point.

126

along the edges of the V. Note that if the collar is to lie flat, you will need to increase several stitches at each shoulder. Read through the description so you have an idea of the shaping technique; then you will find it easy to make this adjustment on the needles. For both versions described here, work the collar back and forth on a circular needle.

For a deep shawl collar, place the back neckline stitches on a circular needle. Work across them in ribbing or garter stitch.

For a shallow shawl collar, begin picking up stitches partway down one side of the V neckline, work across the back neckline stitches, then pick up stitches along the second side of the V neckline until you reach a position opposite where you began on the first side.

For both types, now turn and work across all stitches. At each end of each row, pick up and knit 1 or more stitches through the fabric at the edge of the V shaping; you will work your way down to the point on each side, matching the rate at which you pick up stitches on both sides. By adding 1 stitch at each side, you increase the depth of the collar; by adding several stitches at each side, you reduce depth.

When you reach the point, bind off around the entire collar.

Button-neck closures

This short, open-neckline finish is often called a Henley neckline. Work the body as for a pullover until you reach the point where you

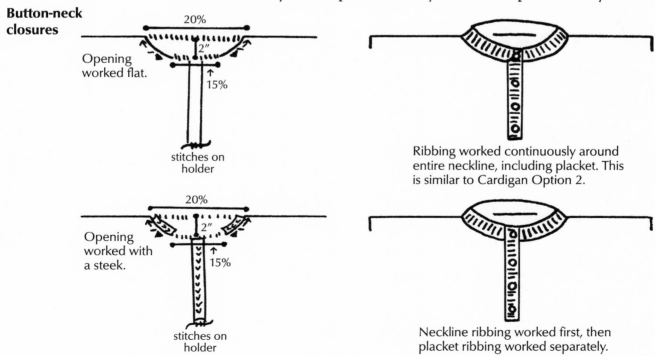

Button-neck closures

Opening worked flat.

20%

2"

15%

stitches on holder

Ribbing worked continuously around entire neckline, including placket. This is similar to Cardigan Option 2.

Opening worked with a steek.

20%

2"

15%

stitches on holder

Neckline ribbing worked first, then placket ribbing worked separately.

127

want the base of the neck opening to begin. This opening is worked in the same manner as a regular cardigan opening, divided or steeked. When you work the bands, remember to work buttonholes in the section that will be on top in the finished garment.

You can pick up the band and work around in one continuous piece: begin at the base of the slit opening, go up around the neckline, then down again to the base of the opening. As you work the band, you will need to shape the two corners where it turns from the front edges to the neckline. Do this with paired increases on every other row.

Or you can begin by working the band around the neck back and forth to the desired depth, then pick up stitches along the edges of the opening on the body plus the edges of the neck band.

No matter which finishing technique you use, there will be a series of stitches at the square base. I join the top overlap to these open stitches with a perpendicular join (see page 97). Then I secure the bottom overlap by grafting or seaming it to the heads of the stitches I joined to the first overlap.

Boat necklines

The early, traditional boat neckline was a wide, straight opening, finished off with a short garter-stitch band worked in the round on the front and back. The contemporary boat neckline is also a flat opening, but it is usually finished with a turned-under facing.

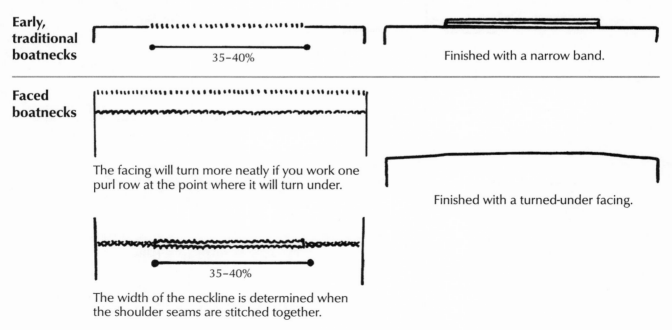

Early, traditional boatnecks

35–40%

Finished with a narrow band.

Faced boatnecks

The facing will turn more neatly if you work one purl row at the point where it will turn under.

Finished with a turned-under facing.

35–40%

The width of the neckline is determined when the shoulder seams are stitched together.

Work the sweater up to the shoulder, then work one purl row so that the fabric will turn neatly when you are finished, and keep knitting to make the facing. If you've worked in the round with an armhole steek, bind off the stitches of the steek as you start the purl row. Then work the facing flat. To reduce the bulk of the facing, I like to knit it on needles smaller than those I am using for the body.

When the facing is about 1 inch deep, turn it under and secure each of its stitches to the sweater body. If you secure the stitches with a half-graft, you will avoid the bulk of a bound-off edge that would make a ridge on the sweater. (A half-graft uses the technique on page 62 to join a set of open stitches to a set of secured stitches.)

After you have turned under and stitched the facings, turn the garment inside out and sew the shoulder seams in as far as you would like. The stitch for this seam resembles a cross stitch, an open herringbone stitch, or a tailor's hem stitch. On the reverse, back-stitch around the side of a purl stitch on one fabric edge and then back-stitch the same way around the corresponding stitch on the adjoining side. Progress this way across the shoulder, joining matching purl stitches from the foldline. The sewn stitches should be on the inside of the fabric, with only a bar joining purl stitch to purl stitch on the right side.

Square necklines

Begin a square neckline by placing groups of stitches at the center front and center back on holders as you work the body. The number of stitches is normally the same for both pieces, although the front neckline is usually deeper than the back neckline. The number of stitches must also be the width of your finished neckline plus the width of the ribbing on each side. For a finished neckline width of 6 inches trimmed with a 1-inch ribbing, set aside 8 inches' worth of stitches on the front and on

Square necklines

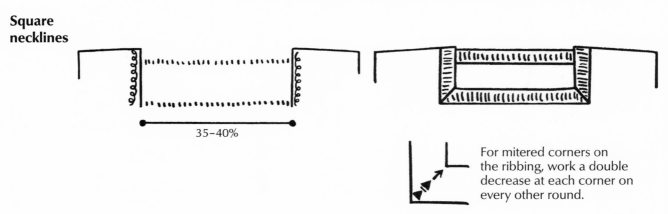

35–40%

For mitered corners on the ribbing, work a double decrease at each corner on every other round.

the back (4 inches on each side of the center line). The stitches on the front will often be reserved at a depth of 2 to 4 inches; those on the back will be at a depth of ½ to 1 inch. After reserving these stitches, work the remaining stitches of the front and back straight to the shoulderline.

After joining the shoulders, work a band around the neck edge, using the reserved front and back stitches along with stitches that you pick up along the vertical edges of the neckline opening (about 2 stitches for every 3 rows). For mitered corners, work a double decrease at each corner on every other round.

Scoop necklines

A scoop neckline is based on the square neckline, but has a curve in each corner. A portion of the neckline stitches is removed to the holder at the depth of the neckline. The remaining number of stitches required to reach the full neckline width is decreased out on subsequent rows. You can make a sharp curve at the corners by decreasing on every row, or a shallower curve by decreasing on every other row.

Variations

These are only the basic neckline styles for sweaters, intended as a starting point for your ideas. For example, instead of leaving the back neckline straight, I like to add a shallow scoop that helps the neckband of my choice follow the contours of the neck and shoulders. Experiment, combine techniques, and vary the shapings until you find the styles you like best—your imagination is your only limitation.

**Scoop
necklines**

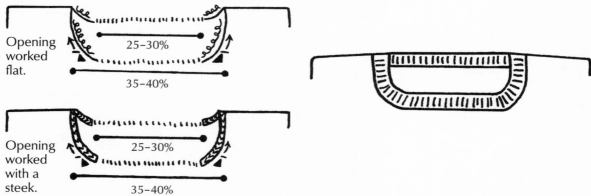

Opening worked flat.
25–30%
35–40%

Opening worked with a steek.
25–30%
35–40%

Color Stranding

Many color patterns in knitting are produced through color stranding, which involves working with two or more colors at a time. The color or colors not in use lie loosely on the back of the fabric. Color stranding dates back to the earliest known samples of knitting. It is often referred to as *Fair Isle* knitting, although Fair Isle is only one type of color stranding.

Color stranding is most easily worked in the round. Intricate patterns can be devised that require no more than two colors in any row. This self-imposed design limitation makes the work proceed quickly, although some knitters with good yarn-handling skills work patterns with three or more active colors.

To produce smooth color-stranded work, you need to become adept at controlling the tension of the strands that run across the back of the fabric. There are many ways to accomplish this, several of which will be described here. Become familiar enough with the technical possibilities that you can always work comfortably and produce high-quality results.

In some parts of the world, knitters carry the yarn in the Continental style, with both yarns tensioned around the left forefinger. Should one of the color floats need to be secured on the back of the fabric, just snake the needle tip around the float to bring the working color into position across the floating yarn.

In other locales, the yarns are both carried in the right hand, in the English manner, with one on each side of the forefinger. With the yarns in this position, the yarn on top of the finger is lifted to knit while the yarn on the underside of the finger is scooped up to knit. To secure a float, the positions of the two yarns are reversed. If the yarns are reversed alternately, top-to-bottom and then bottom-to-top, the two yarns do not become twisted.

Most knitters find the simplest way to work color stranding is to use both hands for carrying yarn—for example, one color in the right hand

Handling several colors

and the other in the left. This technique is believed to have evolved among the Færoese. It's especially useful for working three colors simultaneously, holding two colors in one hand and one in the other.

Developing the skill to manage colors with both hands is worth the effort. Ultimately you want to be able to handle the yarn fluidly with either hand. As you begin to learn these skills, though, you may find it helpful to carry the color that is used most often in your dominant hand and the less-used color in your non-dominant hand; this can also simplify work on designs that have long carries. Practice working several rows of alternate stitches in two colors. When this becomes easy, space the color changes farther apart. Beginners often pull the strand on the back of the fabric too tightly, which causes the fabric to buckle. The yarn not in use must be carried so that it lies smoothly across the back of the fabric, but not so loosely that it sags.

Securing floats

Designs are easiest to work when the color changes occur within a few stitches of each other. If your design requires you to carry the yarn over more than an inch, you will need to secure each float to the back of the fabric about every half inch so it won't snag in use. This is easy if you're carrying colors in both hands. If, for example, the most frequently used color (usually the background) is in your right hand, you need only lift the left yarn up *above the right yarn* and knit the next couple of stitches with the right-hand yarn. Then lower the left yarn to catch it a second time. To avoid color peeking through to the front, try not to catch the yarn behind just a single stitch, because the secured yarn will push that stitch forward and the color may show through on the front. Keep the yarn that floats across the back looser than you think is reasonable, and twist the yarns at staggered locations from one row to the next.

When it becomes necessary to secure a float in the main-color yarn held in my right hand, I usually use the *wrap, wrap, unwrap* technique. After entering the stitch, *wrap* the floating right yarn around the needle tip; *wrap* the left yarn (the color used in the new stitch now being worked) around the needle tip; *unwrap* the floating yarn to take it back into position before drawing the new stitch (with the left-hand yarn) through the loop of the previous round. When feasible, I repeat this maneuver a second time to limit the possibility that the float yarn will peek through.

Managing five colors at once

With practice, you can learn to carry four colors with relative ease—two in each hand. When I need a fifth color, I let that color hang free, manipulating it with my right second finger as necessary. I seldom work

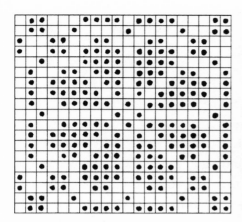

Standard graph paper

Note that the design appears symmetrical. However, knitted stitches are wider than they are tall.

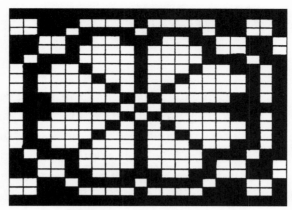

Knitter's graph paper

The same design appears less symmetrical than the version on regular graph paper. This representation is closer to what the knitted fabric will look like.

Standard and knitter's graph paper

with more than three colors any more, two in my right hand, one in my left hand. With three colors, I can outline and highlight a design, which is sufficient for my needs.

Always work out your designs on graph paper; *never* try to work from written row-by-row instructions. You'll also find your designs easier to follow if the graph is colored to match your yarns, not charted in symbols. You can often photocopy a chart and then color over the symbols. Because the standard graph-paper grid is square and knitted stitches are not, many knitters prefer to work on "knitter's graph paper," which is often based on proportions of five stitches to seven rows. When working your pattern, place your chart on a magnetic row-marker (page 40).

Steeks, and knitting in reverse

Let me repeat that color-stranded patterns are much easier to work in the round, instead of back-and-forth. You'll need to use a steek or some other technique to bridge the openings. If you decide to work flat to avoid cutting, you will need to use a locked turning stitch at your selvedges to secure every color that's been used in the row (see page 91). If steeking is not an option, I highly recommend learning to knit in reverse instead of turning the work and purling (see page 200). This way the front side of the fabric always faces you and you can easily watch your pattern.

Norway

During the nineteenth century, beautiful color-stranded sweaters and Norwegian knitting became synonymous. Color-stranded designs were first worked in mittens, then quickly adapted to Norwegian sweaters. In a land of long, dark winters, color stranding doubled the fabric thickness, giving warmth at the same time that it vividly enriched garments with color and pattern. Early sweaters were knitted from woolen or worsted handspun yarns, firmly spun for durability. Woolen sweaters offered greater potential for felting than worsted ones, and felting was a common practice in some areas. The yarns were usually firmly tensioned during knitting, producing a surface like richly embroidered fabric.

As millspun yarns became available, many Norwegian sweaters were made of fine two-ply worsted yarns. The sweaters were knitted in the round, then the armholes were stitched and slashed and the sleeves were worked from the shoulders down. Norwegian knitters today still work in the round and cut their work, but now they typically work each sleeve from the cuff to the shoulder and set it in, using a short facing to cover the cut edge. Today, many recognize the boat neck as representative of Norwegian sweaters.

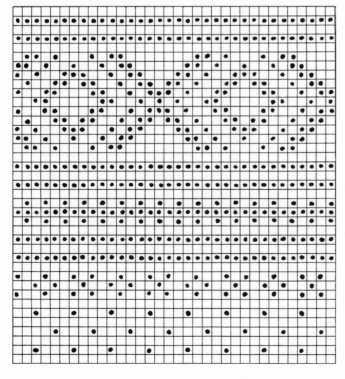

Lusekofte 1

Patterns for upper body.

← This simple repeat of alternating dots is the "lice" patterning used as a background in the body of the sweater and on the sleeves.

134

Lusekofte 1

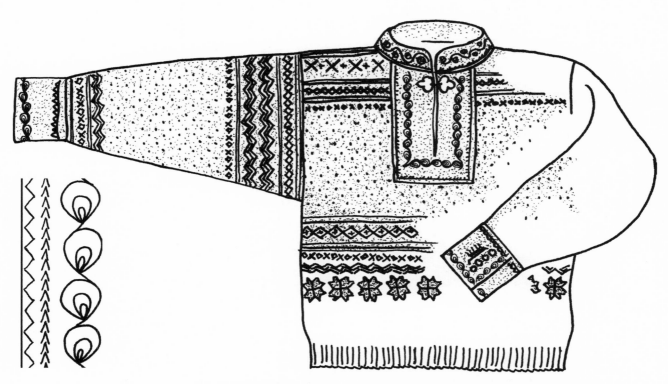

Embroidery pattern for neckline and cuffs. The main elements were typically worked in satin stitch (parallel stitches worked closely together so they cover the fabric surface and produce clear, smooth areas of color).

Patterns for Lusekofte 1 are on pages 134, 135, and 136. The structure shown above follows Plan 6 (pages 92–93).

The lusekofte is the most easily recognizable Norwegian sweater. A classic man's garment, it originated about 1840 in the Setesdal valley and came to worldwide attention as the national ski sweater at the Olympic games of the 1930s. *Lusekofte* means *lice jacket,* referring to the speckled ground pattern. (This same spotted pattern was referred to as *fleas* in Iceland—in both cases, possibly a reminder of bygone days!)

A typical lusekofte began with a lower section in white, which was covered by the high-waisted trousers of the era. Above this, a wide band of black stars or flowers was color-stranded across the white ground. Then the ground color changed to black, crossed by several narrow bands of white geometric designs. The central black ground was decorated with the white flecks, or "lice," and the shoulder areas contained elaborate bands of small geometric designs. Similar bands of pattern were worked at the upper and lower parts of the sleeves, with "lice" in between. The dramatic garment was finished at the cuffs and the neckline with woven and felted black fabric, often heavily embroidered in brilliant colors, and closed along the front opening with pewter clasps.

135

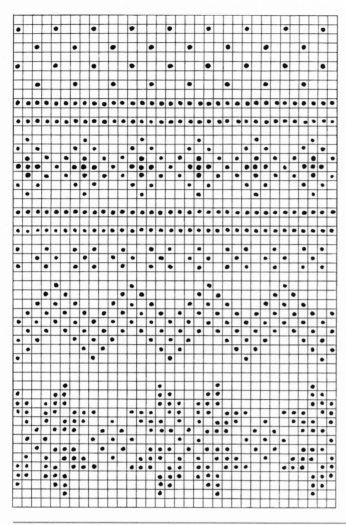

Lusekofte 1

← Patterns for lower body.

The sleeve patterning consists of elements from the upper and lower parts of the sweater body: small bands, lines, and larger zigzags.

Lusekofte 2

The specific sizes for the embroidered elements on a *lusekofte* depend on the sweater you plan to make. These drawings are about half-size for an average adult; photocopy at 200% to return them to their original dimensions, then adjust to meet your needs.

Embroidery patterns for front neckline (→), cuff (↓), and collar (↓↓).

Center back
(place on fold
of fabric)
↓

Work satin stitch within the outlined areas. Experiment with the effects of color and stitch direction.

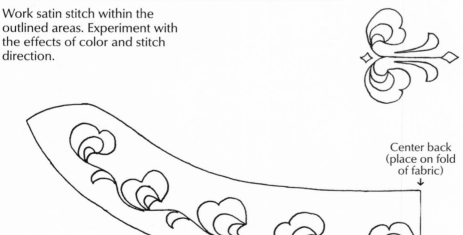

Lusekofte 2

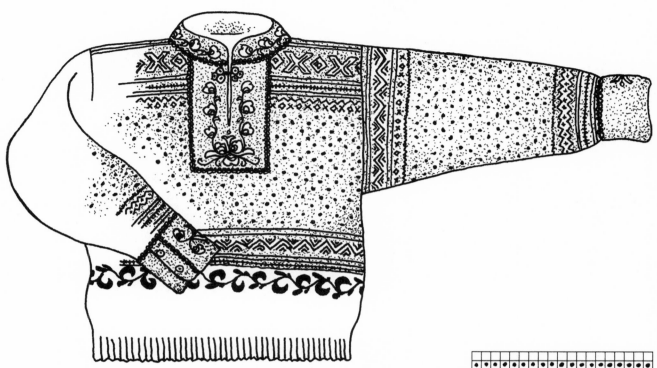

Lusekofte 2

This is a modern interpretation of the traditional lusekofte.

→ Patterns for lower sleeve.

→→ Patterns for upper sleeve.

Patterns for Lusekofte 2 are on pages 136, 137, and 138. The structure shown above follows Plan 6 (pages 92–93).

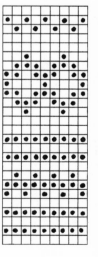

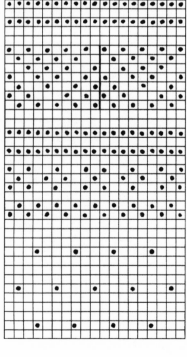

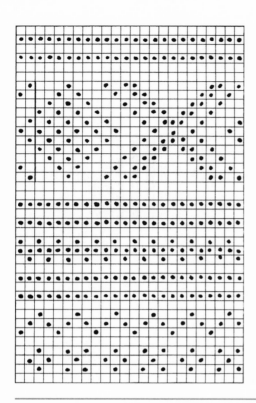

Lusekofte 2

← Patterns for upper body.

→ Patterns for lower body.

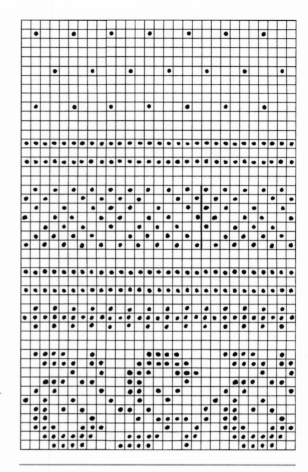

Lusekofte patterns

These extra pattern bands can be combined with stripes and "lice" to create a lusekofte. Or try them in other designs!

More pattern bands appear on pages 143 and 145.

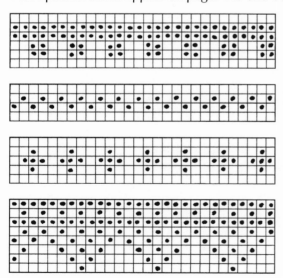

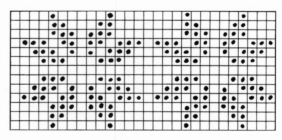

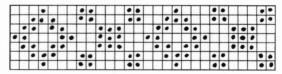

Fana Cardigan

Patterns for the Fana cardigan are on page 140. What about the bottom edge finish? Some of the old ones, worked in stockinette, just rolled forward a bit! But the best of the best used garter stitch for the first few rows, or else began with the twisted-purl edging (page 231). The latter was most often worked in the darker color, or in the two colors of the checkerboard.

In the Fana region, a lovely style of woman's jacket was popular in the latter part of the nineteenth century and the early twentieth century. This cardigan style, usually worked in blue or black with white, was knitted in the round and then the openings were cut, as was typical of all Norwegian color-stranded work. The lower edge had a diced, or checkerboard, band. Next came horizontal stripes of alternating colors with specks of contrasting color in each stripe. A Nordic star design embellished the shoulders. The sleeves repeated the motifs of the body, although the wristbands usually displayed the star pattern, instead of the checkerboard design of the waistband. Bands of woven fabric secured the cut edges at the front and neck, as well as the wristbands. Closures were of pewter.

This regional favorite has recently regained popularity, and the style is being knitted and worn throughout Scandinavia in a wider range of colors.

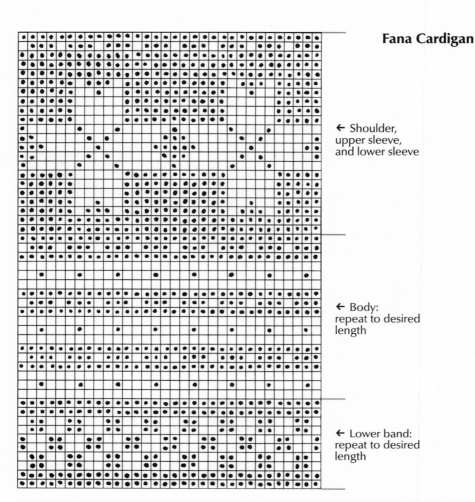

Fana Cardigan

← Shoulder,
upper sleeve,
and lower sleeve

← Body:
repeat to desired
length

← Lower band:
repeat to desired
length

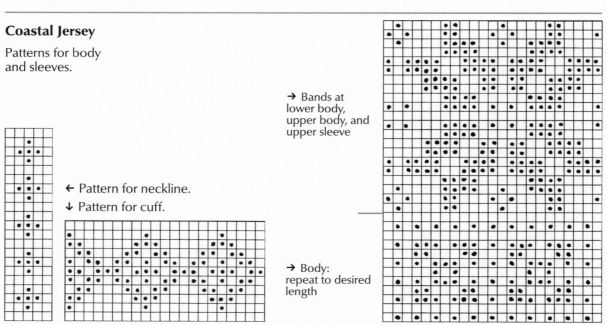

Coastal Jersey

Patterns for body
and sleeves.

→ Bands at
lower body,
upper body, and
upper sleeve

← Pattern for neckline.
↓ Pattern for cuff.

→ Body:
repeat to desired
length

Coastal Jersey

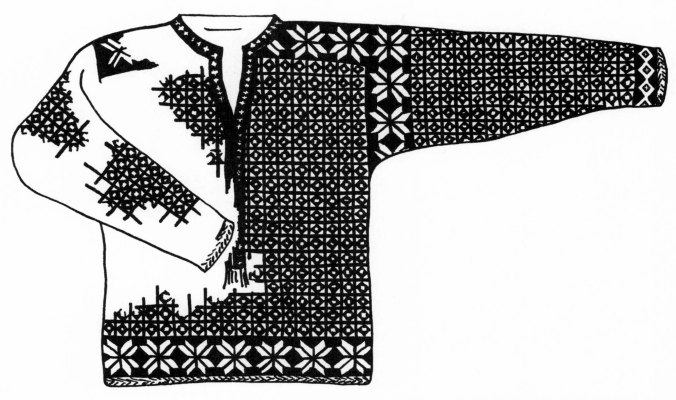

Coastal jerseys from around 1900 incorporated the star pattern at the lower edge, across the shoulders, and at the upper arm, but instead of the lice pattern they had an all-over design, frequently checkered. These sweaters often had a twisted-purl cast-on in two colors, followed by several rows of stitches in alternating colors to control the tendency to roll. The neckline was cut and edged with a decorative woven band.

These garments were worked in the traditional manner, with one exception—a small half-gusset was inserted on the body at the underarm, and these stitches were removed to a holder while the rest of the body was worked. When the time came to work the sleeves, the gusset was not carried into the sleeve; instead, its stitches were incorporated into the sleeve pattern itself.

Patterns for the Coastal Jersey are on page 140. For the twisted-purl edging in two colors, see the commentary on page 231.

Modern Norwegian Sweater 1

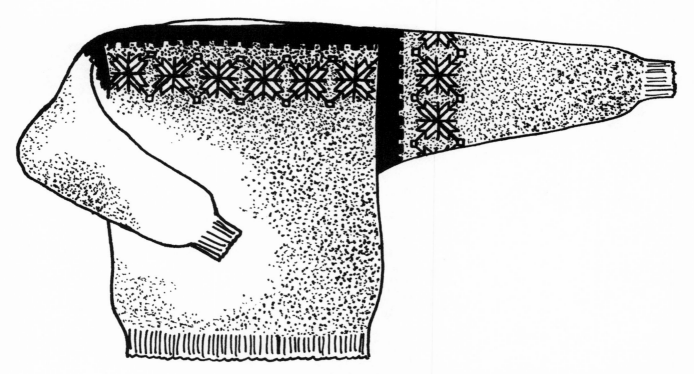

Modern Norwegian sweaters retain the essence of the old designs, but have been greatly simplified. A favorite color scheme consists of a dark blue body and white color-stranded pattern, accented by a red band at the upper edges. This color usage dates to World War II, when the German occupation banned the wearing of red caps. Norwegians added red bands to their sweaters as an expression of national sentiment.

These garments are knitted in the round with no advance provision for cutting the armholes, which are stitched by sewing machine and then cut. The neckline is usually a boatneck. The sleeves are worked from wrist to shoulder, with an extra four to six rows at the top to cover the cut edge of the body—this produces a neat finish on the inside, but adds bulk to the armhole seam.

Color-stranded designs frequently are limited to the shoulder area and the upper arm. In the charts, the motifs are shown in relation to each other and not as individual repeats. The patterns should be centered front and back; make any adjustments for incomplete motifs at the sides.

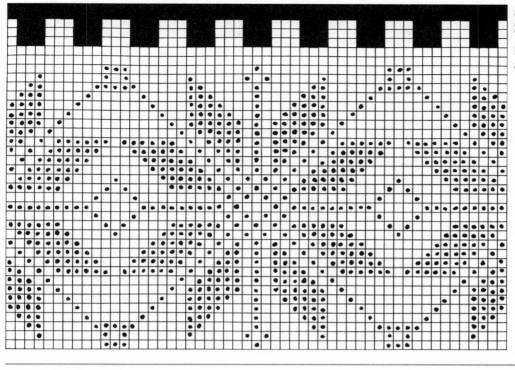

Lusekofte patterns

These extra pattern bands can be combined with stripes and "lice" to create a lusekofte. More appear on pages 138 and 145.

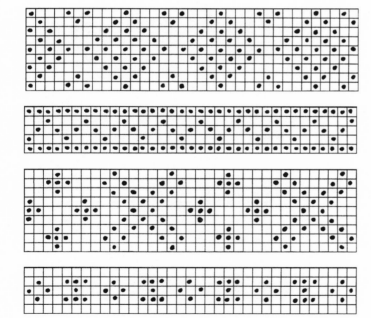

Modern Norwegian Sweater 2, with Hat

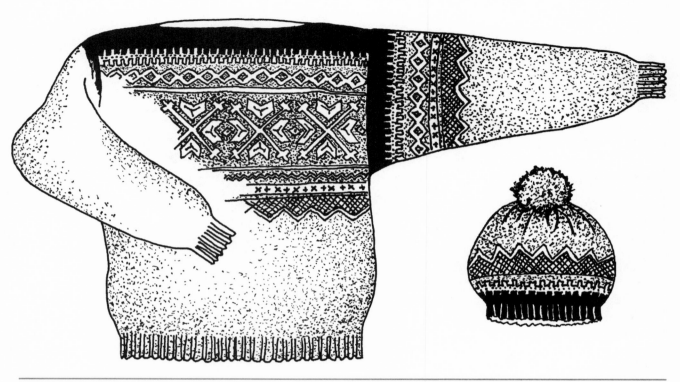

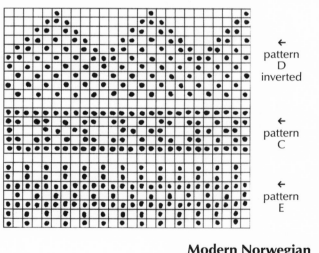

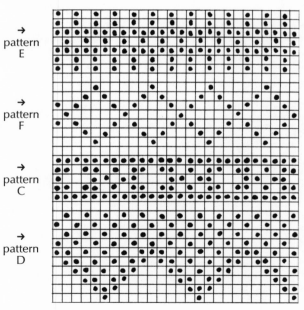

← pattern D inverted

← pattern C

← pattern E

→ pattern E

→ pattern F

→ pattern C

→ pattern D

Modern Norwegian Sweater 2

↑ Patterns for hat.

→ Patterns for upper sleeve.

Patterns for Modern Norwegian Sweater 2 are on pages 144 and 145.

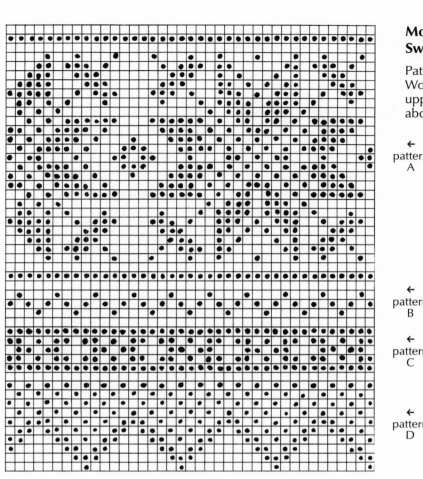

Modern Norwegian Sweater 2

Patterns for upper body. Work patterns F and E from upper sleeve (on page 144) above pattern A.

← pattern A

← pattern B

← pattern C

← pattern D

Lusekofte patterns

These extra pattern bands can be combined with stripes and "lice" to create a lusekofte. More appear on pages 138 and 143.

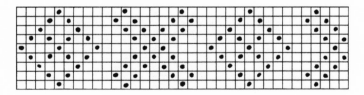

Sweden

Sweden is one of the few countries where the arrival of knitting can be dated. Accounts of historic Swedish knitting credit its introduction to Magna Brita Crasaus, the wife of the newly appointed governor, in the mid-seventeenth century. Before that time, eyed-needle construction techniques that produced similar results were common, but not knitting as we know it today. The earliest sweaters were made of relatively coarse woolen yarns in one color. Color-stranded knitting became popular in the mid-1800s.

Ullared Jersey 1

Ullared Jersey 2

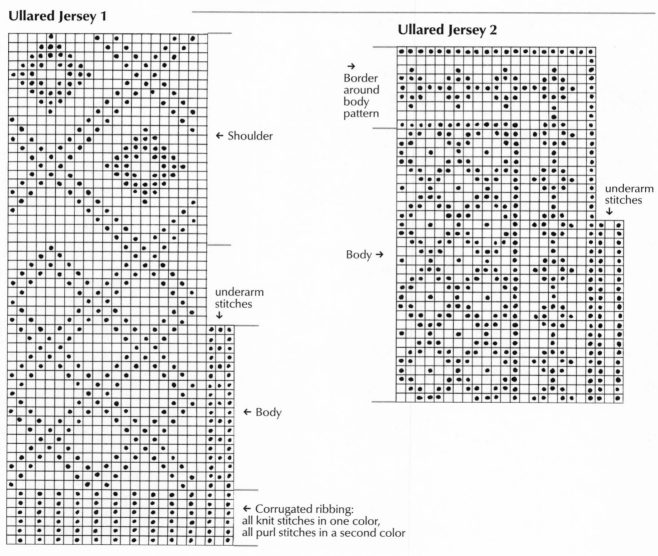

→ Border around body pattern

← Shoulder

Body →

underarm stitches ↓

underarm stitches ↓

← Body

← Corrugated ribbing: all knit stitches in one color, all purl stitches in a second color

146

Ullared Jersey 1, with Decorative Seams

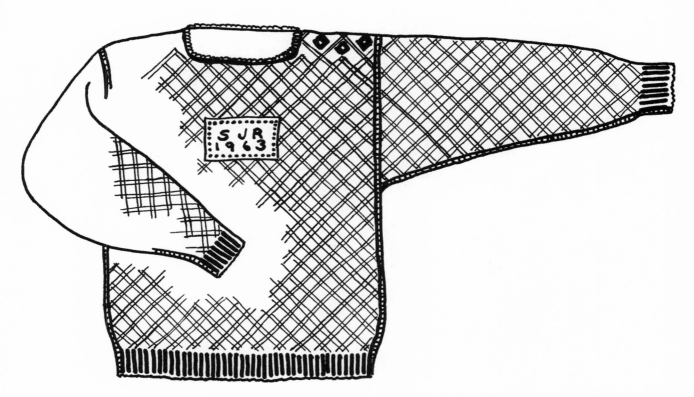

Color-stranding in Sweden became especially popular in Halland, where Ullared jerseys developed. Knitted very tightly in small diagonal patterns, these sweaters were worn chiefly by fishermen and were designed to be both warm and wind-resistant. They shared design features with Danish blouses (see pages 236–38), although the Swedish sweaters involved designs produced with red-and-black color stranding and the Danish garments were worked in a single color and decorated with knit/purl brocaded patterning.

Ullared sweaters often had hip bands of corrugated ribbing, in which the stitches were worked in alternating colors (purl stitches in one color and knit stitches in another). Decorative side seams set off a center body panel of small diagonal patterning, topped by a larger, bolder pattern across the shoulders. The center body section often contained a small rectangle (about 3 by 5 inches) where the wearer's initials and the date

Patterns for Ullared Jersey 1 are on page 146.

Ullared Jersey 2, with Front Panel and Decorative Cuffs

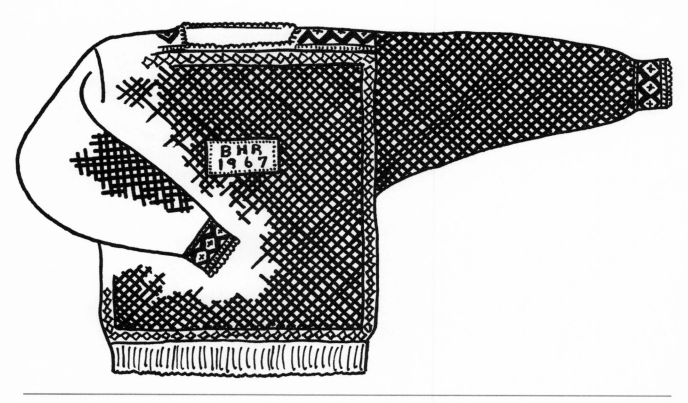

Patterns for Ullared Jersey 2 are here and on page 146.

were knitted into the design. Each sleeve was picked up at the shoulder and knitted to the wrist, continuing the decorative seam treatment and diagonal design of the body. The pattern on the wristband usually related to that of the shoulder. Crocheted edging reinforced the neck opening and the wristbands.

Ullared Jersey 2
Patterns for the cuff and shoulder (shoulder line at the arrow).

shoulderline stitch

Delsbo Jacket

↓ Patterns for lower portions of body and sleeves.

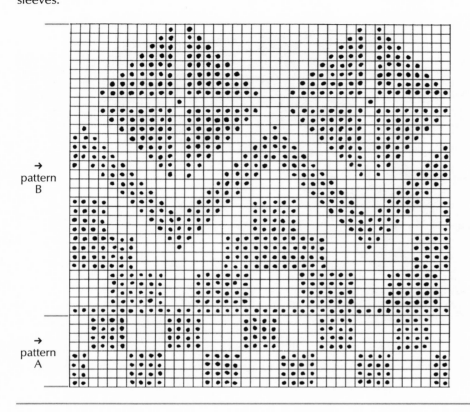

pattern B →

pattern A →

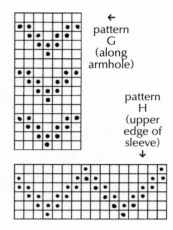

← pattern G (along armhole)

pattern H (upper edge of sleeve) ↓

Delsbo Jacket

The Delsbo jacket for men, with a black or white background and patterns worked in red and green, appeared in the Halsingland area in the nineteenth century.

This short garment begins with a diced (checkerboard) lower band worked in two colors. Although the main pattern itself is constructed in bands, these interrelate and develop into an overall design. They are not just a sequence of bands. Smaller pattern bands occur in the lower areas of the sweater, gradually increasing to very large bands in the upper portions. They feature abrupt changes in color, making the vivid contrasts even more striking.

Like the Ullared jersey, the Delsbo jacket was structurally related to the Danish blouse. It often had a half-gusset and was finished with a square neckline faced with woven fabric, but the side-seam treatment was omitted in favor of carrying the design around the body without interruption. The sleeves were worked from the shoulders down, ending in diced bands at the cuffs. The initials of the wearer and date of the knitting were sometimes worked into the bands of pattern, instead of being placed in a box as on the Ullared sweater.

Patterns for the Delsbo Jacket are on pages 149 and 151.

150

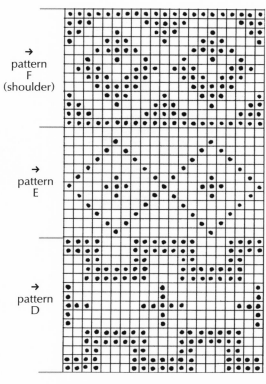

pattern
F
(shoulder)

pattern
E

pattern
D

Delsbo Jacket

← Patterns for upper
portions of body and
sleeves.

↓ Patterns for center
portions of body and
sleeves.

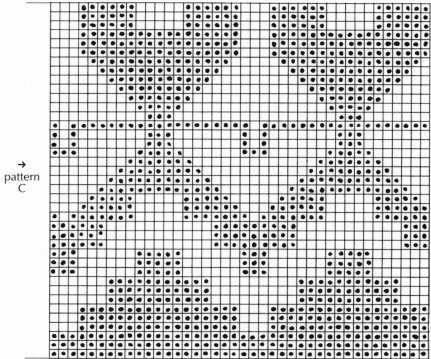

pattern
C

The body patterns are (from
bottom) A, B, C, D, E, and F at the
shoulder. Patterns A and B are on
page 149. C, D, E, and F are here.

Pattern G (page 149) runs along
the armhole, adjacent to patterns
C, D, and E.

The sleeve patterns are (from
upper arm) H, E, D, C, B, and A.
Patterns H, B, and A are on page
149. E, D, and C are here.

151

Bjarbo Sweater

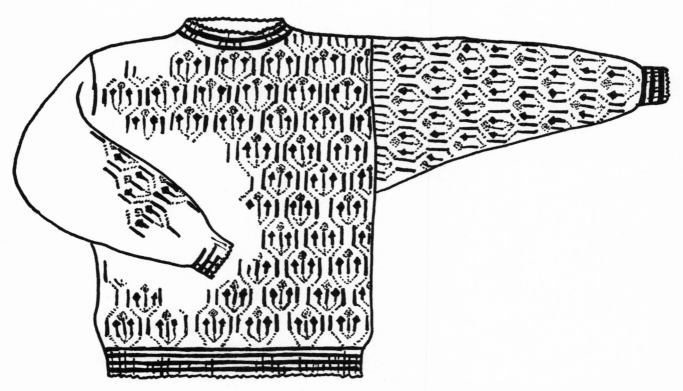

The Bjarbo pattern was worked in red and blue on a cream ground. A sweater of this type often had a hip band worked in garter stitch, with the purl rows worked in one color and the knit rows in another, red or blue against cream. The design is an all-over interlocking pattern with the colors worked in bands. The color changes are similar to those found on Fair Isle; the center portion of a design in one color contrasts with the outer portions, but everything is generally worked on the cream ground.

These garments were knitted in the round. From paintings and photographs, we know that two knitters sometimes worked on the same garment simultaneously. One person would work at one side and the other would follow on the other side. Because the knitting proceeded in a circular manner, each individual worked alternate rows on the body of the sweater. Because the pattern was always the same, this was not as difficult as it sounds.

Bjarbo Sweater

Woman's Jacket with Woven Body and Knitted Sleeves

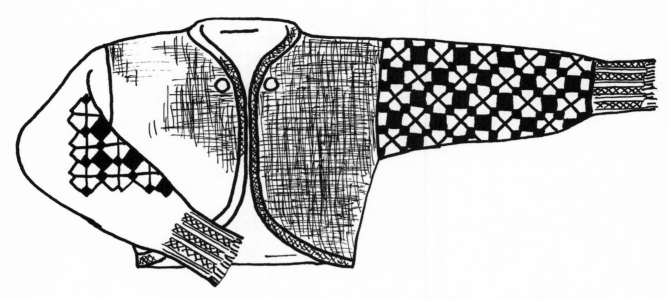

A style of garment worn in some regions by both men and women was made with a woven-fabric body and knitted sleeves in elaborate color-stranded designs. The woman's version was often a snug-fitting bolero style, while the man's was a loose jacket. In early examples, the body usually began as white fabric and the sleeves were knitted in black and white; the entire garment was then dyed red or green, resulting in bright-colored patterns against a black ground. The sleeves were worked in all-over color-stranded patterns with deep cuffs of firmly knitted bands or stripes of small patterns. The tension in these bands of alternating colors was pulled in tight to gather the cuff and provide an elegant finish for the sleeve, which was often edged with fringe.

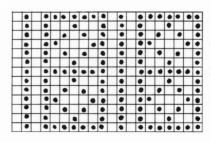

Woman's Jacket

← Pattern for main portion of sleeve.

→ Pattern for cuff.

Man's Jacket with Woven Body and Knitted Sleeves

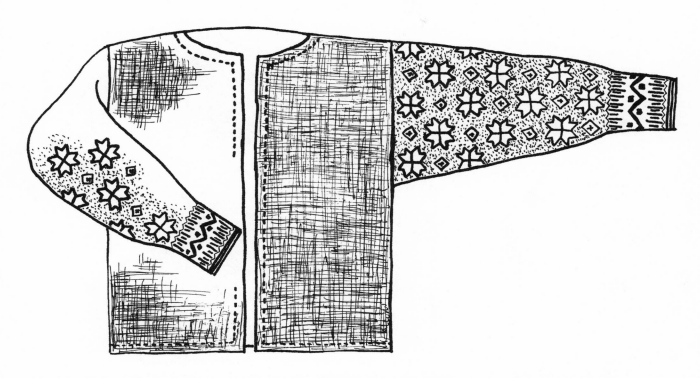

Man's Jacket

← Pattern for main portion of sleeve.

↓ Pattern for cuff.

Bohus Sweater 1

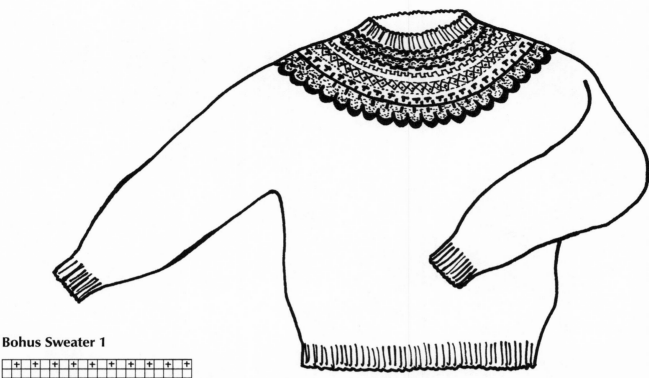

Bohus Sweater 1

Bohus sweaters are twentieth-century garments. In 1939, Emma Jacobsson organized the Bohus Knitting Cooperative in an attempt to alleviate the economic hardships of the times. The aim was to provide local employment through marketing a fashion garment to the world. Although the cooperative ceased operations in 1969, its creative legacy endures.

Instead of continuing with strictly traditional designs, the group created a new direction, initially concentrating on richly color-patterned pullovers and cardigan fronts for women that were made with top-quality wool yarns. But the cooperative became famous for seamless-yoke sweaters worked in fine yarns spun from a blend of wool and angora. Many believe these were the first round-yoke sweaters, and credit their creation in the early 1940s to Ann-Lisa Mannheimer Lunn, the cooperative's primary designer.

Sweaters with circular yokes are now used around the world, but the Bohus garments were unusual in several ways. The designs,

Bohus Sweater 2

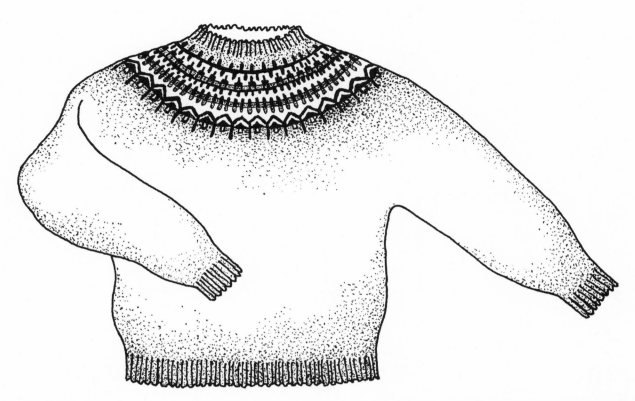

Bohus Sweater 2

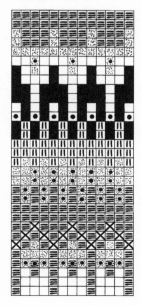

typically composed of small interlocking bands, depend for their effect more on color shading than on dominance of pattern. Sometimes as many as five subtly related colors appear in a single row. In addition, purled stitches worked within the patterns produce delicate textural effects. The appeal of Bohus garments derives from their subtlety of color and pattern, strongly enhanced by the luxuriously soft hand of the wool/angora yarn.

Bohus 2 is a modern interpretation of a sweater with Bohus-style patterning on the yoke.

Great Britain

Among the earliest of the British so-called seamen's jerseys was a garment knitted for both sailors and miners in the dales in North Yorkshire, along the border between England and Scotland. It was made of a heavy woolen handspun yarn called *bump*. Hand knitting was vital to economic survival in these valleys. Records show that local wool was carded, spun, and knitted into jerseys for commercial trade by almost everyone, young and old. Handknitted hosiery for the gentry was also economically important, but the hosiery was made from worsted yarns not of local origin. (Stockings for local use were made of heavy woolen yarns, not fine worsteds.)

Farther north, the series of islands known as Shetland—small in size and population—has been home to extraordinary knitters for centuries. Their creative vision and technical expertise have had a disproportionately large impact on knitting in other parts of the world.

No speckled frocks remain, but related gloves exist in museums.

Speckled Frock 2

→ Patterns from a speckled glove like the one above; used in the sweater on page 160.

Speckled patterns

→→ Patterns from another speckled glove.

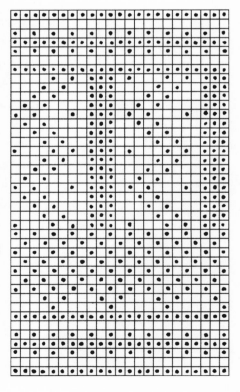

Speckled Frock 1

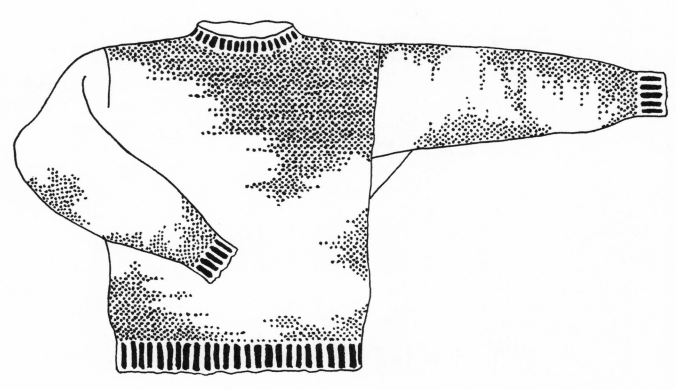

Speckled Frock 1

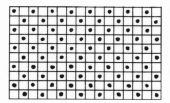

The speckled or spotted pattern alternates light and dark colors in both directions.

There is no pictorial record of the early seamen's jerseys, referred to as *speckled* or *spotted frocks.* Only diaries, letters, and inventories describe their appearance. They were constructed of natural-colored wools in two shades, light and dark, used in alternate stitches, both within each row and between rows. The bands at the edges were probably of corrugated ribbing—that is, ribbing worked with one color for the knit stitches and another for the purl stitches to form a firm, vertically striped welt. These were seamless garments. Once the body had been completed, the shoulders were bound off together, armholes were slashed, and sleeves were picked up and worked down to the wristbands.

By the mid-1800s, commercial demand for speckled frocks in handspun woolen yarn waned, and gansey-style garments with simple textured designs became more popular. But the longstanding tradition of working two colors in alternate stitches was not lost. Patterned

Speckled Frock 2

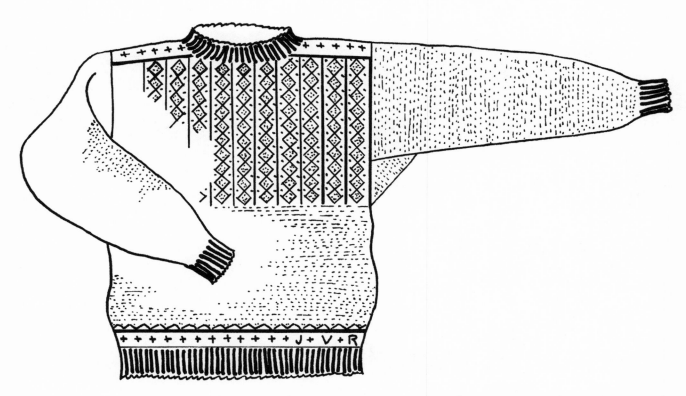

gloves with speckles on the palms and fingers remained popular; several examples have been preserved in museums.

Knitted from the fine worsted yarns that had become available from the early mills, the gloves have a small but elaborate pattern on the back of the hand and a patterned wristband with the name of the owner. The wrist edge is finished with a fringe or a striped welt.

Although we have no specific visual reference for the speckled frocks, little imagination is required to transpose patterns from these very distinctive gloves for use in a sweater. There is no real evidence to indicate that the designs were used in this way, but it is in keeping with tradition that designs were often copied back and forth between sweaters, stockings, and mittens.

Because the gloves were being made when the earliest Fair Isle sweaters were knitted in gansey shaping, using a Scot's steek to form the openings, it is easy to imagine the gloves' designs on a color-stranded sweater of that type.

The patterns for Speckled Frock 2, which were derived from a traditional glove, are on page 158.

Fair Isle sweaters

Fair Isle, Shetland, and Orkney are parts of Scotland that are often left off maps. The long, narrow archipelago to which they belong includes nearly two hundred islands extending into the North Sea. The islands have rich and interrelated traditions of knitting, in part because the several types of native sheep produce fine wools in many natural colors.

Early island knitting of the sixteenth century consisted mostly of coarse stockings, but with the decline of the hosiery trade during the Victorian era the islanders turned their knitting needles to other pursuits—most notably the making of lace shawls (on Unst, part of Shetland) and of color-stranded sweaters adapted from the traditional gansey shape (on Fair Isle). The sweaters involve mostly symmetrical and geometric designs, usually worked in bands over an odd number of rows to allow symmetry. Interestingly, the knitters of Fair Isle and Shetland worked in the round but they didn't use multiple needles in the same way as did knitters in most other areas. They used three long needles, positioning all the front stitches on one and all the back stitches on another, and used the third as the working needle. With short needles, this technique also works extremely well for constructing small tubular elements.

Fair Isle work is unique in the way color is incorporated within the designs. Only two colors are worked in any one row, but the ground color and pattern color shift within a motif, and pattern bands are often emphasized by the color changes. The color shifting within the bands makes the designs appear more complex than other types of two-color stranding.

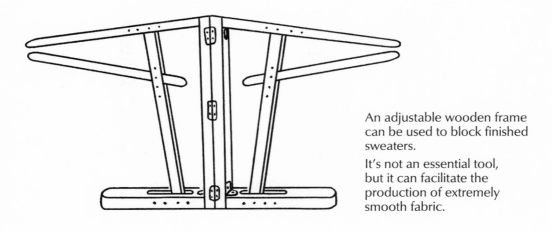

An adjustable wooden frame can be used to block finished sweaters.

It's not an essential tool, but it can facilitate the production of extremely smooth fabric.

There are several stories about the origin of Fair Isle patterns. In 1856, Eliza Edmondston's *Sketches and Tales of the Shetland Islands* suggested that the patterns might be Spanish, learned from Spanish soldiers shipwrecked on the tiny island in 1588—a highly improbable situation. On an island barely able to sustain a native population of fifty inhabitants, starvation must have been more on the minds of the populace than swapping knitting patterns with three hundred Spanish castaways. An even later embellishment of this tale discusses copying the patterns from sweaters on dead bodies washed ashore from the shipwreck. Records indicate that the islanders simply wanted to be rid of the intruders, and descendants of the island people vigorously repudiate all versions of this tale.

According to the islanders themselves, a seafaring native returned home with a woven, patterned shawl, probably from the Baltics. The women adapted its designs to knitting, then developed more complex interpretations. Out of the work that evolved from this source, a "new" folk art was born, probably around 1880. These designs would not have appeared before the middle of the nineteenth century. Why do we think this? Because the oldest surviving pieces were worked in bright, vibrant color combinations not possible before the latter part of that century, when aniline dyes became readily available to the islanders. By the early twentieth century, natural fleece colors became popular for these designs.

Sweaters from this tradition have been, and still are, blocked when the knitting has been completed. The sweater is completely wetted and then stretched on an adjustable frame that holds the sweater taut while it sits to dry in the sun. This evens any variations in tension on the stranding yarns, resulting in a very smooth surface.

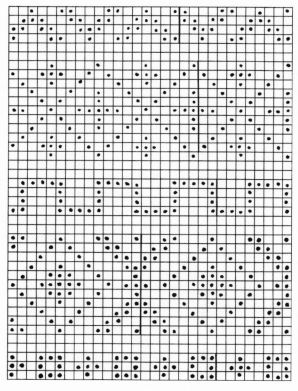

**Fair Isle Sweater
in Gansey Construction 1**

Patterns for lower body.

Fair Isle Sweater in Gansey Construction 1

Patterns for Fair Isle in Gansey Construction 1 are on pages 162 and 164. The structure follows Plan 2 (pages 84–85).

The oldest of these sweaters follow the construction of the typical gansey, omitting the purled side seam so the designs could run continuously around the garment. A corrugated ribbing was used, often worked K2, P2, above which wide and narrow bands of design alternated. The designs were not aligned with each other, but worked in relation to the total number of stitches in the circumference. This allowed the use of any repeat that would fit evenly into the total. (If, in knitting this type of sweater, you choose a repeat that doesn't divide evenly into the total number of stitches, center the design on both front and back and make adjustments in the sequence at each underarm.)

A gusset was worked at the underarm (as described on pages 84–85, but without the purl stitch). The gusset was usually worked in alternating colors, instead of in the larger pattern motif. This eliminated long strands on the inside at the underarm. After the gusset had been half-worked, the stitches were removed to a holder and the area was closed with a steek, which was also worked in alternating colors. The stitches of

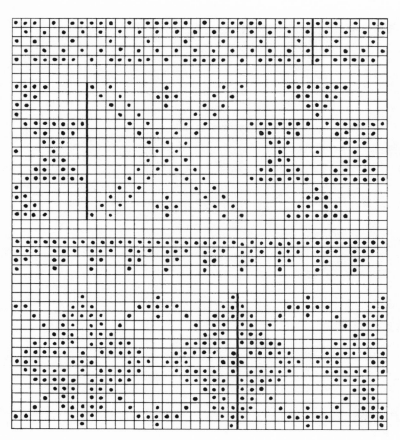

the shoulder seam were either grafted or bound off together on the inside. The steek was slashed, stitches were picked up, and the sleeve was worked down from shoulder to wrist.

The first band of pattern on the sleeve repeated the one located at the center of the armhole, and the remaining bands repeated in order down the sleeve.

**Fair Isle Sweater
in Gansey Construction 1**

← Patterns for upper body.

Fair Isle Sweater
in Gansey Construction 2

Patterns for lower body and lower sleeves. Start with the ribbing at lower right on page 165. The sequence continues on this page, and then on page 166 (upper body and sleeves).

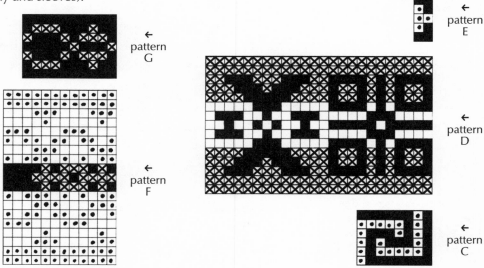

← pattern G

← pattern F

← pattern E

← pattern D

← pattern C

164

Fair Isle Sweater in Gansey Construction 2

The stitch charts for this Fair Isle sweater are shown in order, beginning at the lower right on this page, continuing on the opposite page, and concluding on the following page. Each horizontal stripe represents one full repeat. The corrugated ribbing at the bottom of the sweater is followed by pattern A, and so on. The sleeves, worked down from the armhole, incorporate patterns I through A.

**Fair Isle Sweater
in Gansey Construction 2**

Color key

☐ white

☒ silver tan

⊡ tan

■ brown

Patterns for Fair Isle Sweater in Gansey Construction 2 are on pages 165, 164, and 166, in that order.

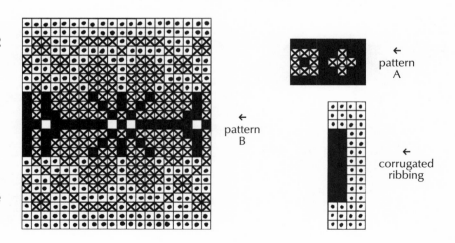

← pattern A

← pattern B

← corrugated ribbing

Fair Isle Sweater
Shaped with Steeks

→ These patterns are used throughout the sweater on the opposite page.

Note the way the large bands are placed so that their motifs alternate vertically as well as horizontally.

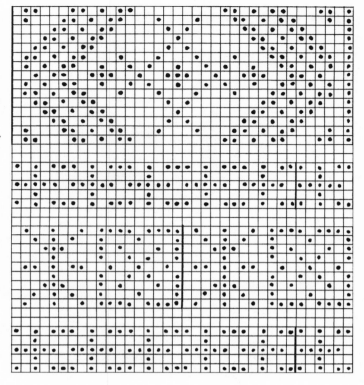

Fair Isle Sweater
in Gansey Construction 2

↓ Patterns for upper body and upper sleeves.

← pattern K

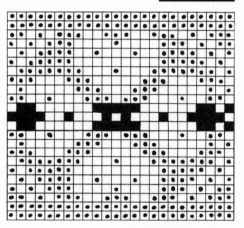

← pattern J

Fair Isle patterns

↓ Extra pattern bands typical of Fair Isle color work.

← pattern I

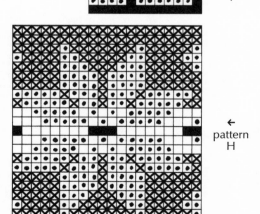

← pattern H

Fair Isle Sweater Shaped with Steeks

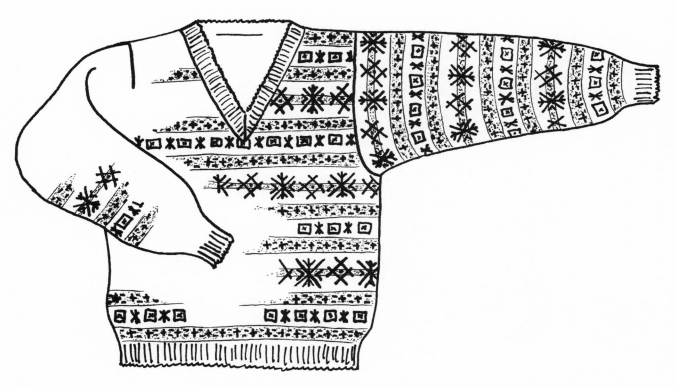

The sweater shown here was shaped with steeks at both sleeves and neckline. Its patterns are on page 166.

In the twentieth century, when shaping became more popular, the gusset was omitted. Instead, a set of platform stitches was set aside at the base of the armhole (see page 92), the opening was steeked, and the armhole was shaped with a series of decreases on each side of the steek. Often these sweaters had V necklines, formed with a steeked opening (see page 87). Decreases were worked on each side of the steek.

Vest with Tesselated Patterns

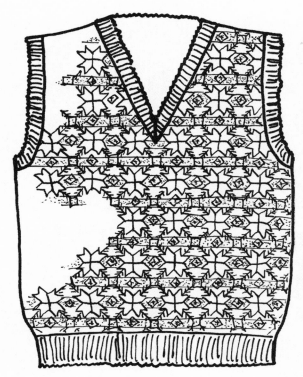

**Vest with
Tesselated
Patterns**

Today, many Shetland-style designs are made
up of all-over interlocking motifs, instead of the
traditional bands. The appearance of bands is maintained even within these patterns because the colors
of the ground stitches change within the designs.
The particular variation shown here is especially
popular for sleeveless vests.

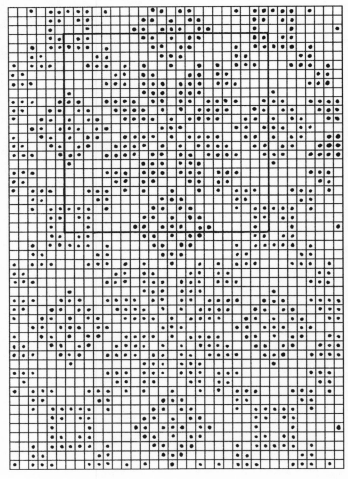

Tesselated patterns

The motifs in tesselated patterns can interlock in different ways.

In the pattern and vest opposite, the stars stack vertically and the diamonds fit between them.

→ In a pattern closely related to the one on the sweater, the stars and diamonds alternate in both directions.

→ In this extra pattern, the motifs nest very closely together.

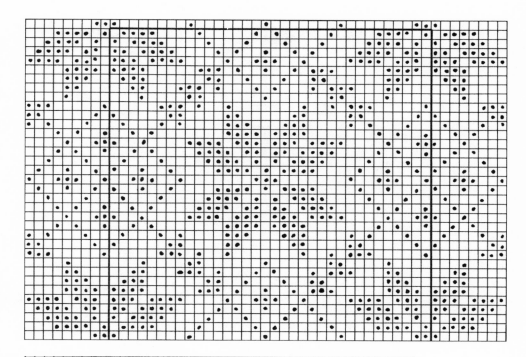

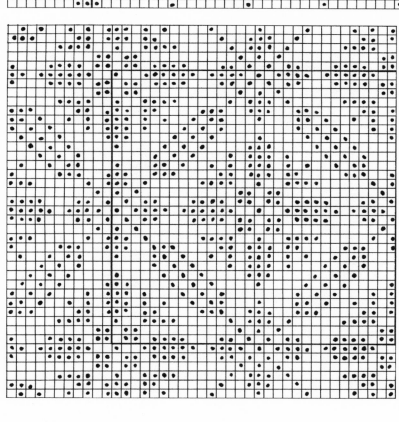

Shetland Yoke Sweaters

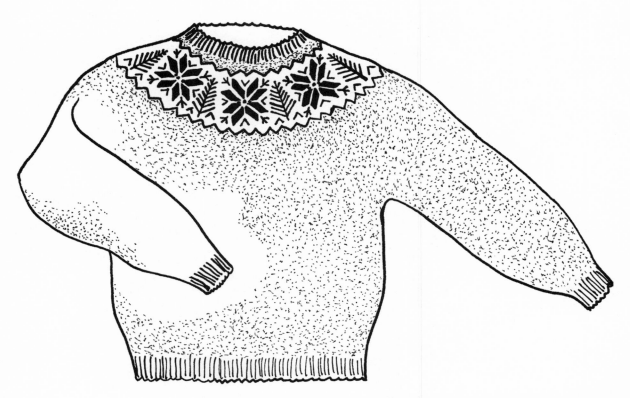

A further evolution of the Fair Isle design produced the Shetland yoke sweater, a garment that has grown increasingly popular in the past half-century. Even though the designs may have originated on Fair Isle, to call the yoke-style garment a Fair Isle sweater is inaccurate. This style is probably a product of all the northern islands in the archipelago that includes Fair Isle, Shetland, and Orkney. It is a marriage of the commercially successful Fair Isle sweaters with Scandinavian yoke sweaters.

Typically, the yoke has one wide pattern band with decreases incorporated between its design elements. This procedure can be simplified by careful selection of a design for the pattern band. If it contains alternating square and triangular pattern elements, the regular rounds of decreases at the edges of the squares will simultaneously taper the edges of the triangles. A Shetland-style yoke can also be worked in several small pattern bands, with the decreases set between the bands.

Shetland Yoke Sweater

→ Patterns for the yoke in the sweater drawing.

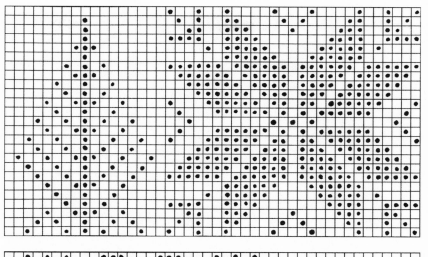

Shetland Yoke patterns

→ Extra yoke patterns.

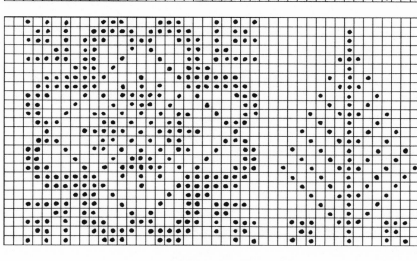

Both patterns show the alternation of "square" and triangular, or wedge-shaped, motifs. This makes it easier to place the decreases without interrupting the design.

Iceland

Transported to this island in the North Atlantic by Viking settlers during the ninth and tenth centuries, the sheep of Iceland are unique. They are genetically the same as their ancestors were more than a millennium ago.

Their fleece consists of two layers. An outer coat of long, silky hairs, measuring between 12 and 19 inches, offers protection from wind, rain, and snow. A shorter inner coat—fine, soft, and fluffy—fills the spaces between the long outer hairs and provides excellent insulation. This inner coat, softly spun in a bulky weight, produces an exceedingly lightweight yarn that traps a lot of air, and can therefore make very warm sweaters.

Hand knitting has long been a tradition and an important activity in Iceland. The craft probably arrived on the island in the 1600s from Dutch sources. One Icelandic jersey dates back to around 1700, and old manuscripts show gridded charts of simple color-stranded designs, which were used on knitted insoles worn in shoes.

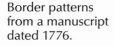
Border patterns from a manuscript dated 1776.

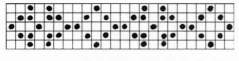

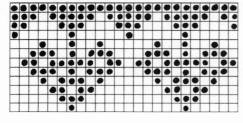

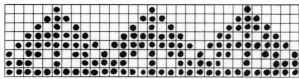

Icelanders

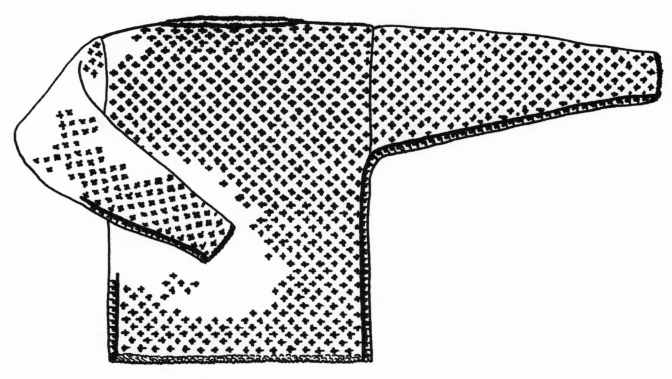

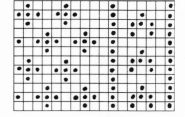

Icelander 1

An Icelandic design with a seam pattern different from, but related to, the body pattern, similar to the patterns in the sweater on this page.

The early workingman's sweater, called an *Icelander*, was a bulky garment knitted in two, or occasionally three, natural colors of wool. It was a simple garment in both shape and patterning, with small, closely spaced geometric designs. Made of heavy woolen yarn, this was possibly the earliest of the "bulky" sweaters. The color stranding provided additional warmth; it doubled the weight of the fabric and made the cloth firm and inelastic. In addition, many of these garments were felted to provide even more resistance to the elements.

The example shown dates from the late nineteenth or early twentieth century.

Little attention was given to edge treatments. The lower edge at the hips began with a twisted-purl cast-on in two colors, and the design started after several rows of twisted two-end knitting (see pages 230–33).

A design feature often found on this type of sweater is a 5- to 7-stitch side-seam panel at the underarms. This panel was often emphasized. Its colors were reversed from those in the body of the sweater, often

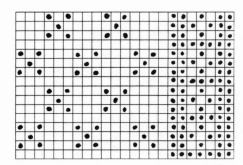

Icelander 2

An Icelandic pattern with colors reversed in the seams.

outlined with the pattern yarn. The design motif in the panel might be identical to that in the rest of the garment or, in an outlined panel, it might be a coordinated design.

To maintain the continuity of the design from body to sleeve, the panel stitches were removed at the underarm and the armhole was closed with a steek (or with a locked stitch incorporating both colors of the row; see page 91). The neck opening, as in this example, was a straight boatneck, with the edge bound off and allowed to roll—not a modern effect after all! The shoulder stitches could be bound off together or grafted.

Traditionally, the sleeves were picked up at the armholes and worked to the wrists. The seam panel design was maintained along the sleeve, and shaping decreases occurred on each side of the panel. There was no cuff on this design; repeating the neck treatment, the sleeves are bound off at the wrists and the edges are allowed to roll. On some sweaters, knitters controlled the tendency to roll by working a few rows of "fleas"—the traditional Icelandic term for alternating stitches in two colors.

Modern Icelandic patterns

→ In this extra set of designs, decreases can be worked in the plain rounds of the yoke, between pattern motifs.

The lower pattern is a coordinating design for the hip band and lower sleeves.

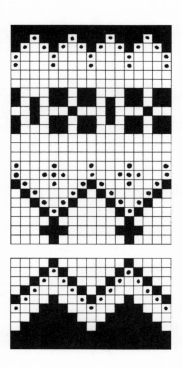

Modern Icelandic Yoke Sweater 1

← Decreases are incorporated into this interlocking yoke pattern.

↓ Pattern for hip band and lower sleeves.

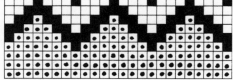

Modern Icelandic Yoke Sweater 1

Patterns for Modern Icelandic Yoke Sweater 1 are on page 174.

When the manufacturing of textiles was first industrialized in Iceland, the wool was often made into *plates* of roving at a mill and returned to the farmer to be spun at home (in some cultures, this package of roving is called a *cheese,* because its shape resembles a round of cheese). The Icelandic term *lopi* refers to both the strand and its package. Unspun lopi is now often used directly for knitting, although this was not the case until 1920, when Elín Guðmundsdóttir Snæhólm, instead of taking the time to spin the yarn, successfully created a lopi scarf on a knitting frame. Her experiments were published, and by 1923 the practice had begun to spread.

Among knitters in the United States, the word *lopi* has become synonymous with the soft, roving-type yarns of Iceland. They are very lightly twisted, but not really spun. The use of lopi in handknitted sweaters increased in popularity during World War II. Today, Icelandic sweaters are characterized by round-yoke patterning in natural-colored lopi yarns. Interestingly, a sweater seen as a national symbol of Iceland has designs that are Scandinavian in influence while the round yoke treatment is an imported idea, based on the popular Norwegian "sunburst" sweaters of the late 1940s, developed when brilliant colors became available.

In 1957, the Alafoss Spinning Mill began to manufacture the unspun "yarns" on a commercial scale, catapulting the hand knitting of lopi sweaters into economic importance. Although hand knitting is no longer financially viable in most cultures, this lofty yarn works up quickly enough to make the handwork profitable. As a result, knitting as a cottage industry contributes to the Icelandic economy. In addition to lopi, spun singles and two-ply woolen yarns are also very popular among knitters in Iceland.

Seamless pullovers are knitted in the round, with full-yoke patterns worked in two or more natural colors. The circular-yoke design is usually complemented by narrow bands of pattern at the hip and wrists. Cardigans are worked flat, because the slashing technique doesn't work well on fabric made with such a fragile and bulky yarn. A locked turning stitch at the center front is recommended (page 91).

Incidentally, the Icelandic yarn marketed in the United States for hand knitting has more twist inserted than the strands available in Iceland. For use within Iceland, the yarn is sold as a plate—a flat, round roll of roving. To create a bulky yarn, the knitter uses the ends from the inside and outside of the plate together; they wrap together loosely with the twist generated by the motion of the knitting itself. Very lightweight garments can be made by working with a single roving from the plate.

If all the looms in the world ceased to produce cloth, and the art of spinning and knitting alone remained, we could still be clothed, both warmly and fashionably.

Mary Thomas
in *Mary Thomas's Knitting Book*

Modern Icelandic Yoke Sweater 2

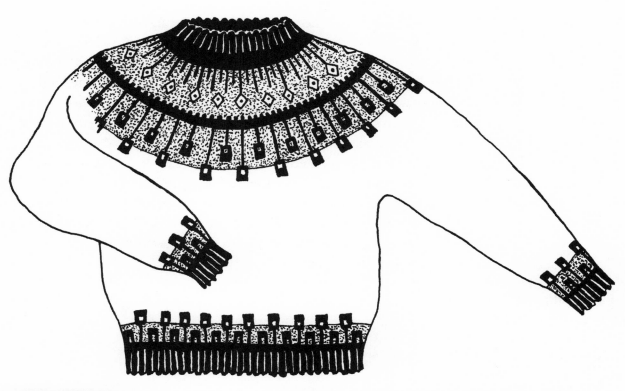

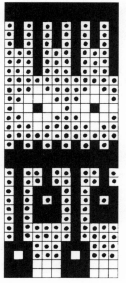

← decrease round 3

← decrease round 2

← decrease round 1

On this sweater, the yoke pattern decreases that shape the neckline are worked in single-color rounds, which eliminates the need to adapt the design to accommodate changing dimensions.

← Pattern for yoke.

↓ Pattern for hip band and lower sleeves.

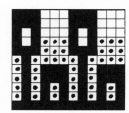

Færoe Islands

The word *færoe* means sheep, and sheep have truly been important in the life of the Færoe Islands since at least the ninth century. Sheep were first brought to the islands by Irish monks, but in the eighteenth century they died out and were replaced with sheep imported from Shetland. The wool was gathered by hand plucking (the local term is *skubbering*), then was both spun and knitted in the grease. The finished garment was scoured and felted simultaneously.

In early times, felted, knitted garments were common for both men and women. The fabrics were often so heavily felted that the knitted structure was almost impossible to see. On festive occasions, men wore jackets cut and tailored from felted, knitted fabric. The women's garments were usually short-sleeved; front openings cut in the fabric were laced with decorative chains.

Færoe jersey patterns

↓ Two all-over patterns.

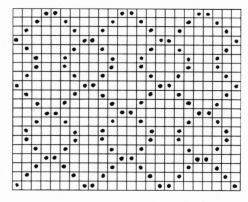

↓ A set of striping patterns.

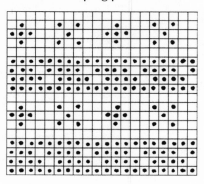

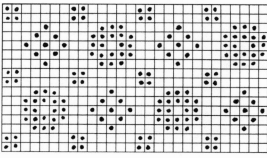

Færoe Jerseys

The Færoe jersey is closely related in design and construction to the old Icelander (page 173); both were likely developments of the mid-eighteenth century. The patterns are small geometric shapes, often worked in narrow bands with ground and pattern colors alternating. Luckily, the old designs were recorded in the early 1900s and labeled with their traditional names. The patterns appeared as samplers in an exhibition in Copenhagen in 1927 and have since been published. The yarn used in these sweaters was a fairly bulky woolen yarn, often felted after knitting, like the earlier garments, to increase resistance to wind and cold.

Færoe Jersey

← Striping sequence for the Færoese jersey shown in the drawing and an alternative dark stripe pattern (↓).

Samiland

Samiland or Sápmi lies within the arctic circle. It extends across the northern parts of Norway, Sweden, and Finland, and into Russia. The Sami are a group of nomadic peoples with locally distinctive variants of language, dress, and craft traditions. They have roamed across political borders, herding reindeer and establishing rich traditions in a territory where even the southernmost sections experience long, dark, bitterly cold winters.

Today, the Sami, like other native peoples, contend with the encroachment of other ways of life upon what outsiders may consider an incredibly harsh environment. Some contributions from the outside world have eased their lives; others have made it more difficult.

Surviving, even thriving, in this austere region of the world, these groups of people developed artwork that depends upon bright colors and elaborate designs, with which they have adorned the tools and clothing they use on a daily basis. Some of their traditional garments are heavily embossed with brilliant embroidery. Knitting does not figure in their craftwork as prominently as other techniques.

Yet the Sami have contributed mittens of a style not found in other countries of northern Europe. They use simple patterns boldly worked in red and blue on a cream ground, with touches of yellow and pale blue. They often use more than two colors in a row to enhance relatively simple patterning. For the mitten cuffs, a two-color cast-on is followed by a zigzag band consisting of two rows of twisted purl stitches, also in two colors, worked in alternating directions. The twisted-purl technique, used for textural embellishment here, also shows up as a major textural patterning device in Swedish two-end knitting (see pages 230–33).

Sami mitten.

Sami-Inspired Tunic Sweater

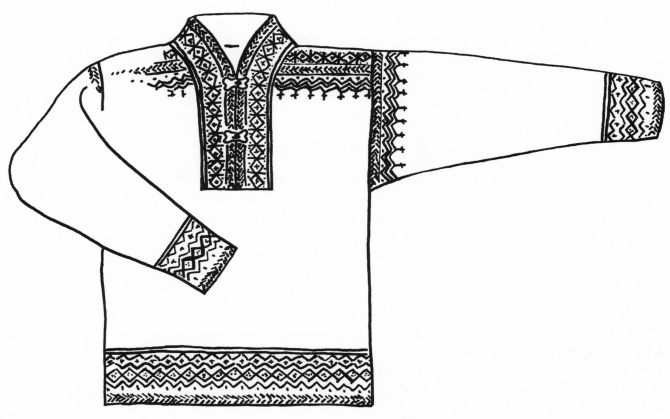

This sweater design combines the appearance of a Sami woven tunic with the patterning of a traditional Sami knitted mitten. The patterns appear on page 183.

The Samis' captivating use of color and design, although not traditionally used to make sweaters, can be adapted for the embellishment of a loosely fitting tunic, shaped like their woven and embroidered garments. Woven Sami tunics are usually red, but a sweater could be worked in primary colors on a cream ground, as the mittens were.

Begin the sweater with the cast-on derived from the Sami mittens, followed by a band of color-stranded pattern. Work the body in the main color, continuing in the round to the underarm. Then either divide the work or steek the armhole above between 3 and 5 platform stitches; at the same time, remove a set of stitches to accommodate a neckband (depending on the yarn, perhaps 3 to 4 inches' worth) and steek the center front opening.

Continue to work in the main color until you've completed about ⅔ of the armhole depth. Then work a pattern band, ending with a double row of twisted purl stitches in two colors to resemble the seam that would appear at the shoulder, on the front yoke of a woven garment (see the center of page 231 for twisted purl stitches). Finish the piece in the main color, shaping the neck at a gentle angle to accommodate the neck band, and graft the shoulders.

For each sleeve, pick up stitches at the armhole, including the platform stitches. Begin the sleeve with a double row of twisted purl in two colors, followed by a band of pattern. Continue in the main color, decreasing at the underarm at regular intervals, and finish with a pattern band and several two-row sets of twisted purl stitches, in two colors, before binding off.

To complete the neck, pick up stitches along the left front, across the back of the neck, and down the right front. You will knit the band and finish the base of the front opening simultaneously, while working a band of color-stranded pattern on the available neck stitches. The pattern needs to fit symmetrically into the neck opening, with its design elements lined up across the edges.

Knit the band back-and-forth. At the end of each row, which will occur at the base of the neckline steek, work into one of the reserved stitches of the body, using an SSK on knit rows and a P2tog on purl rows; the neck-band stitches will consume the body stitches. End with a couple of two-row sets of twisted purl stitches in two colors, immediately before the bind-off row.

Add pewter clasps as a finishing touch on this interpretation of a Sami design.

Sami-inspired patterns

These are extra patterns to be used for Sami-influenced designs.

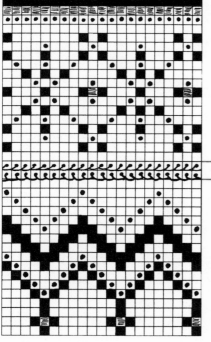

← twisted purl stitches

Sami-Inspired Tunic Sweater

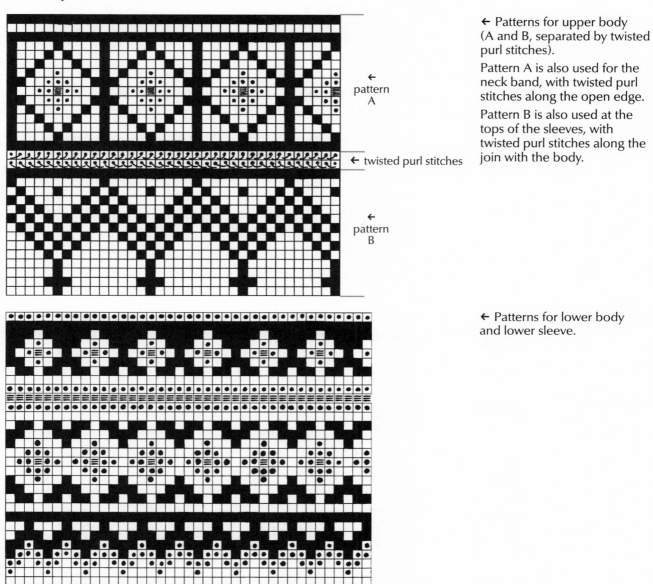

← pattern A

← twisted purl stitches

← pattern B

← twisted purl stitches

← Patterns for upper body (A and B, separated by twisted purl stitches).

Pattern A is also used for the neck band, with twisted purl stitches along the open edge.

Pattern B is also used at the tops of the sleeves, with twisted purl stitches along the join with the body.

← Patterns for lower body and lower sleeve.

Cowichan Sweaters of Canada

The only true folk sweaters of North America are those of the Cowichans, a band of the Coast Salish native people. These garments, widely copied throughout the northern reaches but seldom equaled, are unique for many reasons. They offer some truly grand construction techniques to knitters who are aware only of the European-based American knitting traditions. Even today they are made of handspun yarns. Furthermore, they are always hand knitted, because knitting machines can neither handle the heavy yarns nor duplicate the firm fabric of the classic Cowichan sweater. In this book, I can offer only a glimpse of the many ingenious knitting skills you can learn and adapt from the treasure trove of Cowichan knitting.

In 1864, the Sisters of Saint Ann opened a school for native girls in the Cowichan Valley of Vancouver Island, and they included knitting in their course of study. The native women, already skilled in handspinning, first used their bulky yarns to make stockings, mittens, and caps. Jerimina Colvin, a Scottish settler who emigrated to Canada in 1885, is often credited with showing these women how to apply their knitting skills to making one type of sweater, a turtleneck in one color. Oral tradition offers an alternate story: that a group of Cowichan women traded for a British fisherman's gansey, which they studied to determine the construction techniques necessary for making a sweater.

However they learned to make the garments in the first place, the local knitters began to enhance their sweaters with the geometric designs of their basketry. For the most part, they formed these color-stranded patterns with natural colors of wool grown by the local sheep, although sometimes they made similar hues with natural dyes. With these creative shifts, their acquired craft evolved into a true folk art.

The Cowichans further modified their sweaters to include an unusual shawl collar (see pages 186–87), and they began to incorporate highly stylized representational motifs adapted from other sources.

The sweaters are often done in white and another natural color, although a third color (a heathered blend of the two natural colors) is sometimes used for the ground color within the geometric bands. This heathered yarn served two purposes: it made the sweater aesthetically more interesting and it extended the prized natural-colored wool.

Cowichan is pronounced COW-itch-un and *Salish* is SAY-lish.

184

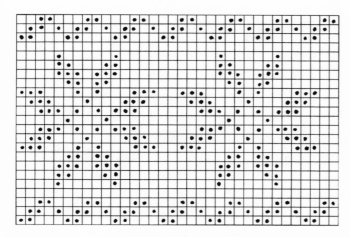

Cowichan patterns

Extra geometric patterns.

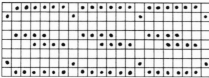

Both the geometric and the pictorial designs were color-stranded and the yarn not in use was woven behind every stitch. This weaving technique eliminated floats across the back of the fabric and permitted the knitter to carry an unused color across any distance required by the design.

The yarns for authentic Cowichan sweaters are handspun. The earliest yarns were produced on large handspindles. The Cowichans then adapted European spinning-wheel technology to accommodate bulky yarns by putting a huge spinning head on the base of a treadle sewing machine. When treadle sewing-machine bases were no longer readily available, they designed a different type of treadle base. The resulting device is known as an *Indian-head spinner* (sometimes *bulk-head* or *bulky spinner*).

The Cowichan women spin thick singles of moderate twist—firm and sturdy, yet lofty in character. They knit this yarn into an extremely hard-wearing, solid fabric. A typical Cowichan knitter uses needles in size 10 (6mm) for yarn that the average Euro-American knitter would work up on size 13 or 15 (9–10mm).

Many commercial adaptations of Cowichan-style sweaters are available today, both as patterns and as garments. Most often the sleeves and yoke are raglan-style, and the yarn is a machine-made, lofty six-ply in which the component strands are held together with minimal twist.

The true Cowichan is always knitted of a soft, bulky, handspun singles, firmly tensioned to produce a sturdy fabric. Authentic, well-made, old Cowichan sweaters are now sought as collector's items. Because they are usually "guaranteed to last through thirty years of hard use," many remain from the early 1900s.

A Cowichan-style shawl collar

The Cowichan-style shawl collar can be worked in a number of ways, but all have a similar foundation: a three-section construction, the back plus two front portions. These parts may be worked in ribbing or garter stitch (garter stitch is favored today). The front sections are usually worked first, and then the back section is both formed and joined to the front pieces as the work progresses.

My favorite collar has two stripes in a contrasting color in each of the three sections, as well as a stand. A collar stand is a vertical portion above the neckline that is worked on the back segment before width is added. The height to which the collar back rises above the base of the neck is determined by the depth of the collar stand.

Traditional collar, beginning with the front sections

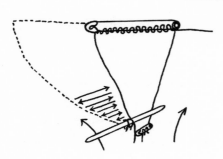

1. Attach the yarn at an inside edge on the center front so the tail can be worked in and concealed. Work back and forth in garter stitch or ribbing, picking up a new stitch each time the neck edge is reached. With one stitch added at the end of every other row in this way, you will have a shallow collar. If you want a deep collar, you must also increase at the outside edge at the beginning of each row. To keep the edge of the collar smooth, make this increase between the first and second, or second and third, stitches from the outside edge. Continue until the collar is as deep as you would like it.

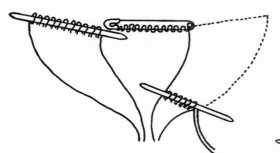

2. Leaving the first section on a holding needle, repeat the same process on the other side of the front. After this section has been completed, leave its stitches on a second holding needle.

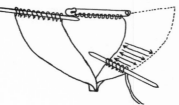

If you are working a pullover, overlap the second side by picking up through the back of the initial stitches of the first side.

186

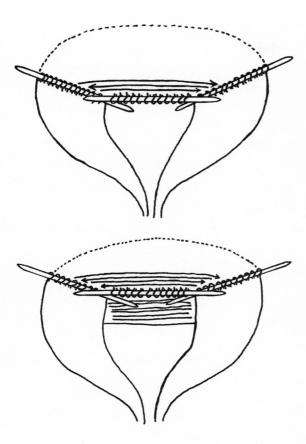

3. Put the back-neck stitches on a third needle and, with a fourth needle, begin working back and forth. To build the collar stand, which should be between 1 and 2 inches deep, the first few rows are joined by knitting the last back-collar stitch and the next front-collar stitch with the appropriate decrease for the structure (garter stitch or ribbing). When the collar is the desired depth, join the back to the front by adding a stitch from the collar front at the end of every row.

4. Continue to work across the back neck, adding one stitch from the collar front at each side. This increases the collar back by one stitch at the end of every row, first from one side front and then from the other side front.

5. Proceed in this manner until all the front-collar stitches from both sides have been incorporated into the collar back. Bind off the back-collar stitches. The finished collar, especially with stripes, is lovely in fit and appearance.

Unique Cowichan shoulder join

Some of the most creative knitters use a shoulder join unique to these sweaters, a double bind-off technique. It requires three needles: a short, straight cable needle (called the working needle) in a size that matches that of the body needles; one needle to hold the back shoulder stitches; and one needle to hold the front shoulder stitches. With the strand of yarn *between* the two shoulder needles, you will rotate the working needle first clockwise to the front, then counterclockwise to the back, slipping it back and forth so its tip comes within working distance of the stitches on the two holding needles, alternating between front and back.

Double bind-off shoulder join using three needles

1. Knit 1 stitch on the front needle.

2. Rotate the working needle counterclockwise to the back.

3. Purl 1 stitch on the back needle.

4. Rotate the working needle clockwise to the front needle to knit 1 stitch.

5. Pass the first knit stitch over the second knit stitch to bind off 1 stitch on the front.

6. Rotate the working needle counterclockwise to the back needle to purl 1 stitch.

7. Pass the first purl stitch over the second purl stitch to bind off 1 stitch on the back.

8. The bind-off alternates: K1 and pass over on the front, then P1 and pass over on the back.

Continue until all but the 2 final stitches, 1 on the front and 1 on the back, have been removed. These 2 stitches can be set aside to be used in forming the collar stitches or knitted together, pulling the yarn end through this final loop to close it. (Look on the wrong side—the double bind-off looks like stockinette!)

Cowichan Pullover with Geometric Patterns 1

The early geometric designs were most often worked in five horizontal bands. A wide center band dominates the body of the sweater and is repeated on the upper arms. Narrower pattern bands repeat on both sides of the center band. The first and fifth bands consist of stripes incorporated into the hip ribbing and the collar.

The pullover is knitted in the round to the underarm, where a few stitches may be added for ease. The work is divided and the back is worked to the shoulders. The front is further divided into two equal sections (sometimes one or two stitches are set aside to begin the collar), and a V neck is formed as these front portions are worked up. On older sweaters, the stitches at each shoulder were bound off together. The sleeve stitches are then picked up around each armhole and worked to the wrist.

Cowichan Geometric Pullover 1

← Large band on body and sleeves.

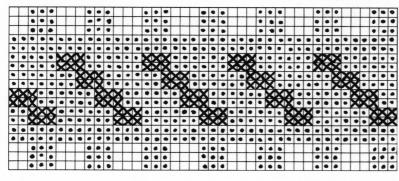

← Smaller band on body and lower sleeves.

Cowichan Pictorial Cardigan

→ Main sleeve patterns. The center three elements also appear across the yoke.

→→ Bird for sweater front; mirrored on opposite side.

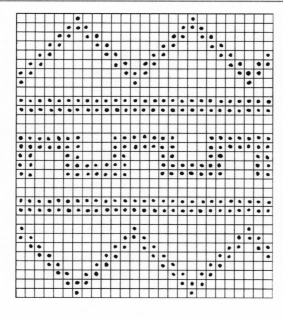

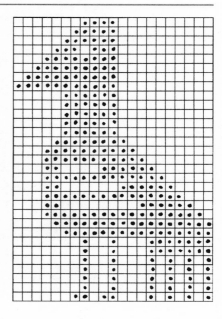

191

Cowichan Pullover with Geometric Patterns 2

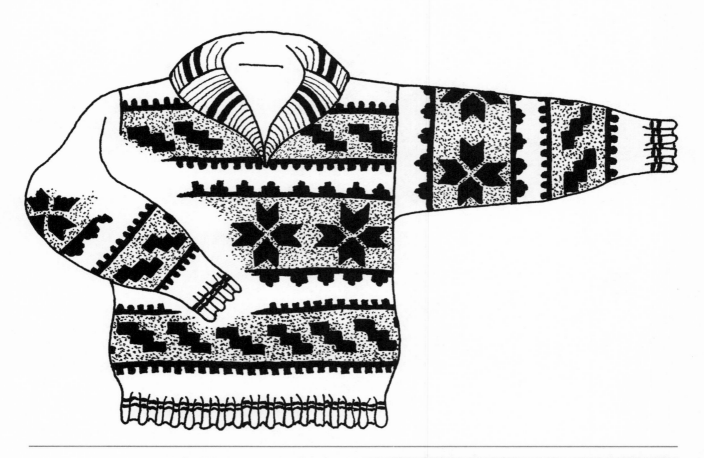

Cowichan Geometric Pullover 2

→ Large band on body and sleeves.

↓ Smaller band on body and lower sleeves.

Cowichan Cardigan with Pictorial Motifs

The large bird on the right in the drawing appears on the back of the sweater. Patterns for the Cowichan Pictorial Cardigan are on pages 191 and 194.

When Cowichan knitters use non-geometric designs—for example, representations of local flora and fauna, or ideas from outside sources like embroidery books—the center band is replaced by a pictorial design. This is bounded on one or both sides by smaller geometric pattern bands, and the stripes appear as before at the hip and in the collar. Despite the pictorial motif on the body, the sleeves usually have a wide geometric band, like the center band of an all-geometric sweater.

The early sweaters were pullovers, but many are now cardigans. Early sweaters were always knitted in the round; many traders slit a pullover and inserted a zipper to make a cardigan. The best Cowichan knitters frown upon cutting, preferring to work the bodies of their cardigans flat and the sleeves in the round. When a representational design is used, the cardigan front is handled as two separate units, each side a mirror image of the other. The design itself might be an adaptation of the design on the back of the garment or it might be complementary but totally different.

Because most Cowichan cardigans have a zipper, the first stitch of every row is slipped, and the slipped stitch is followed by two stitches in garter stitch.

For a buttoned front, on the other hand, an overlap is required. The overlap must be at least 5 stitches wide to accommodate an appropriately sized button (the buttonholes are worked as K2, bind off 2, K1). The edge/overlap stitches form part of the base for the shawl collar (pages 186–87) and are reserved on holders while the shoulders are completed.

Cowichan Pictorial Cardigan

→ Pattern for lower body and lower sleeves.

→ Large bird for back. Note that the banding on the wings and the tail structures of the large bird and the small bird vary slightly among the drawings and charts (pages 184, 191, 193, and here). You can similarly modify patterns to suit your stitch and row counts, or just because you want to.

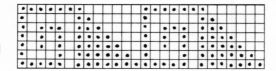

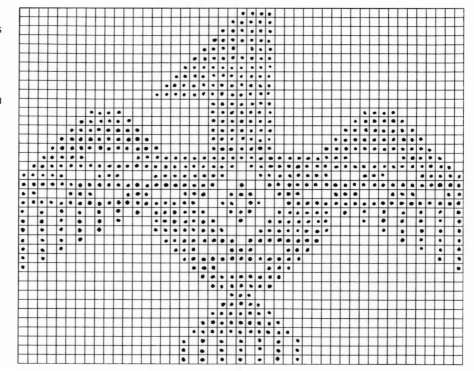

American Folk Art Designs

Although knitters in the United States lack a distinctively national knitting tradition, we have an abundance of folk art motifs that can be readily adapted for color-stranded knitting. In the 1980s, a folk art look has emerged using stylized figures in bands of color-stranded patterns. The figures, copied from other folk art media, often include hearts, birds, and tulips.

The style I prefer for displaying these motifs is a boxy vest worked in a bulky yarn with little or no shaping, very loosely fitted. The neckline can be a straight boat style or a widely fitting crew (pages 128 and 123).

I use a wide, deep, unshaped armhole that complements the straight lines of the vest. The underarm consists of a straight platform of stitches, between 4 and 5 inches wide. This permits the armband to drop straight from the edge of the shoulder. The armhole must be as much as 10 to 12 inches deep to provide sufficient space for the width of the armband, for which K1, P1 ribbing, garter stitch, and seed stitch are appropriate choices.

To work the armband, divide the underarm stitches into two equal parts. Beginning in the middle, work to one side. Then pick up stitches around the edge of the armhole, ending at the bottom of the far side; then work the remainder of the reserved underarm stitches. You will need to decrease 2 stitches at each corner on every other row (a double decrease). If you are working in ribbing or seed stitch, a slight modification of the balanced double decrease keeps the pattern in order and makes a nice design element: slip 2 together knitwise, K1, then pass both slipped stitches over together (S2tog, K1, P2SSO).

Folk Art Vest 1

Patterns for upper body.

Another American folk art design—a sheep-motif sweater worked in intarsia—appears on pages 210–11.

195

Folk Art Vest 1

Folk Art Vest 1

← Patterns for middle body.
↓ Patterns for lower body.

Patterns for the upper body
are on page 195.

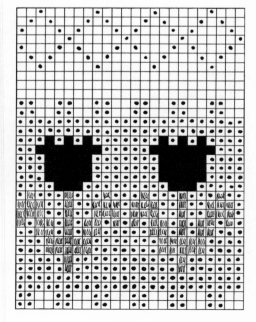

196

Folk Art Vest 2

A note about adapting designs to your own size applies to all the patterns in this book, but can be demonstrated easily with this particular combination of charts, and with such an intricate combination of motifs the placement of the designs is critical to the effect.

The interlocking pattern bands for Folk Art Vest 2 mirror at the center stitch (marked with ↑ on the chart sections). Note the variation at the outer edges of the side tulips.

At 5 stitches to the inch, this vest as charted will measure about 32 inches in circumference. At 4 stitches to the inch, it will be about 40 inches around. Using your yarn's gauge and your desired circumference, adjust or adapt the patterns to achieve symmetry.

Folk Art Vest 2

← Patterns for upper body. Patterns for the middle body and the lower body are on page 198.

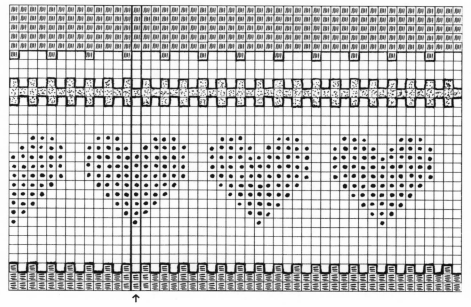

Folk Art Vest 2

↓ Patterns for middle body.

↓↓ Patterns for lower body.

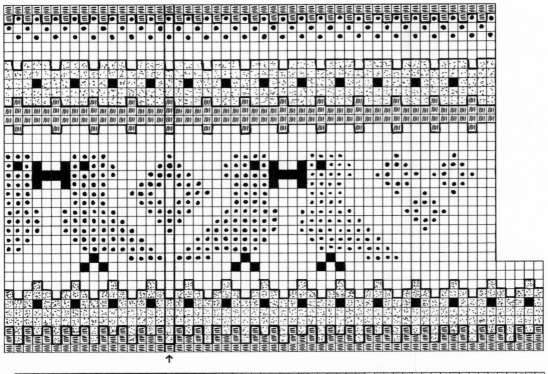

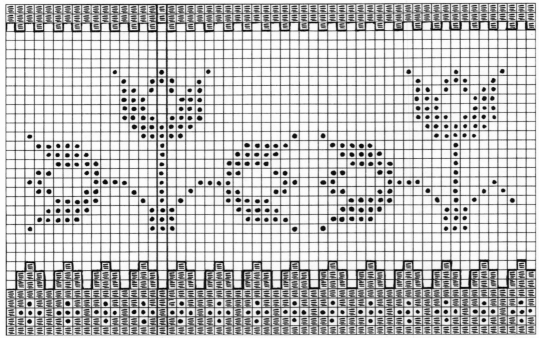

198

Intarsia

For many years, I refused to consider intarsia patterning as a legitimate aspect of knitting. After all, it had no basis in the folk tradition and I am not a "fashion" knitter. Then my fascination with sock knitting began—and I discovered a long and illustrious history of intarsia patterning in the folkwear of South America, Eastern Europe, the Middle East, and Central Asia!

But I was right in one regard: intarsia is not a circular technique. The pattern must be worked flat. Nonetheless, there are a number of intriguing ways to work intarsia in a "seamless" garment. All involve working rows back and forth in each section of color while interlocking adjacent sections.

I will detail four techniques that I have found to be most useful for forming connected areas of color in sweaters: a two-step color-stranding process; the yarn-over join; and two types of invisible join. Two of these methods come from South America; one is from Eastern Europe; and one developed in both South America and Eastern Europe.

Incidentally, I have now embraced intarsia with a passion!

Motifs

The word *motif* has two meanings, and the move from color stranding to intarsia requires a shift from one to the other. Structurally, these meanings acquire a world of difference.

In color-stranded knitting, a motif is a *recurring thematic element.* The bands and other patterning arrangements of color stranding are composed by grouping, and often alternating, individual motifs. Motifs form in repetition as yarns are carried all the way around the sweater.

In intarsia, a motif is a *single unit.* Here, *motif* can refer to a single leaf on a sleeve, a bird with outstretched wings on a sweater back, or each of two reindeer that face each other across the front opening of a cardigan.

In intarsia, the colors that form an isolated pattern element (*motif* in the second meaning) are not carried around the entire circumference of the garment.

Knitting in reverse

For knitting intarsia patterns in the round, the skill of knitting in reverse (i.e., backward) is not essential, but it is important. If you can knit in reverse, you may not want to turn the work on alternate rows. When you knit in reverse, the face of the pattern is always toward you, which makes it much easier to see what is happening. Once you learn to knit in reverse, your progress with intarsia patterns will be both faster and more relaxed.

Knitting usually proceeds from right to left (the next stitch to be worked lies to the left of the stitch just worked). Reverse knitting proceeds from left to right, and the next stitch to be worked lies to the right of the stitch just worked. Many left-handed knitters are familiar with working this way.

Working a standard knit stitch in reverse

1. Enter the stitch with the left needle tip from left to right, behind the right needle tip.

2. Wrap the yarn from back to front, coming up and over the left needle tip. Draw the yarn wrap through the loop on the right needle to form the new stitch on the left needle.

3. Here the new stitch ison the left needle, and the right needle is being withdrawn from the old stitch.

Maintaining a consistent gauge

Your gauge may change when you shift from knitting circularly to knitting flat. This may cause uneven fabric when you work intarsia (flat) areas in a basically circular garment. Here's how to avoid the problem.

If the difference is significant, information presented in the discussion of Eastern, Western, and combined knitting (Chapter 4) holds the answer to your problem. Wrapped in the standard manner, the purl/reverse-knit stitch requires more yarn than the standard knit stitch. When you wrap the yarn in the non-standard manner, this disparity disappears. So consider adapting the way you wrap the yarn when you form a purl stitch (when working a section flat) or a reverse-knit stitch (when knitting in reverse).

When you make this adjustment, the new stitch will be mounted with the leading side of the loop on the back of the needle. On the next row, you will need to knit each of these stitches through its back loop to produce a standard knit stitch.

Wrapping a *purl stitch*, coming over the needle tip from back to front, makes a new stitch with the leading side of the loop on the back of the needle. (This is the combined method on page 46: Western stitch mount and Eastern yarn wrap.)

Wrapping a *reverse-knit stitch*, coming over the needle tip from front to back, also makes a new stitch with the leading side of the loop on the back of the needle.

In *either case*, to form an open knit stitch on the next row you knit the new stitch through the back loop with a standard wrap.

Intarsia techniques

Two-step intarsia technique

This method works well for designs where the main color appears within, as well as surrounding, the motif pattern. Each motif is worked in two steps.

A technique from both Eastern Europe and South America. Suggested for use in the sweater on page 209.

Step 1. Color-stranded row (one pass, right to left):

Color-strand the design in the pattern color(s) and the main color. At the left side of the motif, drop the pattern color(s).

Using the main color, complete the round. Step 2 begins when you reach the righthand edge of the motif.

Step 2. Two-pass row:

First pass, main or background color (right to left): Continue with the main color and work across the motif by knitting all the main-color stitches in the motif and slipping as to purl all the stitches in the motif color(s). The main color is at the left side of the motif; drop it there for the moment.

Second pass, motif color(s) (left to right): Working from the left side, knit in reverse (or turn and purl back). Pick up the pattern color(s) so that they come up and over (across) the main-color yarn. Now work all the pattern-color stitches and slip as to purl all the main-color stitches (those that were worked on the first pass of this step).

At the right side of the motif, drop the pattern color(s). They are now in position to knit the next color-stranded row.

To complete the round, return to the left side of the motif to pick up the main color and continue to knit around the circumference until you reach the right side of the motif again. Repeat steps 1 and 2 until the motif is complete.

Yarn-over join

A technique from South America. Suggested for use in the sweater on page 210.

This technique is useful for knitting blocks of color like those used in the representational patterns of many contemporary sweaters made in Bolivia. Hand knitted in glorious, earthy tones from alpaca yarns, these sweaters are a fine addition to a long tradition of knitting.

This join is not totally invisible (there is a slight thickening at the join), but this process is useful any time the pattern does not encircle the sweater. To make the join as unobtrusive as possible, position the joining point under an arm or at the center back, and/or use the main color as the first and last color of the round.

Each section of the design requires a separate color bobbin (or center-pull butterfly).

1. Start at the join (the beginning of the row) with the first color; yarn-over and knit to the first color change. Drop the first color.

2. Reach under the first-color strand to bring up the second color (twisting the yarns), and knit the second color across its section.

3. Drop the second color. Reach under the second-color strand to bring up the third color (twisting the yarns), and knit the third color across its section.

4. Continue in this manner around the circumference, working up to the last stitch of the *row*. Complete the *round* with an SSK decrease, joining the yarn-over from the beginning of the row with the last stitch. Turn.

5. Yarn over and purl back around the garment, dropping and twisting the yarns as before at each color change. Purl up to the last stitch of the *row*. Complete the *round* with a P2tog decrease, joining the yarn-over at the beginning of the row with the last stitch.

You can also knit in reverse (see page 200), with the design always facing forward. Working in this manner, the last stitch is joined with the yarn-over as a K2tog (in place of the P2tog when purling).

Invisible join 1

This intarsia technique has its roots in Andean knitting, specifically in the cuffs of socks from Bolivia and Ecuador. With this technique, there is no visible join, because the connecting points for the rows shift, following the path of one of the color changes. This technique is not difficult, although it can be confusing on the first attempt.

As on the previous technique, the sweater is worked back and forth, not in circular rounds, and after each knitted row you can work the next row either by turning and purling back or by knitting in reverse.

A technique from South America. Suggested for use in the sweater on page 212.

To begin, knit the first row of the intarsia design in the standard manner, twisting the colors as usual at each color change. When you finish this round, continue the work in rows throughout the design portion, as follows:

1. Turn the work so that the purl side faces you. When you do this, all of the yarns will be at the right edges of their color sections, in working position.

2. You will purl the first row from right to left. As you begin the row, twist the yarn of the first color section with the yarn of what will become the last color section for this row. This sets you up to make the join at the end of the row, the invisible join or "seamless" part of this technique.

Note that the yarn for the first color section is where it needs to be, at the right edge of its area. Yet the yarn for the last color section in the row is also at the right edge of its area, which is not where it *apparently* needs to be in order to be part of this twist. Twist these two yarns together anyway, allowing the yarn of the last color section to float across the face of the stitches until it reaches the twisting point. Don't worry about the float. It will disappear at the end of the row. You are now ready to begin purling.

3. Work this first row as usual. As you purl the row, at each color change you twist the yarns in the standard manner: bring the new color under the old, then drop the old section's color and continue with the color of the new section.

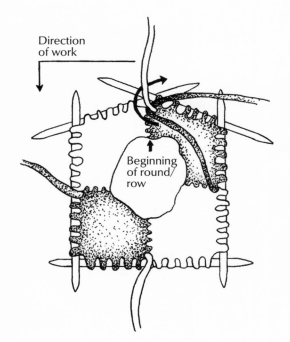

Direction of work

Beginning of round/ row

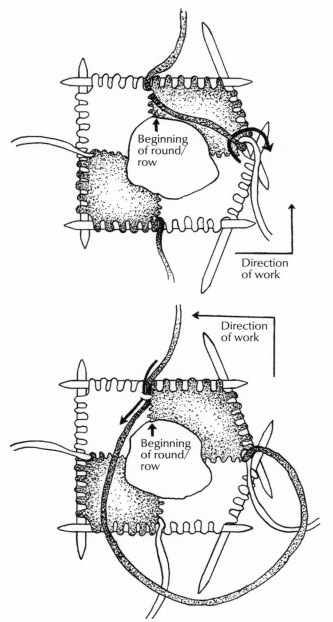

Beginning of round/ row

Direction of work

Direction of work

Beginning of round/ row

4. At the last color section, the final yarn does not appear to be available for use, because it is secured at both ends. Instead, you have a float that originates in the stitches of the previous row at the color change and travels across the section before being secured in the twist at the start of the row. To twist the yarns of the second-to-last and last sections, slip the yarn of the second-to-last color through the floating loop of the last color. This produces the standard twist at the last color-change point.

5. To complete the final section, create a working length of yarn with which to knit by pulling on the float of the last color. The yarn slides easily through the twist that secures it to the beginning of the row. Pull the looped yarn until enough is free for you to knit comfortably, even though the yarn's far end is not completely loose. Beginning with the end that comes out of the last stitch of the previous row, work this final section.

6. At the turning point of the beginning of the row, eliminate what remains of the yarn loop by pulling the excess back through the twist. The first and last sections of this row have been invisibly joined, and the piece is again circular.

7. When you turn the piece to work in the other direction, continuing the intarsia portion of the garment in rows rather than rounds, repeat this process of setting up the end of the row by twisting the colors of the first and last sections right at the start. Note that when you change directions, you will be working with different "first" and "last" colors—the color that was first is now last.

This South American invisible technique is ideally suited for joining in a vertical line. If your pattern elements have a fluctuating edge, you have two choices. If the design allows, you can keep the joins along a vertical line by placing the join down the middle of a section of color (the same color will be used for the first and last stitches of the row). Or you can keep the join at a color change by shifting the starting point of each row according to the design. To make a color change shift to the left, at the end of the round slip the stitches from left to right until you reach the new starting point. To make a color change shift to the right, complete the round and then slip stitches from right to left to go back to the new starting point. If slipping these stitches produces a long float across the back of the piece, secure that float on the next row. To do this, take the needle tip under the float before working a stitch. Work the stitch and then draw the needle tip back under the float. When you knit the following stitch, the working yarn will cross the float and secure it.

And, yes, this technique can be readily applied to the knitting of argyle patterning on socks or sweaters, because the color changes only shift by one stitch at a time, progressing to the left and then back out to the right. No long floats!

Invisible join 2

Recently, I discovered a "new" old way of working seamless intarsia on a pair of footlets believed to be of Eastern European origin, probably from the Balkans. This has become my favorite intarsia technique. It is very easy, especially when the designs on the front and the back are separate units. I find it especially useful for pictorial designs, including the bulky Cowichan-style pullovers (traditionally color-stranded).

Once you understand the process, the work becomes incredibly simple. I suggest that you become familiar with the technique through a small sample. In your test use two different colors of yarn: what I call the original color for the back of the "garment" and a contrasting color for the front.

To eliminate the need to slip stitches back and forth, work on two circular needles. When you start, needle 1 will hold all the stitches. You will move all the stitches onto needle 2 in two steps. In the next pass, you move them all back to needle 1, and so on.

Working circularly, begin by working a few rounds of ribbing followed by a few rounds of stockinette. At the beginning of the next round, divide the stitches in half and with the contrasting color knit the half of

A technique from Eastern Europe. Suggested for use in the sweaters on pages 214 and 216.

the stitches on the near side of the circle (knit side facing you). Use the original color to work the second half, on the far side of the circle (purl side facing you).

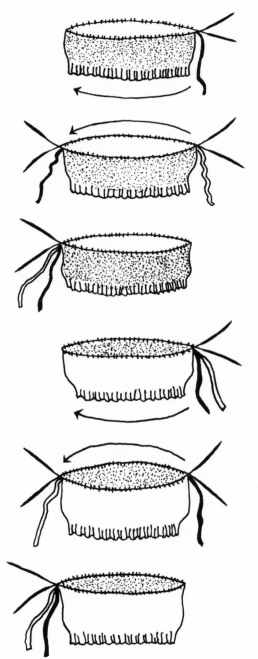

1. With the contrasting color, knit across the stitches on the near side of the circle (front of the sweater) from right to left. Drop the working yarn on the left side. Half the stitches will be on one circular needle and half on the other. Your work is off by half a round.

2. Return to the beginning of the round. With the original color, purl across the far side of the circle (back of the sweater), using the other end of the working needle. (If you would like to continue your work on the face side of the fabric, turn the entire tube so the far side faces you and knit in reverse on this row.) The round is now complete, and all the stitches are on one needle.

3. Turn the work to bring the tips of the needles to the right.

4. Twist the contrasting and original yarns together. Using the original color, knit across the near side of the circle (back of the sweater). Half of the round is complete; the stitches are on two needles.

5. Return to the beginning of the round. Using the contrasting color, purl across the far side (front of the sweater). (If you would like to continue your work on the face side of the fabric, turn the entire tube so the far side faces you and knit in reverse on this row.)

6. The round is complete and all the stitches are on one needle.

7. Turn the work to bring the tips of the needles to the right (ready for step 1).

Repeat these seven steps. When you finish the fabric and work the ends in, close the gap at the beginning of the first round with the tail of the contrasting yarn.

207

Once you understand the technique when working with two colors, it's simple to insert intarsia patterns. You can divide the work into units anywhere—not just between front and back, and even within a unit of pattern—because there is no jog at the dividing point.

If you work isolated units, as in the falling leaves sweater (page 214), you will use two strands of yarn of the same color that come from separate balls. When working in this way, I use yarn markers to divide the work into the two units (for example, the front and the back of the sweater). The yarn markers are scraps of yarn about 6 to 8 inches long and unknotted, so they have 3- to 4-inch tails. I will weave the tails behind a row, then in front of a row, in order to secure the markers that track the division points for the continuing rounds.

Sweater with Two-Step Intarsia Motif

One llama/alpaca motif is for fine yarns (→) and one is for medium-weight yarns (↓). Either would make an excellent sweater, but look at how much more character the fine motif has!

This version has been charted for use with fine yarns. It is 41 stitches wide and 77 rows tall.

This simple version has been charted for medium-weight yarns. It is 17 stitches wide and 38 rows tall.

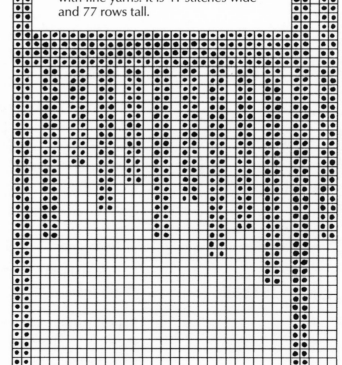

Sweater with Two-Step Intarsia Motif

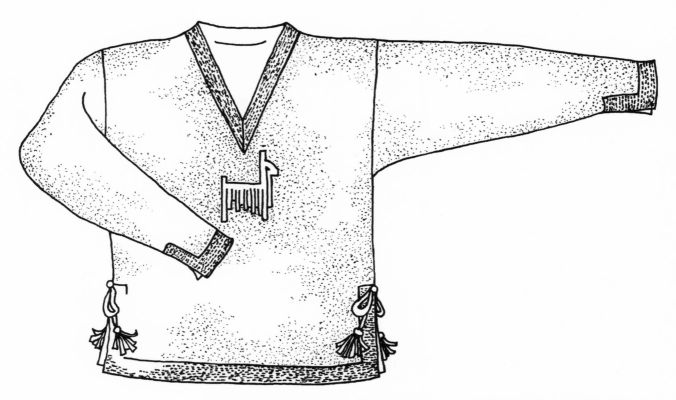

The two-step intarsia technique is described on page 202.

Motif knitting is credited to Bulgaria, yet we find the identical two-step intarsia technique practiced by the native peoples of South America.

Many South American ponchos and sweaters feature images of llamas or alpacas, and the possible variations are endless. Simple, tunic-style sweaters, like the one shown here with a single motif at the point of the V neckline, have been around for years.

In all but a few rows, the background color is incorporated into the pattern. On the body rows where it is not part of the design, the main color must be woven loosely onto the back surface of the fabric.

Fine yarns are most suitable for this sweater. Luxury fibers, like llama or alpaca, spin up most effectively into fine yarns. So you might consider making a llama of llama.

Sweater with Yarn-Over Join

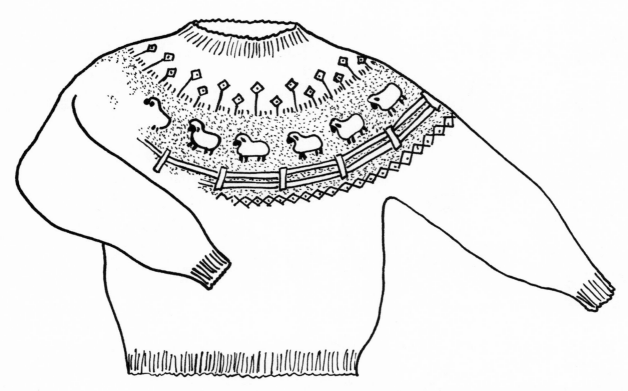

Many knitters in North America, especially handspinners, like to knit sheep into their sweaters. These sheep come in many varieties, and are often surrounded by color-stranded patterning. The sheep themselves—whether one or many—are usually best worked as individual units, to eliminate long floats on the back.

The particular rendition of a sheep sweater shown here is ideal for the yarn-over join. In this case, the join should be positioned at the center back.

The yarn-over join is described on page 203.

Sweater with Yarn-Over Join

These patterns can be used to try a variety of color-handling techniques. Instructions for the full-yoke structure shown in the sweater drawing opposite are on pages 103–07. There are plenty of solid-color rows within which to work the decreases (as described on page 174).

Sweater with Invisible Join 1 (South American)

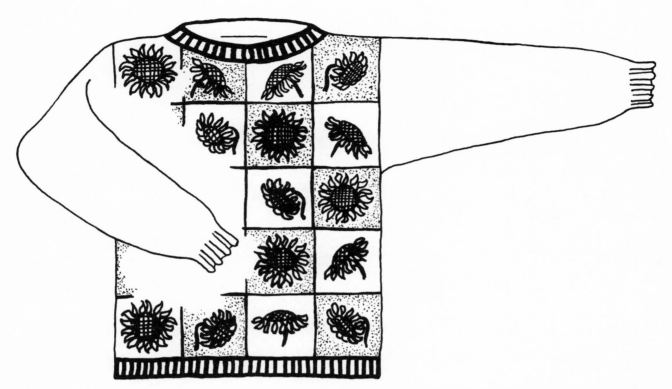

Squares of many colors are a good way to utilize small quantities of yarn. In this design, the ground colors are earthy shades, common to vegetal dyes, and natural-colored wools, many of which have been overdyed to increase the color range.

This patterning style is typical of some of the earliest sweaters to come from South America, both cardigans and pullovers. The floral patterning in traditional sweaters usually involves smaller design elements than my bold adaptations of sunflowers. Use a medium-weight yarn to maximize the realism of the blossoms. Although there are only three flower charts, you can evoke an illusion of greater variety by reversing some and by using many shades to work them, from pale yellow through rich orange to russet red.

Because the design appears only on the front, the best solution when working the garment circularly is to place an invisible join at one underarm. The size of the blocks can be increased to make larger sweaters, or decreased to make smaller sizes.

Invisible join 1 is described on pages 204–05.

Sweater with Invisible Join 1

Three sunflower patterns worked in many color combinations will produce the effect of a garden. The lines on the drawing indicate the joins between squares, not a line of a contrasting color. However, you can add lines of contrasting color, if you like!

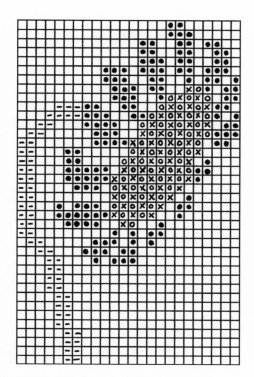

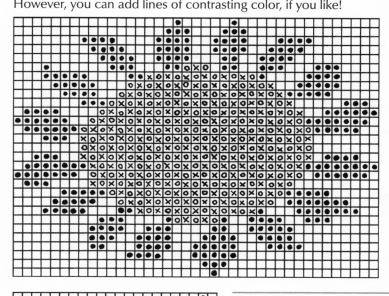

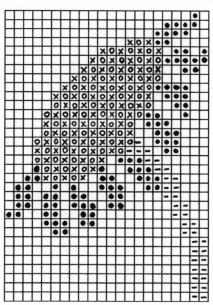

Sweater with Invisible Join 2 (Eastern European)

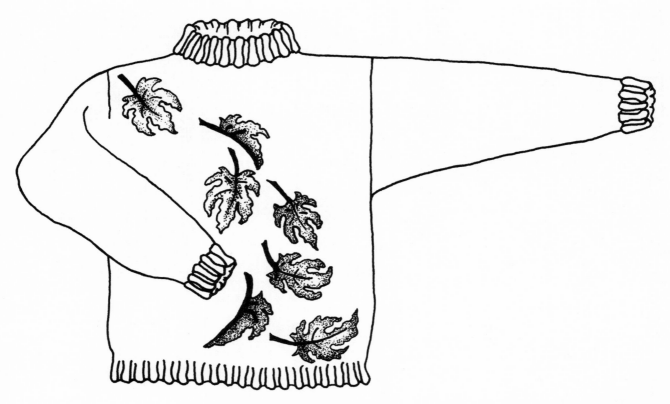

I have not seen invisible join 2 used in sweaters, but it is the ultimate technique for many intarsia patterns. Most intarsia patterning can be divided easily for the front and back at the underarms, as can this design with one of my favorite themes: maple leaves in their autumn colors. This turtleneck sweater is suitable for medium- to heavy-weight yarns.

The background colors are the same front and back, but they are worked from separate balls of yarn. On the front, the intarsia patterning is worked in the standard manner, with a small butterfly or bobbin for each color.

Although only two variations of the leaf pattern are offered, you can develop an endless variety from these baselines, like the leaves of a real maple tree. Use a full range of colors, from a yellow dappled with green to a red shading into brown. Reverse the patterns; increase their size; change the curvature. Alter the placement of the leaves to accommodate any size of garment.

Invisible join 2 is described on pages 206–07.

Sweater with Invisible Join 2

Use these leaf patterns in a variety of colors, change their orientation, and chart variations.

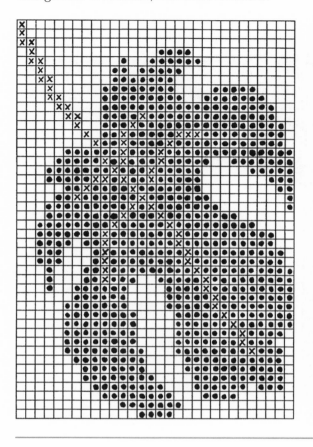
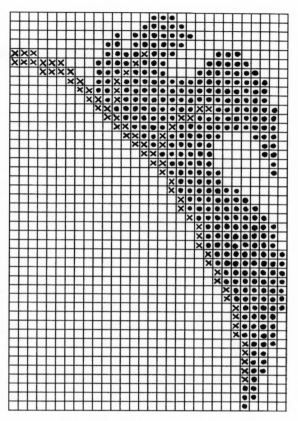

Modern Interpretation of Bolivian Patchwork Sweater

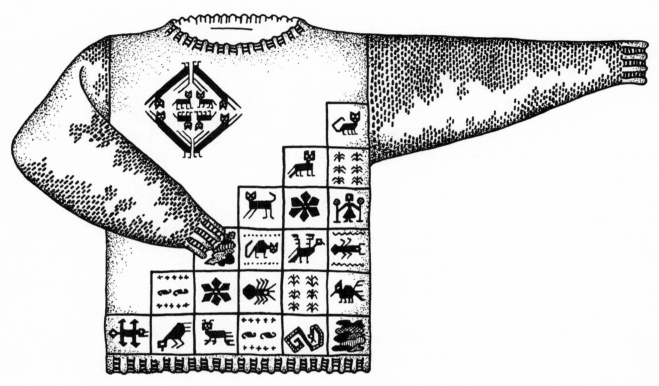

Modern Patchwork-Style Sweater

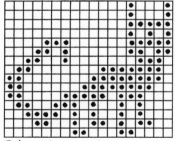

Column 1, square 6

Consider using invisible join 2, described on pages 206–07. The sweater patterns are on pages 216–19.

To remain valid, traditional knitting designs and techniques must be dynamic, never static. This sweater, with age-old designs found on knitted caps and arm-warmers from mountainous Bolivia, is my interpretation of the patchwork block sweaters that evolved in South America. Yet the sweater is a knitter's hybrid: its construction technique is Eastern European.

The yarn of choice is spun from soft, warm alpaca, grown in Bolivia. Natural alpaca colors are augmented by overdyeing with colors from native plants plus indigo and cochineal, a palette that yields an awesome range of muted shades, not of high contrast and sharp focus.

Each block consists of 36 stitches, planned for construction in a fine to ultrafine yarn (working up at between 8 and 12 stitches to the inch). The garment size is determined by the dimensions of the squares. The backgrounds of the squares are different colors.

The sweater body is stockinette, worked in the round. The edges are worked in a ribbing variation where rounds of K2, P2 alternate with straight knitted rounds. The sleeves carry out this theme of subtle textures by alternating rounds of K2, P2 with rounds of P2, K2. The patchwork blocks on the sweater front can be repeated on the back of the sweater, or the back can be plain (typical of South American garments, and much simpler).

This garment is ideal for the intarsia technique of knitting the front and purling the back (invisible join 2, described on pages 206–07; always twist the yarns at the sides). The squares are intarsia and the design on each square is color-stranded. The lines around the squares in the drawing indicate color shifts, not outlining, although outlines could work!

Modern Patchwork-Style Sweater

The charts for the patchwork squares are marked according to these location numbers keyed to the sweater drawing. Columns are numbered from right to left and squares from the bottom ribbing up. Column 1, on the right in the drawing, contains six squares. Column 6, on the left, contains one square.

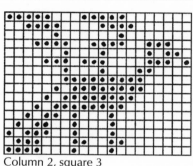

Column 2, square 3

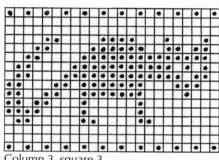

Column 3, square 3

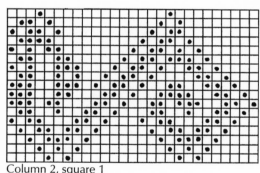

Column 2, square 1

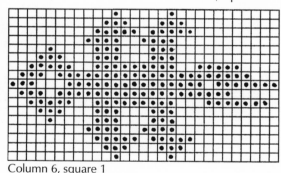

Column 6, square 1

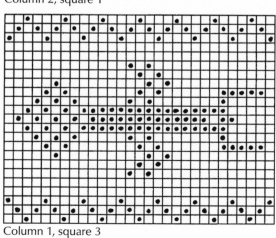

Column 1, square 3

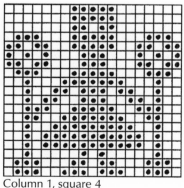

Column 1, square 4

↓ Texture pattern for sleeves.

↓↓ Texture pattern for edges.

217

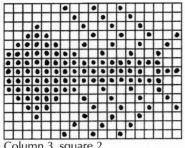

Column 3, square 2

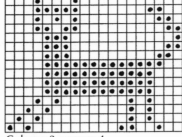

Column 3, square 4

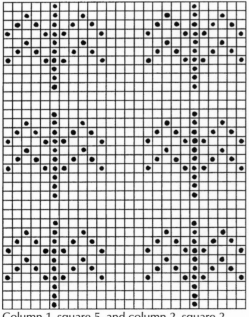

Column 1, square 2

Modern Patchwork-Style Sweater

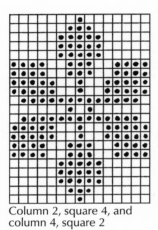

Each of the charts in this lower group appears twice in the sweater.

Column 2, square 4, and column 4, square 2

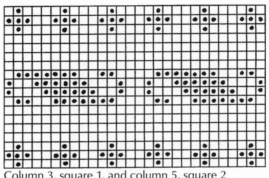

Column 3, square 1, and column 5, square 2

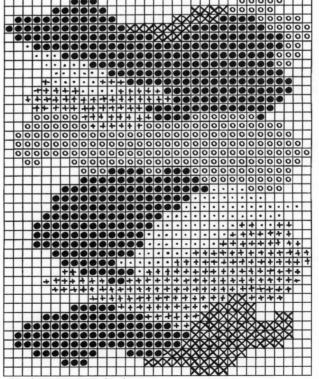

Column 1, square 5, and column 2, square 2

Cloud mass in mixed colors:
Column 1, square 1, and column 4, square 3

218

← Eight-cat motif on upper body.

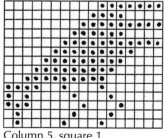

Column 5, square 1

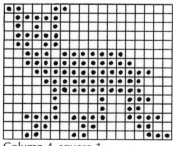

Column 4, square 1

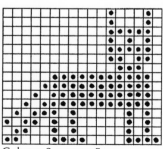

Column 2, square 5

Texture

Textured patterns range in difficulty from very simple knit/purl sequences to laces to basic or intricate traveling-stitch patterns to complex embossed designs. The work of making knitted textures is relatively easy to master, but reading the instructions can be a mind-boggling experience!

Charting textured patterns

Charting the designs on graph paper with a system of symbols gives an easy-to-follow visual representation of the design. When diagramming textured patterns, I use standard graph paper, preferably four or five squares to the inch, because the symbols are easier to read than on knitter's graph paper. The chart shows just the basic moves, because most textured knitting requires little more than variations of knit and purl stitches.

In situations requiring maneuvers other than those in my list (pages 72–73) or someone else's, you can adapt symbols for a particular use. As an example, here's how to adapt the symbol for a *make-one raised increase,* Ϙ. If the pattern calls for a *bar increase* (knit through the leading side and then again through the trailing side of the stitch), you can add a bar to the symbol, so it reads Ϙ. Or the same Ϙ increase can be adapted to read Ϙ to signify a *raised purl increase.*

Making a chart from line-by-line written instructions

Written directions for textured designs are usually given for flat knitting. To work in the round or to make it easier to remember how the stitches fit together to form the pattern—to free yourself from dependence on the page and to learn the skill of "reading" your growing textile instead—you will want to translate any directions from words to symbols, in the form of a chart.

The written directions for flat work name the stitches as they appear to the knitter, not with reference to the face of the fabric. Your chart will graphically represent the face side of the fabric. You will quickly learn to "think" as a knitter in this way, and your freedom will expand profoundly. On page 222–23, a series of illustrations shows how to move from line-by-line directions to a chart.

To make the translation from written directions as easy as possible, chart all the right-side rows first, working from right to left across each row. Then fill in the wrong-side rows, working from left to right and making sure you use the symbols for the actions as they would be performed from the right side. As an example, a wrong-side purl stitch appears on the right side as a knit stitch. The correct notation for these reverse rows is much easier to figure out once you've established part of the pattern by way of the right-side rows.

Once you have your charts, there will be times when you will need to use them to work back and forth. Remember to work each stitch according to the appearance you want on the face of the fabric. Some pattern elements, like bobbles or lace edgings, must be worked back and forth. In charts for these items, row numbers placed on the right or the left side of each row will indicate where the row starts.

A word of caution: when transcribing a pattern from written instructions, always check to see if the pattern begins on the right or wrong side of the fabric. If the pattern begins on the wrong side, begin by charting the even-numbered rows, as demonstrated in the example on the next pages, and then fill in the odd-numbered rows.

Simple knit/purl designs

Often referred to as *damask* or *brocade,* purl designs on a stockinette ground have been used to decorate knitted fabrics for a long time. The earliest use of pattern on garments for the upper classes occurred in silk frocks with elaborate knit/purl motifs. These probably inspired the common folk in Denmark to invent their damask blouses.

The designs depend on subtle surface texture rather than bold relief. Sometimes the designs were made to stand out more prominently by alternating single purl and knit stitches (what we call seed stitch) within the sections of the pattern. The knit stitch below each purl of the seed stitch can be worked through its back loop; this twists the knit stitch,

Charts for simple knit/purl (brocade) mesh patterns.

which in turn makes the subsequent purl stitch tighter and therefore more distinct.

This type of textured knitting was probably inspired by woven damask fabrics, although many designs were also related to embroidery motifs. Knitting, being a latecomer among textile construction techniques, has always been notorious for copying designs from other textile sources. Early folk knitters tended to lift design ideas from just about any surface embellishment, just as knitters do today.

Damask or brocade designs require a simple system of charting: dots to designate purl stitches on a plain ground.

Embossed or sculptured designs

Textured designs featuring embossed or sculptured surfaces—such as traveling stitches, cables, bobbles, trellises, and honeycomb structures—require moving stitches or groups of stitches across the surface,

---

Example of charting from line-by-line instructions

Here are written instructions for a pattern stitch, along with a step-by-step demonstration of how to chart it. Practice with simple patterns like this until you become familiar with thinking about face-side effects of reverse-side maneuvers.

Multiple of 5 stitches plus 2.

Row 1 (wrong side) and all other wrong-side rows: K2, * P3, K2; repeat from *.

Row 2: P2, * K3, P2; repeat from *.

Row 4: P2, * K2tog, yarn-over, K1, P2; repeat from *.

Row 6: Repeat row 2.

Row 8: P2, * K1, yarn-over, SSK, P2; repeat from *.

This pattern is "Single Eyelet Rib," from Barbara G. Walker, *A Treasury of Knitting Patterns.*

1. To see how the repeats fit together, set up a grid with two repeats (5 × 2) plus 2 balancing stitches (total 12 stitches). Because the repeat is 8 rows, the grid is 8 rows tall (or 16, if you want to see how the vertical repeats fit together).

so the stitches end up in a different order. These three-dimensional designs appeared in Spain in the latter half of the eighteenth century, although they may have developed earlier elsewhere—perhaps in the Islamic world. They reached heights of intricacy first in Bavarian traveling stitches of the nineteenth century and later in the Aran knitting of the twentieth century.

Traveling stitches involve units where one stitch (or occasionally two stitches) moves over a single stitch. A traveling-stitch pattern contains many units that move in each row. *Cables* involve the movement of stitches in groups of two or more, with one or more intervening rows between the rows in which stitches move.

Traveling stitches

Traveling stitches provide surface texture by moving diagonally left or right from round to round. These stitches lie on top of the fabric, in sharp relief from the background. If the stitch that moves is twisted (by working it through the back loop), the raised effect is more pronounced.

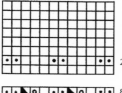

2. Because row 1 is a wrong side row, begin by charting row 2, working from right to left (the direction of face-side knitting progress).

3. Next chart the other right-side rows: 4, 6, and 8 (noting that row 6 is the same as row 2).

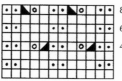

4. Now go back to row 1. Work from left to right on the grid. The first action is K2; these stitches will appear on the face as purls, so mark them that way. The second action involves P3, K2, repeated twice. This will appear on the face as K3, P2, repeated twice, so mark the stitches that way.

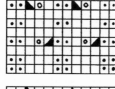

5. The same sequence appears on rows 3, 5, and 7, so they can be filled in to match row 1.

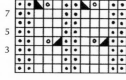

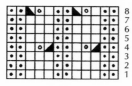

6. The finished chart. Mark the repeats if you like.

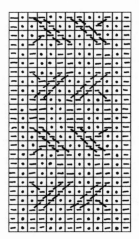

Chart for pattern formed with traveling stitches.

This type of work often highlighted and bordered the brocade patterns of Danish blouses, and later achieved complex heights in the Bavarian waistcoats popular in the alpine regions of Austria and Germany.

Traveling stitches are usually worked as knit stitches. In Western and combined knitting, they travel over a purl ground, and in Eastern knitting they travel over a knit ground. The stitches themselves are most often twisted in Western and Combined knitting and are worked open (not twisted) in Eastern knitting.

The traveling stitches move left or right over the surface of the fabric, changing position on every row. Work of this type is, ideally, a circular technique that originated in sock knitting. However, it is not difficult to work flat as long as you remember that the stitches travel to left or right on *every* row.

Stitches are usually worked singly or in groups of two and do not require the use of a cable needle. The work is charted with a slash from one row diagonally to the next, showing the direction the stitch travels. The diagonal line shows the new position of the stitch in the working row relative to its position in the former row. A word of caution when working twisted traveling stitches back and forth in flat knitting: both the knit stitch on the face of the fabric and the purl stitch on the reverse side must be twisted.

The stitches can be worked out of order (going beyond the first stitch to work the second stitch, then working the second stitch before moving any of the stitches to the right needle). Or you can change the order before working the stitches. I now work only in the latter method, because it is easier on my hands.

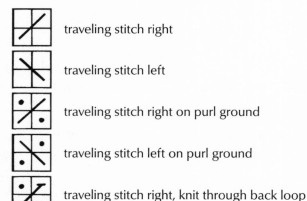

traveling stitch right

traveling stitch left

traveling stitch right on purl ground

traveling stitch left on purl ground

traveling stitch right, knit through back loop (twisted)

traveling stitch left, knit through back loop (twisted)

Method 1: Stitches worked out of order

To work a left cross—that is, a stitch leaning to the left on the surface—go behind the first stitch and work the second stitch; then work the first stitch, and slip both completed stitches off together. To work a right cross, go in front of the first stitch and work the second stitch; then work the first stitch, and slip both completed stitches off together.

224

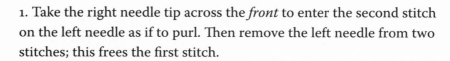

Method 2: Changing the order of the stitches before working them

To move the second stitch on the left needle to the *right* in front of the first stitch:

> 1. Take the right needle tip across the *front* to enter the second stitch on the left needle as if to purl. Then remove the left needle from two stitches; this frees the first stitch.

> 2. The second stitch is on the right needle tip. Take the left needle tip across the back to enter the freed first stitch from left to right.

> 3. Bring the second stitch (on the right needle) across the front of the first stitch, placing it back on the left needle tip.

🢐

To move the first stitch on the left needle to the *left* in front of the second stitch:

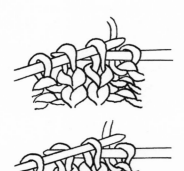

> 1. Take the right needle tip *behind* the first stitch on the left needle to enter the second stitch as if to purl. Remove the left needle from both stitches; this frees the first stitch.

> 2. With the second stitch on the right needle, take the left needle tip across the front to enter the free stitch from left to right.

> 3. Place the second stitch (now on the right needle) back onto the left needle.

🢐

In each of the above cases, the stitches are now ready to work in the new order. They can be twisted by knitting through the back loop or left untwisted. The former method was traditional in Eastern Europe and the latter in the Middle East.

225

The fine points of twisting stitches

When the knit stitches are twisted, they are tightened and become more distinct, especially on a purl ground. Traditionally, the knit stitches are twisted by knitting through the trailing side of a standard stitch mount. This results in a crossed knit stitch that leans to the left. I like to make all crossed stitches traveling to the left (or in the left half of a repeat) in this manner. However, I make my twisted knit stitches traveling to the right (or in the right half of a repeat) lean to the right by adjusting the stitch mount. I place the leading side of the loop on the back of the needle (non-standard stitch mount) and knit through the front of the loop (the trailing side). This results in a twisted knit stitch that leans to the right. Although I use traditional alpine patterns, I like the symmetry provided by adapting the directional cross of the traveling stitches.

Cables

The *simple cable* was probably the earliest embossed work, and also the most widely adapted among many cultures. The cable is an extension of the traveling stitch; instead of a single stitch crossing the surface, a group of stitches is carried to another position. This move requires an auxiliary needle, such as a cable needle. A group of stitches is removed from the left needle to the cable needle without being worked. One or more stitches beyond these are worked, then the stitches on the cable needle are moved back into position on the left needle and worked, or are worked directly off the cable needle, to complete the sequence.

To work a cable leaning left, place the stitches on the cable needle and hold them in front of the work. To work a cable leaning right, hold the stitches on the cable needle behind the work.

To chart cable patterns, use diagonal lines within the working row, one on each side of the group being realigned. The direction of the diagonals corresponds to the direction in which the stitches lean.

Trellis, honeycomb, and intricate *braided* designs are composed of elaborate cables. The basic working technique is still only a matter of removing a series of stitches to an auxiliary needle so they can be worked in a different order.

An elaboration of the cabling technique is the *divided cable,* in which the two sections are divided by one or more stitches that are worked in their original positions. To accomplish this, you must cable twice. The regular cable movement removes a series of stitches to reverse

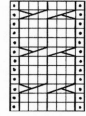

Right cable,
three-over-three.

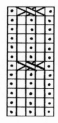

Divided cable. Every sixth round involves the following two cable movements: P1; slip 2 stitches to cable needle and hold in front; K1 from left needle; slip 2nd stitch on cable needle back to left needle and purl it; K remaining stitch from cable needle; P1.

226

their order, with the left cable stitches removed to the front and the right cable stitches removed to the back. In the divided cable, you must change the working order twice to maintain the position of the center-most stitch or stitches.

Fine points of knitting cables

Some knitters have a problem with loose edge stitches on cabled patterns. The solution again lies in adapting the manner in which the purl stitches are wrapped. A standard purl stitch requires more yarn in the wrap than does a standard knit stitch. To eliminate the disparity, the yarn for each purl stitch should be wrapped over the needle tip from back to front (producing a purl stitch with a non-standard stitch mount). The resulting stitch will have the leading side of the loop on the back of the needle and must be worked through the back of the loop on the next round.

Purl stitch, non-standard stitch mount

1. Entering to purl with leading side of the loop on the back of the needle.

2. Wrapping the yarn to form a new stitch, with the leading side of the loop on the back of the needle.

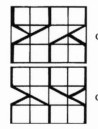 cable right (cable needle to back; leans right)

cable left (cable needle to front; leans left)

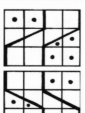 cable right over purl

cable left over purl

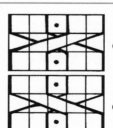 divided cable right

divided cable left

Patterning with increases and decreases

There are countless ways to increase and decrease to create a seemingly infinite number of pattern-stitch variations. Increases and decreases can be used to alter the outlines of design units, or to form sculptured units (for example, bobbles). It's difficult to give general guidelines about how to choose the right increase or decrease for a particular pattern element, although directional lean of the increase or decrease always corresponds to the direction of the outline of a design feature.

In most cases, the number of stitches within a row remains constant, and the number of increases in any given row equals the number of decreases in that row. Some lace stitches and heavily textured patterns are exceptions to this principle. Charting designs with variable stitch counts on graph paper requires flexibility in the use of the basic symbols. You are the only one who needs to be able to read your notations!

For example, a bobble is worked within one row, but its development requires the knitter to work several little rows back and forth within that row before proceeding. (The ability to knit in reverse greatly simplifies making bobbles!) On a chart, a bobble would appear as ●, with a separate section, rather like a footnote, showing how to work the bobble.

To make a bobble in a designated stitch, work one or more increases into that stitch; then turn the fabric and work those new stitches (likely two or three or five); turn the fabric again and work another row just across the bobble stitches; turn and work back. On the final

An all-over bobble pattern. Instructions for working the bobbles themselves (indicated by the circles) are given separately, and often in words.

Individual bobbles can be worked in many different ways. At right are two possibilities, either of which could be used with the all-over bobble pattern charted above. If you are using a source pattern, look for instructions—or experiment!

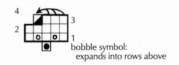
bobble symbol: expands into rows above

Bobble alternative 1, with its translation

Row 1: In the foundation stitch for the bobble, K1, yarn-over, K1, yarn-over, K1.

Row 2: Turn and P5 (or knit in reverse).

Row 3: K3, K2tog.

Row 4: Turn and pass 2nd, 3rd, and 4th stitches individually over the 1st stitch (1 stitch remains).

Turn and and continue round.

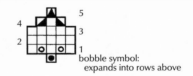
bobble symbol: expands into rows above

Bobble alternative 2, with its translation

Row 1: In the foundation stitch for the bobble, K1, yarn-over, K1, yarn-over, K1.

Row 2: Turn and P5 (or knit in reverse).

Row 3: K5.

Row 4: Turn and P2tog, P1, P2tog (or knit in reverse, decreasing 2 stitches).

Row 5: Balanced double decrease (slip 1, K2tog, PSSO).

228

bobble-forming row, all of the stitches are decreased back to a single stitch. Then work on the row continues in the normal direction. The overall stitch count for the row has not changed. To pull the bobble snug against the surface, twist the final stitch of the bobble on the following row.

The fine points of charting intricate embossed patterns

A final note on charting intricate embossed patterns: it's hardly possible to chart some of these designs without having to use an asterisk to refer to additional instructions. But the primary purpose of charting is to clearly define the position of each design segment in relation to the whole garment and to other pattern elements. The chart represents continuous rows across the pattern or patterns, so that it's easy to see at a glance what comes next. To simplify a chart for, say, an Aran sweater, use a contrasting color to draw vertical lines between pattern units. Put split-ring markers on your work to correspond to these lines, and you'll find it much easier to maintain order while your work is in progress.

Also, because the number of stitches and rows in a repeat varies from pattern to pattern, it helps to draw lines across the chart to mark the vertical repeats. If the patterns have different numbers of rows in their repeats, use a magnetic row-marker for each pattern unit (see page 40).

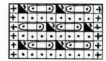

This intriguing pattern has many names, including *blackberry, trinity, cluster,* and *bramble stitch.* The stitch count varies from row to row. Even patterns of this type can often be charted with symbols. The effort is always worthwhile.

Two-end textured designs

Two-end knitting is a traditional Scandinavian technique that fell into disuse late in the nineteenth century. At this time, for some unknown reason (perhaps a charismatic personality?), there was a mass conversion from right-hand to left-hand carry of the yarn. Although two-end knitting *can* be worked with the yarn in the left hand, those proficient in the technique and knowledgeable of tradition will tell you it is, and always has been, worked with the yarn in the right hand.

In recent years, there has been a groundswell of interest in reviving this technique, particularly in Sweden. There, in keeping with the old way, it is commonly used to make accessories, like mittens, gloves, and caps, and occasionally to construct sleeves for woven garments.

The name implies, correctly, that the technique involves working with two strands at once, often the two ends from a single ball of yarn (except, of course, when two colors of yarn are being used). At first glance, old stockings and mittens constructed with the two-end process may appear to have been knitted in stockinette stitch. Closer examination shows that stitches were actually formed with two strands, used alternately.

True two-end knitting was worked with both ends held in the right hand, the strands separated by the first two fingers. The yarn for each new knit stitch must come from beneath the strand used for the previous stitch. The two yarns twist around each other, making a firm, double-thick fabric. This requires frequent stops to untwist the working strands. Alternating purl stitches produce the pattern: a float that rides on the surface and partially covers the knit stitch just below.

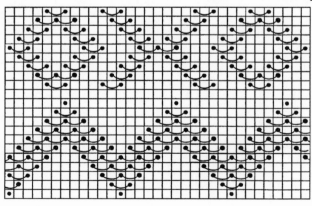

Twisting the yarn with every stitch elongates the knit stitches and reduces elasticity in the fabric. For these reasons, I prefer to work a simplified version of the technique. It resembles color-stranding, because the two-end technique is necessary only in the patterned rows. Although this process lets me use the decorative purl-stitch/float patterning, it is *not* true two-end knitting. It is a hybrid that I find more suitable than the traditional technique for making sweaters as we know them today.

> **Construction detail: Two-end finishes for edges**
>
> An effective way to keep cast-on/bound-off edges from rolling is to make several rounds of twisted two-end knitting, worked in the traditional way with the twist between stitches.
>
> You can create a decorative edge by using two colors and carrying the strands on the front of the work, alternating the directions in which you twist them.

230

Twisted-purl edging in two colors

The only time I twist alternate stitches is for a twisted-purl edging in two colors. The cast-on must be adapted to accommodate the alternating colors. There are many ways to cast on in two colors, but my favorite is an easy way based on the right-hand carry of the twisted-loop cast-on (page 53). The instructions here are brief, because they assume you understand the single-color version of this cast-on. Be sure that you are comfortable with the basic version before you expand your skills to include the two-color variant.

Tie the two strands together, one with a long tail (three times as long as the piece to be cast on). With the knot snug against the needle, use the long tail to form a twisted loop on the left index finger, alternating the two strands coming from the balls when drawing a loop onto the needle. The initial twist is captured in the color of the long tail coming from the knot, appearing immediately below the colored loops on the needle.

These five drawings are a reminder of the twisted-loop cast-on, right-hand carry, described fully on page 53.

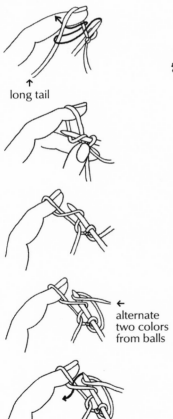

↑
long tail

← alternate two colors from balls

Casting on in two colors

After the stitches have been cast on, the edging is worked as purl stitches in alternating colors; the floats between the stitches ride on the face of the fabric. On the first round, the yarn for the new stitch (matching the color of the first stitch on the needle) must come *under* the yarn of the previous stitch. On the second round, the yarn for a new stitch is twisted *over* the yarn of the previous stitch. This results in a braided effect that can also be utilized within the main body of the work as long as you work a set-up row of knit stitches in alternating colors.

Patterning with two strands of the same color

Other than the twisted braid, the designs are worked in two strands of the same color, hence the name *two-end knitting*. Any number of geometric patterns can be interpreted with the use of the techniques described and illustrated in the stitch sampler and chart. The classic O–X–O patterns shown opposite and on page 232, popular in Norway, are good examples of how a design may look when working with two yarns of the same color.

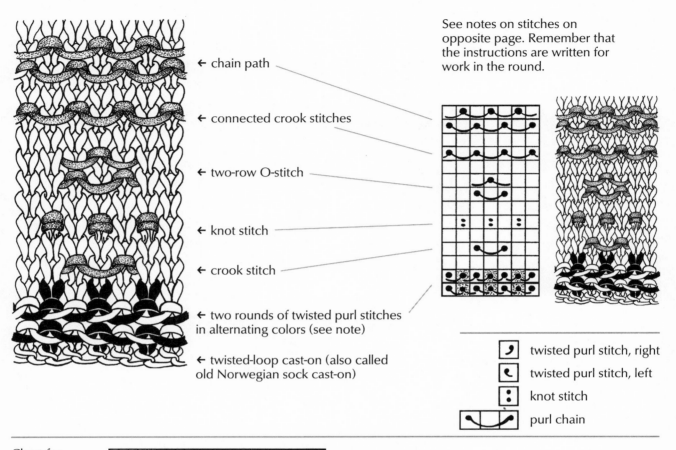

← chain path

← connected crook stitches

← two-row O-stitch

← knot stitch

← crook stitch

← two rounds of twisted purl stitches in alternating colors (see note)

← twisted-loop cast-on (also called old Norwegian sock cast-on)

See notes on stitches on opposite page. Remember that the instructions are written for work in the round.

﹂	twisted purl stitch, right
ﻉ	twisted purl stitch, left
⋮	knot stitch
⌣	purl chain

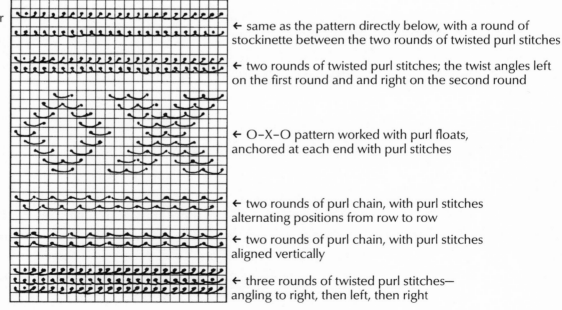

Chart for another sampler of two-end knitting pattern types.

← same as the pattern directly below, with a round of stockinette between the two rounds of twisted purl stitches

← two rounds of twisted purl stitches; the twist angles left on the first round and and right on the second round

← O–X–O pattern worked with purl floats, anchored at each end with purl stitches

← two rounds of purl chain, with purl stitches alternating positions from row to row

← two rounds of purl chain, with purl stitches aligned vertically

← three rounds of twisted purl stitches— angling to right, then left, then right

Two rounds of twisted purl stitches in alternating colors

On the first round, the strand for the new color must come *under* that of the previous color. On the second round, the strand for the new color must come *over* that of the previous color.

Chain path

Two rounds of connected crook stitches with knit above purl, purl above knit.

Knot stitch

In lieu of purling with only one strand as in brocade patterns, the purl stitches are worked with two strands, creating designs of great depth. This requires knitting the two ends at the same time on the previous row; these knit stitches become the purl head on the next row.

Crook stitch

1. Knit one stitch with first strand, knit one stitch with second strand.

2. Bring first strand forward, purl one.

3. With first strand remaining forward to float on the face of the fabric, knit one with second strand.

4. Purl one with first strand; take yarn back.

5. End the sequence by knitting one with second strand, knitting one with first strand.

Two-row O-stitch

First row:

1. Knit one with first strand

2. Knit one with second strand.

3. Purl one with first strand, leaving it forward to float on face of fabric.

4. Knit one with second strand.

5. Purl one with first strand; take yarn back.

6. Knit one with second strand.

7. End the sequence by knitting one with first strand.

Second row:

1. Knit one with first strand.

2. Knit one with second strand.

3. Bring second strand forward; knit one with first strand.

4. With second strand forward, purl one with first strand.

5. With second strand forward, knit one with first strand.

6. Take second yarn back; knit one with second strand.

7. End the sequence by knitting one with first strand.

Denmark

The Danish brocade blouse, called *natrøje* or *night shirt,* is the oldest sweater-like garment thought to have been worn by common folk. However, there is some question about when it became part of the peasant costume.

The pieces that have survived appear to have come from the upper classes. We surmise this because most of the examples in museums are copies of silk knitted garments worn by royalty, and mentioned in estate inventories as early as the 1690s. Instead of silk, they are made of fine worsted yarn or even silk-wool blends. These are not items of clothing you'd expect to find among the working classes. Apparel that made its first appearance in royal wardrobes would first have entered the wardrobes of the upper classes before filtering down to the population at large. We do know that by the mid-eighteenth century the brocade blouse had made that later transition and had been incorporated into Danish women's folkwear.

Regardless of its precise history, the brocade blouse offers splendid inspiration for knitters today. The garment came in many forms, sometimes appearing with a short body and short sleeves and sometimes as a long blouse with long sleeves.

Plan 1 (pages 82–83) describes the basic structure of the brocade blouse. It was worked from the lower edge, where the hem sections began as separate front and back units. These were most often decorated with a diced pattern of small, alternating squares of knit and purl stitches. After between 1 and 1½ inches had been worked, the two parts were joined at the sides and worked in the round to the armhole, which included a small half-gusset. The garment was then divided into front and back sections and worked separately (back and forth) to the shoulder. A square neck opening was shaped on the bodice front. On early pieces, the lower front neckline was often decorated with an appliquéd overlay of woven brocade fabric. The entire neck edge was then bound with a strip of woven fabric.

The all-over brocade knitted pattern used on the body and sleeves was usually copied from woven damask fabrics. Occasionally, twisted traveling stitches in an interesting ribbon-fold pattern were included. False seamlines on the sides consisted of two purl stitches; on either side

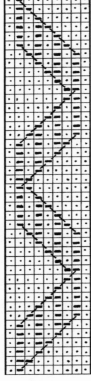

Ribbon-fold pattern.

of these stitches, for emphasis, the knitter might incorporate decorative bands in knit/purl patterns or twisted traveling stitches. These decorative bands were carried all the way to the shoulder, where the front and back stitches were bound off together on the inside.

Knitters' mysteries

An interesting parallel in both construction and patterning exists between these blouses, worn exclusively by women, and the ganseys of Great Britain, worn exclusively by men. Both feature a split welt, side seamline, gusset, and similar working technique. Was there a connection between the two—and which came first?

See the Amager Island Blouse on page 239 for another intriguing example of the tangled, and tantalizing, history of knitting.

Amager Island patterns

Extra patterns for the knitted sleeves of Amager Island blouses.

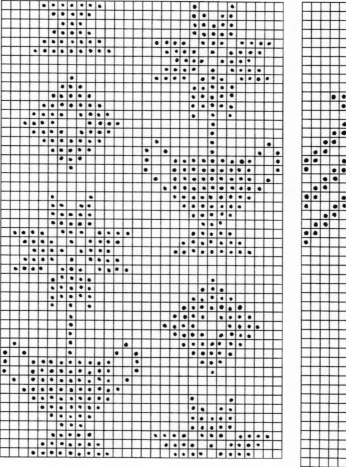

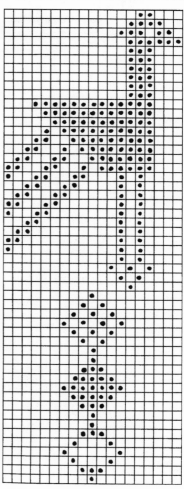

Danish Brocade Blouse, Short Version

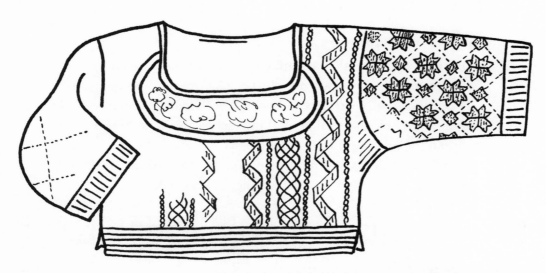

Patterns for the Danish Brocade Blouse, Short Version, are on pages 236 and 237. The structure for both Danish blouses follows Plan 1 (pages 82–83).

The sequence below shows one-half of the pattern for the bodice of this blouse, with the center at the left edge of the chart and the side at the right edge of the chart. The chart for the other half of the pattern is the mirror image. This produces the subtlety of having the traveling stitches reverse directions on opposite sides of the centerline. The effect works on all the individual elements of the design, but is most striking on the ribbon-fold pattern (see also page 234).

pattern A (ribbon-fold) pattern B pattern D (diamond mesh) pattern B pattern A (ribbon-fold) pattern B

Danish Brocade Blouse, Short Version

Pattern for bodice.

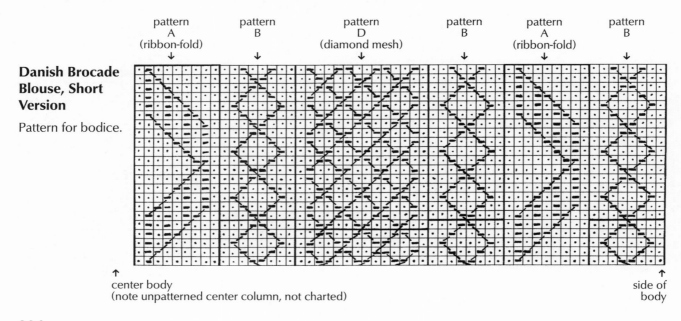

↑ center body
(note unpatterned center column, not charted)

↑ side of body

Danish Brocade Blouse, Long Version

→ Pattern for body and sleeves.

Notice the way the simple zigzag lines form a mitered corner. Adjust the placement of the center pattern to produce this effect at all corners.

  twisted stitch, knit through the back loop

traveling stitch right on purl ground

traveling stitch left on purl ground

→ diced welt

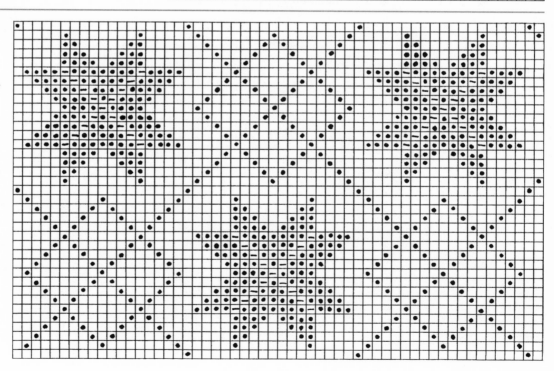

Danish Brocade Blouse, Short Version

Pattern for sleeves.

Danish Brocade Blouse, Long Version

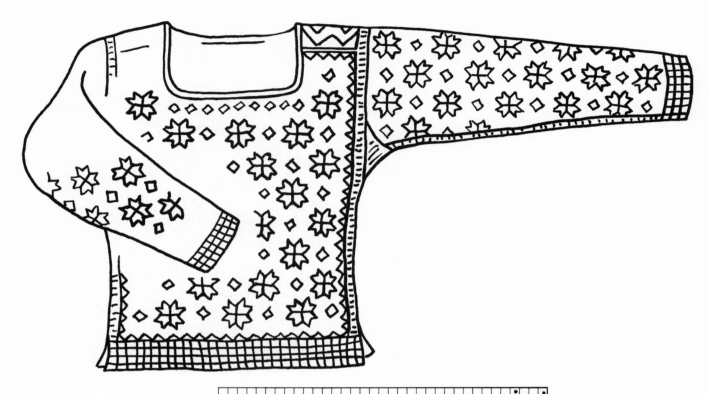

→ shoulderline stitch

Danish Brocade Blouse, Long Version

← Patterns across shoulders. These connect at their lower edge with the main body/sleeve patterns on page 237.

↓ Patterns at lower edge of front neckline.

Patterns for the Danish Brocade Blouse, Long Version, are on pages 237 and 238. The structure for both Danish blouses follows Plan 1 (pages 82–83).

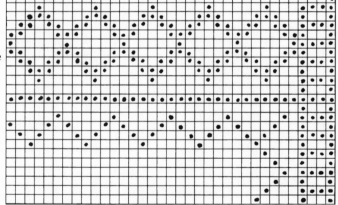

Amager Island Blouse

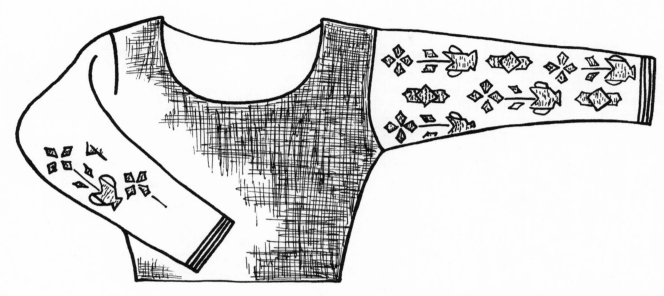

Here's another puzzle about the history of knitting styles and techniques. In 1521, a group of wealthy Dutch farmers settled on Amager Island, off the coast of Denmark. Their well-dressed wives wore bodices of indigo blue or black woven fabric with knitted sleeves worked in complex knit/purl patterns. Some of the patterns were probably copied from stocking "clock" patterns, the vertical designs worked in the area above the heel gusset. Other designs—peacocks, crowns, stars, flowers—might have come from embroidery patterns, because these Dutch Amager women were known to excel in fine needlework.

Although the garment was part of the regular costume of this group, the women themselves did not knit. Knitting wasn't considered suitable for women of their social rank, so their knitting was done by their Swedish maids. A similar cloth-bodice jacket with knitted sleeves, color-stranded instead of textured, was once part of the Swedish national costume.

Where did the garment originate—with the Dutch Amager, or the Swedish maids? And how did the patterning evolve, from color-stranding to brocade patterning or vice versa? These are intriguing questions.

Patterns for the Amager Island Blouse are on page 240. Extra Amager Island patterns are on pages 235 and 240.

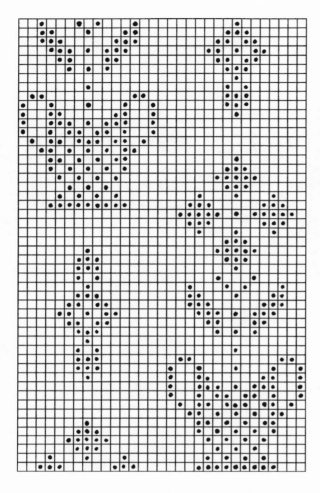

Amager Island Blouse

← Pattern for knitted sleeves.

Amager Island patterns

→ Extra patterns for the knitted sleeves of Amager Island blouses.

Great Britain

In Great Britain, *gansey* refers to a seaman's jersey. The term apparently originated on the Channel Islands of Guernsey and Jersey; both islands' names describe a pullover sweater, with *gansey* a slang term to describe pullovers in general.

A standard construction technique was followed in making these seamless garments. The cast-on incorporated double yarn for durability. The sweater began with a short welt in two sections, one each for the front and back. After the welt had been worked to about 1 to 1½ inches deep, the two units were joined and the garment was knitted in the round to the underarm, with full gussets added for ease. The work was again divided at the armholes into front and back sections. On some, a shoulder strap at each side provided depth for the neck opening; others had a small half-gusset at the neck edge. The sleeves were picked up and worked just short of the wrist, with the edge bound off in doubled yarn.

Simple knit/purl patterns were worked on the upper chest; in time, this patterning became more elaborate. First cables were added and the patterned area was extended to the upper arms. Later, the entire body and sleeves were patterned. In early times, specific patterns could be used to identify people of a particular village, but over the years ideas were copied from place to place and lost their regional distinctness.

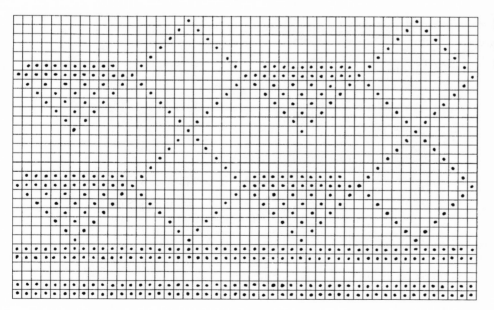

Early Gansey patterns

Extra patterns for early ganseys.

The earliest ganseys were not necessarily made of the yarn identified with this style of sweater today, a fine, five-ply, navy worsted often called *seaman's iron.* Early ganseys were made from a coarser two-ply woolen yarn. Multiple-ply fine knitting worsteds didn't come into common use until the advent of spinning mills. Worsted yarns were commonly used to make hosiery for the upper classes; the gansey developed as an outgrowth of hosiery knitting, so the use of a similar yarn was natural when it became available.

On the islands of the Outer Hebrides, particularly Eriskay, the gansey reached new heights of textured design. Early Hebridean ganseys were similar to those of the rest of Great Britain, although the pattern elements were distributed differently. There is little doubt that a more ornate style developed during the early twentieth century. These newer designs may have been influenced by Aran patterns, which Heinz Edgar Kiewe first brought to public attention in the 1930s. Regardless of their origin, these garments are distinctly Hebridean in character and a highly developed folk art. Even today, these fine ganseys are still produced by hand for sale.

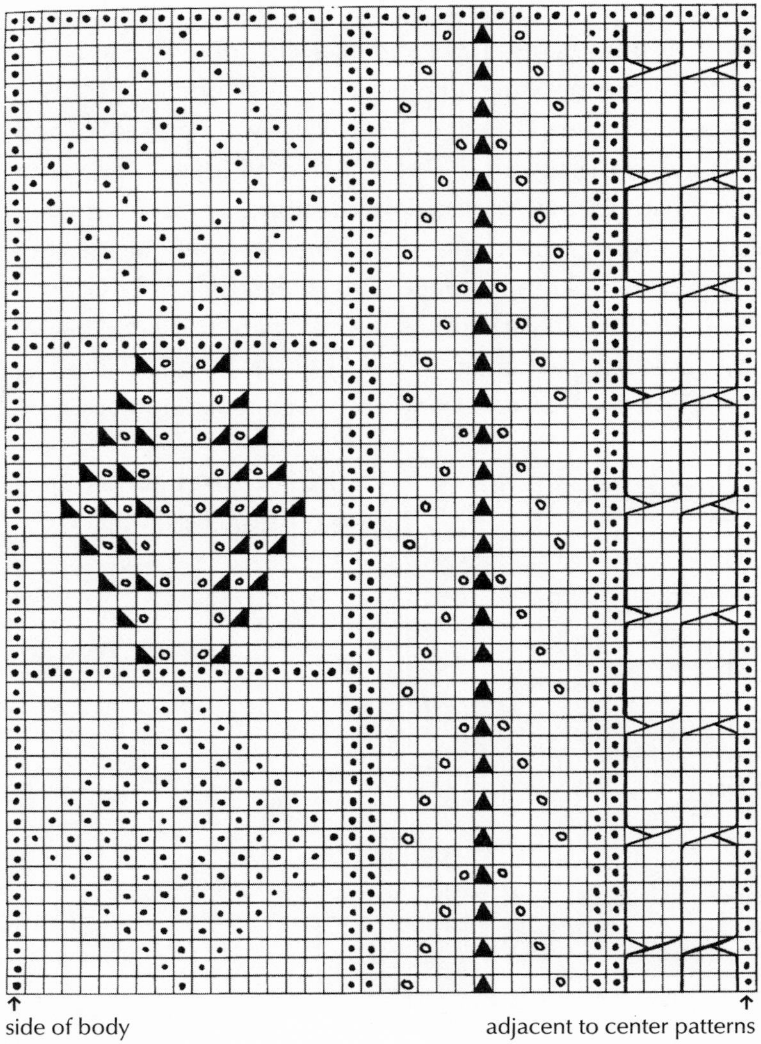

Hebridean Gansey 1

Side patterns for upper body. This chart goes to the left of the upper body pattern on page 251. Its mirror image (shown on page 249) goes on the right side.

side of body   adjacent to center patterns

242

Early Gansey with Simple Knit/Purl Patterns

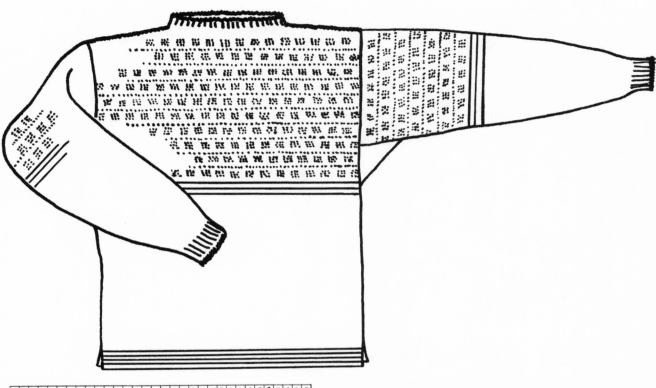

Early Gansey with Simple Knit/Purl Patterns

Pattern for upper body.

Patterns for the Early Gansey
in the drawing are on this
page, with extra patterns
both here and on page 241.
The structure shown above
follows Plan 2 (pages 84–85).

Early Gansey patterns

Extra combination for an early gansey.

Ganseys with Extended Panels

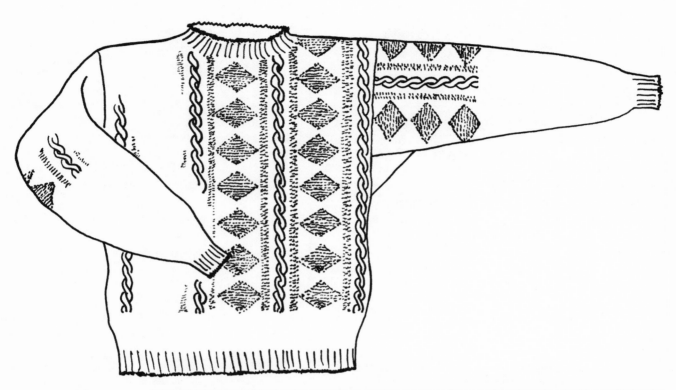

Gansey with Extended Panels 1

Patterns for body and sleeves.

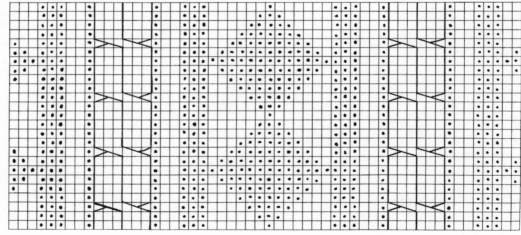

Patterns for a second extended-panel gansey are on page 245.

Gansey with Extended Panels 2

These are patterns for an alternative gansey design, similar to the one on page 244. They show how to adapt panel width to the available number of stitches. For example, the horizontal block units on the sleeve are 10 stitches wide and on the body they are 12 stitches wide.

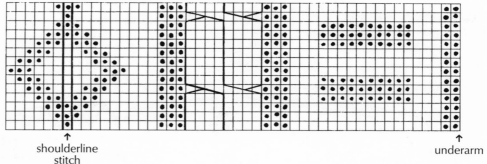

↑ shoulderline stitch

↑ underarm

↑ Patterns for upper sleeve. The patterns mirror around the shoulderline stitch.
↓ Patterns for upper body. The patterns mirror around the center-front stitch.

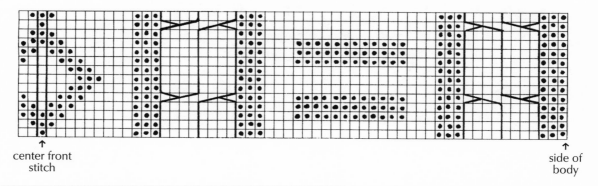

↑ center front stitch

↑ side of body

Gansey with Vertical Panels 2

These are patterns for an alternative gansey design, similar to the one on page 246. Arrange a sequence and modify stitch counts to fit your own requirements.

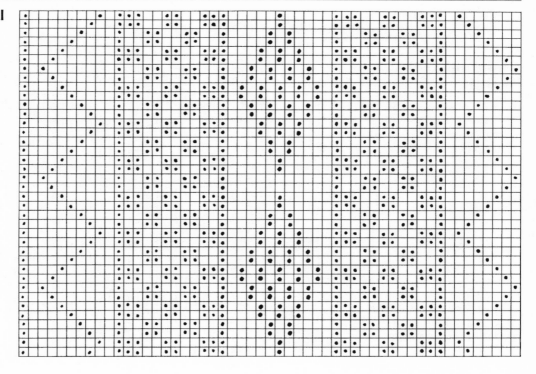

Ganseys with Vertical Panels

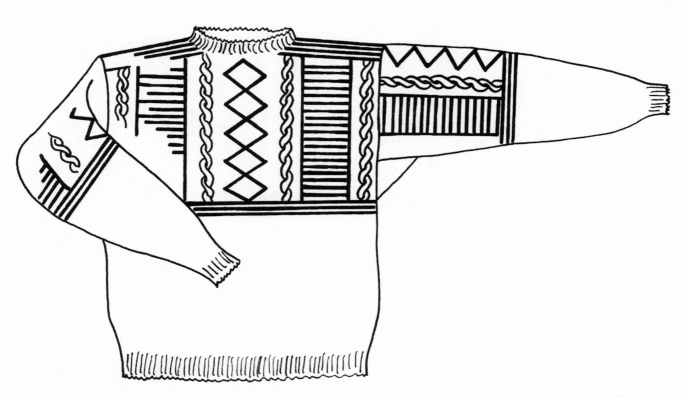

Gansey with Vertical Panels 1

Patterns for body and sleeves. The cable at the far right appears on the body, but not the sleeves.

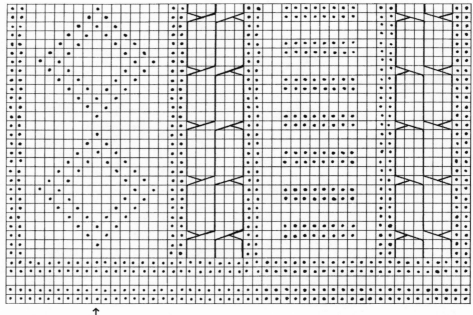

Patterns for Gansey with Vertical Panels 1 are on this page, with patterns for a second vertical-panel gansey on page 245.

↑
center stitch

Gansey with Horizontal Panels

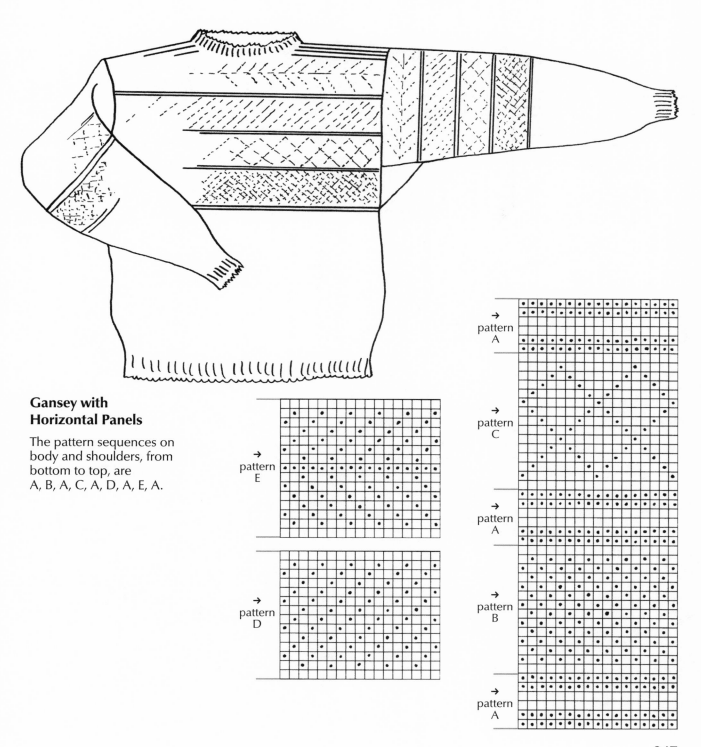

Gansey with Horizontal Panels

The pattern sequences on body and shoulders, from bottom to top, are A, B, A, C, A, D, A, E, A.

→ pattern E

→ pattern D

→ pattern A

→ pattern C

→ pattern A

→ pattern B

→ pattern A

Ganseys with Continuous Shoulder Straps and Sleeves

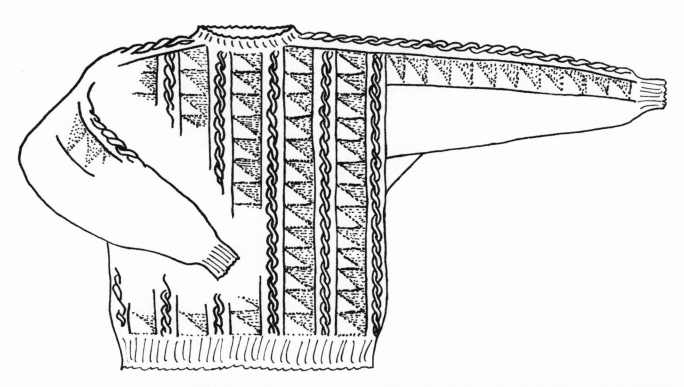

**Gansey with
Continuous
Shoulder Straps
and Sleeves 1**

The structure follows
Plan 8 (pages 96–97).
Patterns for this gansey
appear on this page,
and patterns for a
second shoulder-strap
gansey appear on the
bottom of page 249.

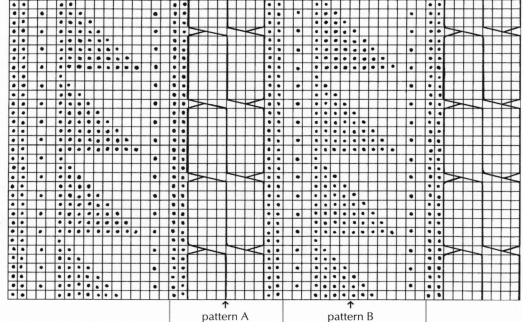

pattern A   pattern B

Hebridean Gansey 1

→ Side patterns for upper body. This sequence goes to the right of the upper body patterns on page 251. Its mirror image (shown on page 242) goes on the left side.

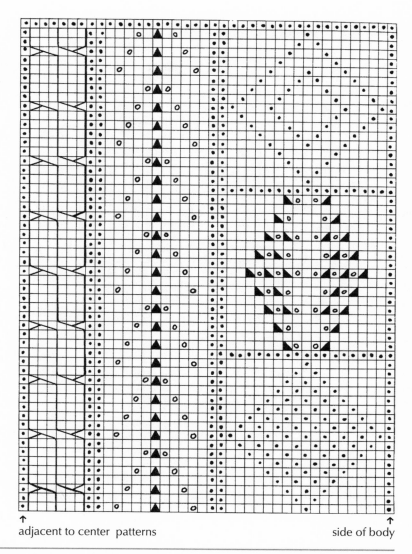

↑ adjacent to center patterns

↑ side of body

Gansey with Continuous Shoulder Straps and Sleeves 1

← Patterns for body and sleeves.

The body alternates patterns A and B, with an instance of B aligned on the center front and back.

Pattern A begins at the neckline, forms the shoulder strap, and extends to the cuff. On the sleeve itself, A is bordered by B.

Gansey with Continuous Shoulder Straps and Sleeves 2

→ These are patterns for an alternative gansey design, similar to the one on page 248.

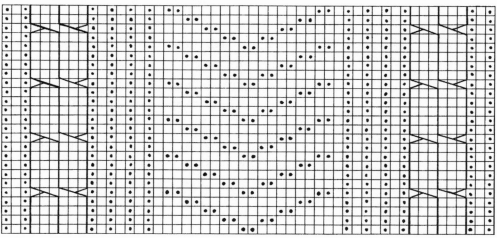

Hebridean Ganseys

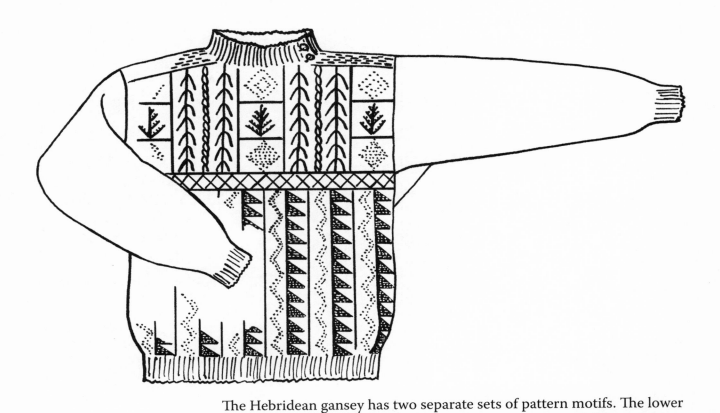

Patterns for Hebridean Gansey 1 appear on pages 242, 249, and 251, and patterns for a second Hebridean gansey appear on pages 252–53.

The Hebridean gansey has two separate sets of pattern motifs. The lower body has simple knit/purl patterned panels; it is divided from the yoke by a horizontal welt, often in a mesh pattern of small diamonds. The yoke is more complex, with vertical panels divided into square blocks of different patterns and the panels themselves sometimes divided by cables. Today's Hebridean sweaters have become more elaborate in the square blocks of the yoke, with patterns that often include openwork. The shoulder straps are worked as flaps at the top of the sweater front; the straps are bound off together with corresponding sections of the upper back to close the shoulder. A simple mesh design often decorates the straps. The collar is picked up and knitted back and forth, and includes an underlap to allow for buttoning. The sleeves of older styles were often plain stockinette stitch, but today they often repeat the patterns of the lower body.

Hebridean Gansey 1

→ Center patterns for upper body. These are flanked on either side by the patterns on pages 242 and 249.

↓ Mesh pattern for shoulder straps.

↓↓ Patterns for lower body.

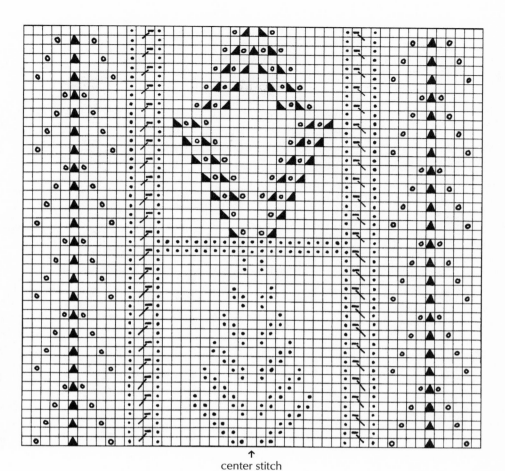

↑
center stitch

←
a mesh pattern
of diamonds

251

Hebridean Gansey 2

This page and the next contain patterns for an alternative gansey design, similar to the one on page 250.

→ Patterns for upper body. The design includes patterns A, B, C, B, C, B, A across the yoke area.

↓ Mesh pattern for shoulder straps.

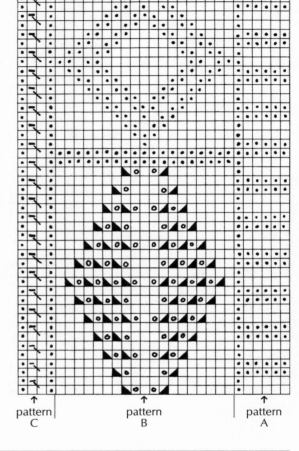

pattern C   pattern B   pattern A

[C]aminante, no hay camino, se hace camino al andar....

Antonio Machado
(1875–1939)

252

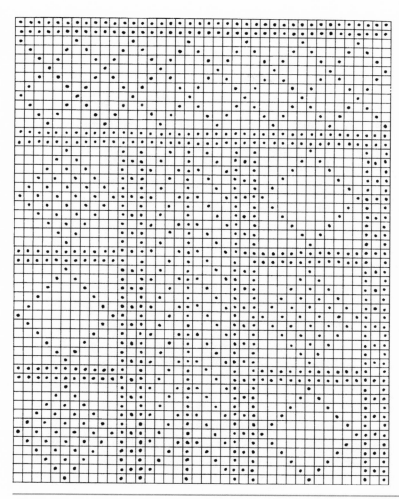

Hebridean Gansey 2

Patterns for lower body.

[W]alker, there is no road,
you make the road by walking....

Antonio Machado
(1875–1939)

253

The Netherlands

Coastal villagers of the Netherlands depended on the sea for their livelihood. Dutch fishermen began to wear sweaters by the mid-nineteenth century, both handknits of local origin and frame-knitted garments imported from England and Belgium. The knitters of the fishing villages apparently adapted the designs of knitters in Great Britain, their neighbors to the west, while the basic shaping was similar to that used in Scandinavia to the north. But the Dutch fisherman's sweater developed a distinctive style, some elements of which were associated with certain geographical areas.

The common practice was for each fisherman to have two sweaters, one made of thick yarns, heavily felted, for wear on the sea, and one of finer yarns, often elaborately patterned, for wear on shore.

They were knitted of a common and inexpensive domestic wool yarn called *sajet*. Because the local sheep were raised primarily for meat, their wool was short and coarse, requiring the firm twist for which the yarn was named. The yarn was dyed in several colors, including blue, beige, gray, and black; the most popular was called *Nassau blue* after the Dutch royal family. (The royal family comes from the House of Nassau-Orange, and this color features prominently on their flags.) This particular color was dark blue with red fibers spun in, giving the knitwear a reddish heather tone. *Sajet* became less popular after World War II, when knitters no longer had to be so thrifty and many began to choose the newly available synthetics.

Knitters of old did not knit by "measurements," or even percentages, as we do today. Knitwear was worked according to simpler systems of proportions, a folk process that can serve us as well. The methodology has produced countless elegant, well-fitted garments for centuries of needleworkers and it has given me many years of knitting pleasure.

The boxy shape of the seamless fisherman's sweater was based on division by thirds, both in length and in width. Of the total length, two-thirds became the body to the underarm and

Sajet is pronounced sah-YET. This Dutch word historically meant *firm twist* and its contemporary meaning is *worsted*.

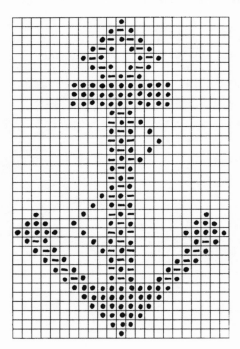

Single-Motif Sweater 2

This is an alternative pattern for the sweater style on page 258.

254

one-third became the armhole. The garment was knitted in the round, beginning with a K2, P2 ribbing. The patterns were mostly knit/purl designs with simple cables. The work was divided into front and back at the armhole and worked flat to the shoulder. Three to five platform stitches were allowed for ease at the underarm (see description of platform stitches on page 92).

Of the total width, the outer thirds became the shoulders and the center third became the neckline. The front neckline stitches were removed about 2 inches below the top of the shoulder, but the neck opening wasn't shaped.

The shoulders were bound off together, and the sleeves were picked up at the armholes and worked down to the wrists. The neckband, worked in ribbing, often contained eyelets for a drawstring that produced a snug fit. Pompons frequently decorated the ends of the drawstring.

Many Dutch fisherman sweaters resembled British ganseys, with textured patterns across the upper body and all-over cabled patterns. Others were patterned like samplers. Some bore only a single motif at center front, usually a God's-eye or anchor. Dutch textured sweaters are represented here by the latter two distinctive types.

Dutch Sampler-Style Sweater 1

→ Patterns for upper body and shoulder of the sweater on page 256.

→ shoulder pattern

→ pattern F

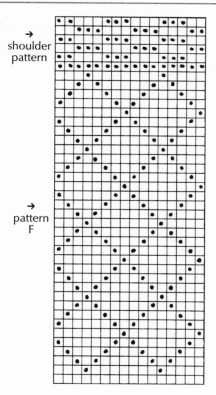

Dutch Sampler-Style Sweater 2

↓ Patterns for upper body and shoulder of the sweater on page 257.

→ shoulder pattern

→ pattern F

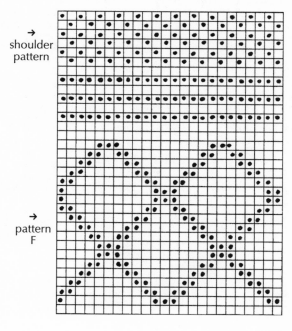

Dutch Fisherman's Sweater, Sampler-Style, 1

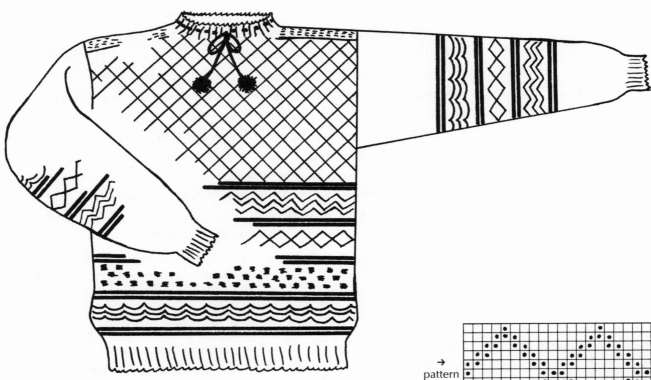

Dutch Sampler-Style Sweater 1

The body, knitted from the K2, P2 ribbing up, includes patterns A, B, A, C, A, D, A, E, A, F, and shoulder.

The sleeves, knitted from the top down, include patterns A, B, A, D, A, E, and A.

Patterns for the upper body (F) and shoulders of Sampler-Style Sweater 1 appear on page 255.

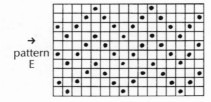

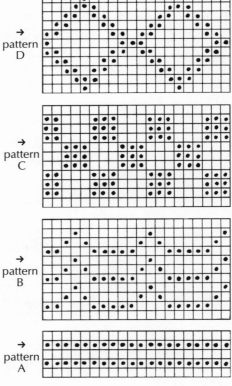

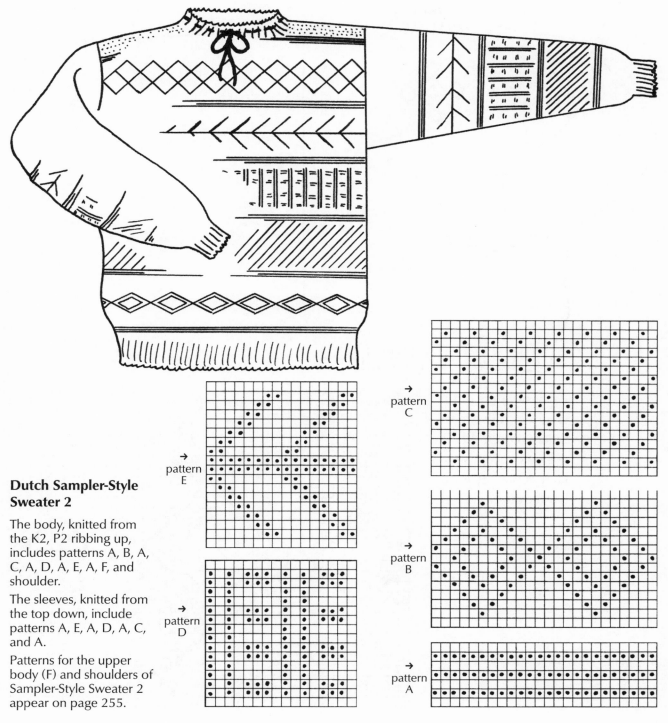

Dutch Sampler-Style Sweater 2

The body, knitted from the K2, P2 ribbing up, includes patterns A, B, A, C, A, D, A, E, A, F, and shoulder.

The sleeves, knitted from the top down, include patterns A, E, A, D, A, C, and A.

Patterns for the upper body (F) and shoulders of Sampler-Style Sweater 2 appear on page 255.

→ pattern E

→ pattern D

→ pattern C

→ pattern B

→ pattern A

Dutch Fisherman's Sweater with Single Motif

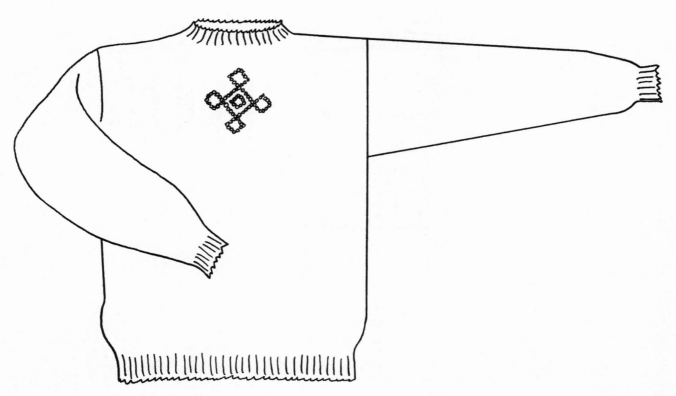

Early sweaters of the single-motif style were machine-knitted. The design concept was later copied by local handknitters.

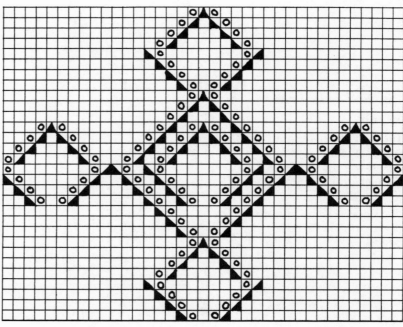

The pattern at right is a God's-eye. Another single-motif pattern, an anchor, appears on page 254.

Ireland

Off the coast of Ireland lie three islands, the Arans, home of the Aran fishing shirt. No other type of knitted garment has had more mythical qualities attributed to it, nor more controversy surrounding it. Although many early knitted garments are documented through letters and cottage-industry inventories, not so with the Aran. Until recently, its history has been largely unwritten.

We know that the Aran fishing shirt was first brought to public attention in 1936. Heinz Edgar Kiewe recorded and photographed this remarkable garment, and then proceeded to devote thirty years to collecting patterns that he commissioned Hebridean knitters to construct for him. In studying old documents and Celtic art, particularly the Book of Kells, Kiewe developed a theory that dated the Aran sweater to antiquity, and he gave names to various patterns that reflected early Christian religious significance.

It's easier, though, to justify a more recent origin for the Aran sweater—to argue, in fact, that this type of sweater is a product of the twentieth century. In the first place, there are no written records of its earlier existence. Second, the sweaters are knitted of natural white yarn—an impractical color that was astutely avoided by most early folk knitters. Furthermore, some knitters in the 1940s clearly recalled that the typical British gansey style was traditionally knitted on the islands, not the fishing shirt with its heavily embossed patterns. Fortunately, Gladys Thompson recorded these garments and her research has been published for posterity.

It now appears the Aran mystery was solved in the 1980s by Rohana Darlington, a Churchill Scholar whose work is acknowledged in other sources. Intrigued by a statement on an accession card in the Dublin Museum that Aran knitting came from America, she personally contacted a local knitter who could, indeed, verify this information. According to oral history, two young women from the Aran Islands went to Boston in 1906 with plans of emigrating to the United States. There they expanded their skills, learning richly patterned knitting from a "foreign" immigrant, most likely from Austria. Deciding to return home, they took their new knitting skills with them, combined the patterns with the traditional gansey structure of their homeland, and shared

Aran patterns

Extra patterns for Aran sweaters.

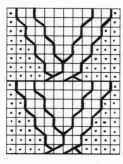

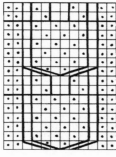

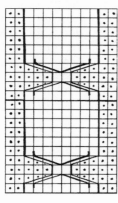

this approach with others. The embossed patterning developed rapidly as the fishing shirts found a ready market. In this account, the Aran fishing shirt became part of European knitting through an American connection!

Ultimately, however, whether the craft displayed in these garments developed in ancient or modern times becomes irrelevant. These sweaters—with bobbles, cables, and interlacing stitches providing deep surface relief—are distinctly Aran, and they are lovely. They are knitted of a thick, creamy woolen yarn called *bainin* (pronounced *bawneen* and meaning *natural*), and they feature deeply embossed patterns.

Further controversy concerns the way in which the sweaters were constructed: have they always been knitted in sections and sewn together (as they often are today), or were they originally worked in the round? Museum specimens in Dublin were made by contract workers, thus the construction is not necessarily the same as that of the originals. Thompson stated that the earliest Aran garments were most likely knitted in the round, and most authorities on traditional knitting agree with her. The shift to working in flat pieces occurred as the designs became more complex. Although based on similar techniques, many of the complex modern designs have evolved a long way from the early Arans.

Aran Fishing Shirt 1

The arrangement of panels across the body is D, C, B, A (center), B, C, D.

The sleeves include patterns A, B, D (which extends to the shoulder strap), B, and A.

↓ Pattern for center panel of body, also used on sleeves.

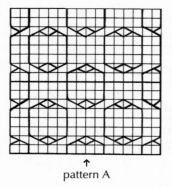

↑
pattern A

→ Patterns for side panels of body; B and D are also used on the sleeves. The large dots indicate bobbles, worked according to the sequence in the small chart (→ →).

↓ Fancy ribbing for skirt (bottom of sweater body).

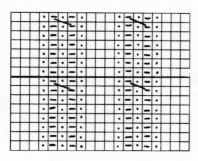

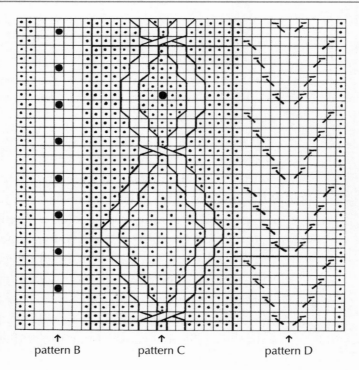

↑
pattern B

↑
pattern C

↑
pattern D

Bobble sequence (worked at large dots). Line-by-line description on page 228, lower right.

Aran Fishing Shirts

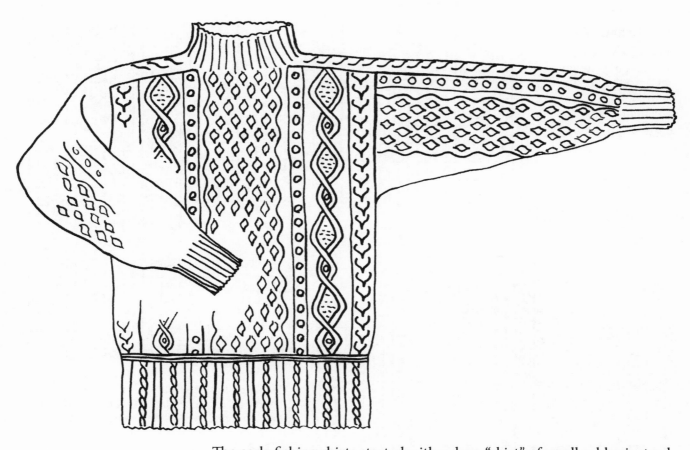

Patterns for Aran Fishing Shirt 1 are on page 260; patterns for an alternative shirt are on page 262. Both follow Plan 9 (pages 98–99), a traditional boxy shape that includes a cabled "skirt" at the lower edge of the body; deep cuffs and neckband; and shoulder straps.

The early fishing shirts started with a deep "skirt" of small cables instead of a ribbed welt. This skirt was separated from the main body by a ridge of purling or garter stitch. The body included a center panel equal in width to the front neckline, flanked on each side by vertical pattern panels. The sleeves were knitted with deep cuffs of ribbing, which sometimes included small cables; each sleeve contained a vertical panel that ran along the outside of the arm and extended to the neck, forming a shoulder strap. The sleeve panels generally repeated some portion of the body patterning, although the elements were not necessarily in the same order or of the same width. The neck band was a deep ribbing, sometimes with cables, that reached to the chin.

The charts on this page were designed for a sweater similar to Aran Fishing Shirt 1, but worked in bulky yarn (7 wraps per inch calculated at a gauge of 3½ stitches per inch). The needles will be approximately size 10 (6–6.5mm).

Aran Fishing Shirt 2

These are patterns for an alternative design, similar to the one on page 261.

→ Patterns for body.

↓ Patterns for sleeves.

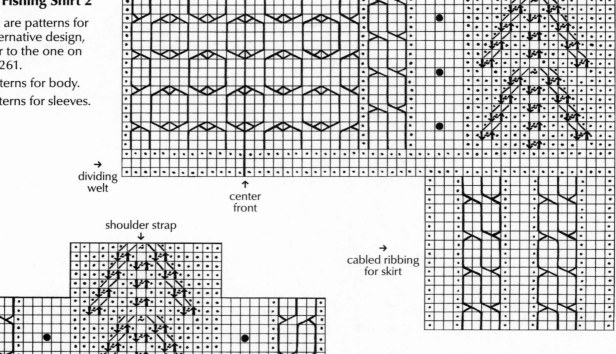

→
dividing
welt

↑
center
front

→
cabled ribbing
for skirt

shoulder strap
↓

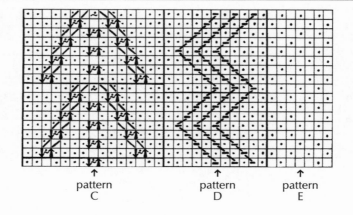

The large dots on both sleeve and body charts indicate bobbles, worked according to the sequence in the small chart on page 260.

This combination of symbols, used frequently in one of the panels, means P1, yarn back, slip one stitch purlwise, yarn front, P1.

Aran with Square Armholes

Side section of body panels.

↑
pattern
C

↑
pattern
D

↑
pattern
E

Aran with Square Armholes

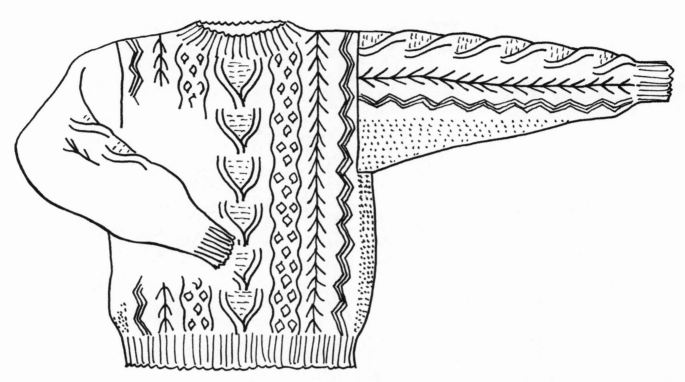

Later Aran sweaters often omitted the shoulder strap; instead, the body pattern continued across the shoulders. The shoulder line was sloped for a closer fit, and the cabled skirt was also omitted. Knitting in the round was replaced by flat-knitted sections seamed together during finishing.

Aran with Square Armholes

→ Center section of body panels.

Patterns for the Aran with Square Armholes are on pages 262–63. The structure follows Plan 7 (pages 94–95).

The arrangement of panels across the body is E, D, C, B, A (center), B, C, D, E.

The sleeves include patterns E, D, C, A, C, D, and E.

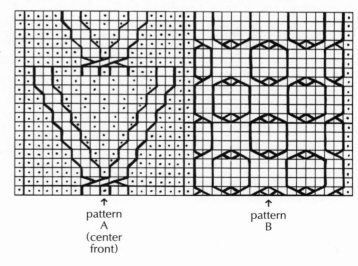

pattern A (center front)

pattern B

Raglan-Style Aran

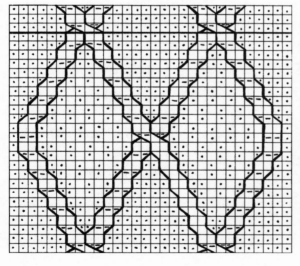

Today's Arans are usually raglan-style. The commercially produced sweaters lack spontaneity in their patterning, and many are worked in bulky yarns that limit the number of stitches and thus the pattern complexity.

Raglan-Style Aran

← Center body panel.

→ Side body panels.

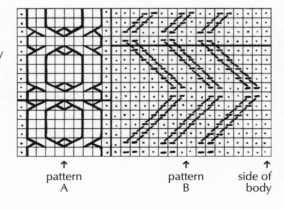

↑ pattern A   ↑ pattern B   ↑ side of body

Patterns for the Raglan-Style Aran are on pages 264–65. The structure follows Plan 11 (page 102).

Aran patterns

Extra patterns for Aran sweaters.

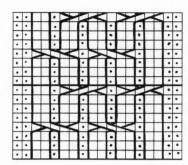

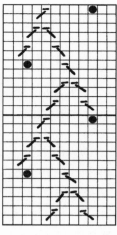

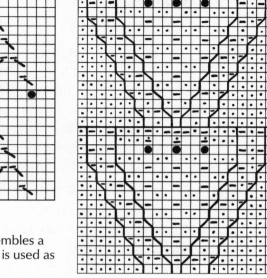

Bobble sequence for both patterns at left (positions indicated by large dots).

Row 1: In one stitch, K1, yarn-over, K1, yarn-over, K1.

Row 2: Turn and P5 (or knit in reverse).

Row 3: K3, K2tog.

Row 4: Turn and pass 2nd, 3rd, and 4th stitches individually over the 1st stitch (1 stitch remains).

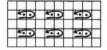

This texture pattern resembles a series of tiny bobbles. It is used as a background filler.

Round 1 and all odd rounds: K.

Round 2 and all even rounds: K1; P2; with yarn in front, return these 2 stitches to the left needle; take the yarn around both stitches to the back; slip the same 2 stitches back to the right needle. Repeat across panel.

Raglan-Style Aran

→ The main panel along the sleeve is a narrow adaptation of the center-front panel. It is bordered on both sides by panels A and B, as in the side body.

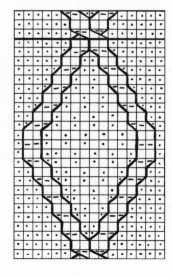

Norway

Initially, two-end knitting was often found in thick woolen mittens and stocking tops. During the nineteenth century, knitters in the Sunnhordland region of Norway applied this technique to jackets. These garments were knitted from two strands of yarn, both of the same color (mitten bands were often worked in two colors). The yarns twisted together between knit stitches, so the result was a very firm, non-elastic garment of double thickness. The jackets have bands of textured patterns, created by bringing one strand forward, purling it, allowing the float to travel across the surface of a knit stitch, purling it again, then returning it to the back.

For more information on two-end knitting, see pages 230–33.

Two-End Jacket of Sunnhordland

Two-End Jacket of Sunnhordland

→ Patterns used horizontally at center of body, and also at upper edge of sleeve.

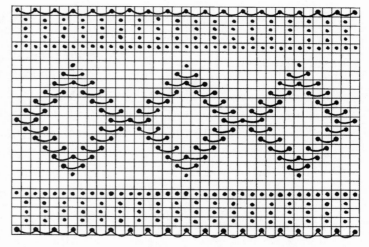

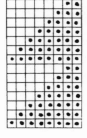

← Pattern used on body along edges of armholes.

→ Patterns used at lower edge of body, along front opening edges, and at lower edges of sleeves.

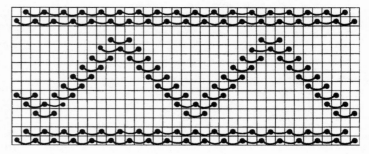

Austria and Germany

The alpine regions of Austria and Germany produced beautiful traditional styles that have much in common with the work of the Aran Islands. In fact, these alpine sweaters are probably the forerunners of the Aran fishing shirt. While the Aran is made of a heavier yarn in bold patterns, Bavarian garments are made of finer yarns in many panels of greater intricacy.

The Bavarian designs are richly textured and embossed with twisted traveling stitches, a style of patterning that first appeared in elegant stockings. As in other cultures, the designs migrated from hosiery to other items of clothing, in this case to waistcoats and jackets. We have found little information about the earliest of these garments, but we can assume that they were usually close-fitting. They come from the land of the dirndl skirt, where a jersey-style sweater would be out of place! Furthermore, the construction of clothes from felted-and-cut knitted fabric was a common practice in this region; some of the early, tailored "boiled wool" jackets might well have been made of felted and brushed knitted fabrics, as they are today. Working the fully shaped pieces flat and then seaming them together is a carryover from this earlier tailoring tradition, rather than from the circular work of patterned stockings, as we might expect.

Bavarian knitted vests and jackets for women are snugly shaped, waist-length cardigans with scooped necks and richly patterned panels. Typically, panels of traveling-stitch motifs adorned each side of the center-front opening and were repeated down the center back. The rest of the garment was often worked in simple all-over knit/purl patterns. On especially elaborate pieces, the entire garment, including the sleeves, was worked in vertical panels of traveling stitches. The way these patterns matched at the seams demonstrates the precise work of master knitters.

Men's vests and jackets were usually slightly longer and less elaborate than the women's, and often omitted the center-back panel, although some were richly patterned throughout.

Woman's Bavarian Waistcoat

Patterns for sides of body. Pattern B is also used as an all-over texture on the sleeves.

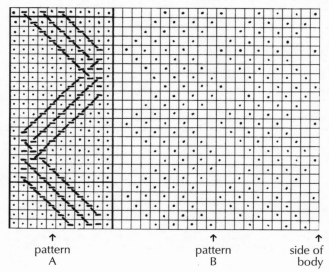

pattern A   pattern B   side of body

Woman's Bavarian Waistcoat

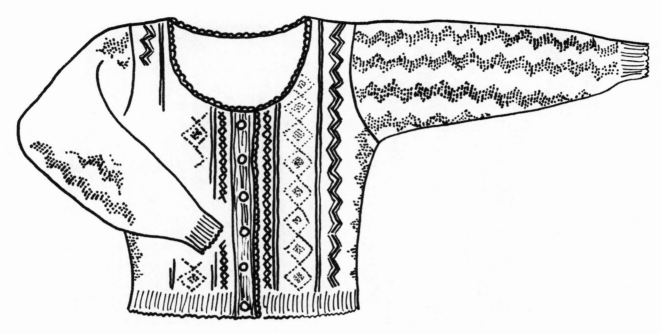

Woman's Bavarian Waistcoat

↓ Patterns on either side of cardigan opening.

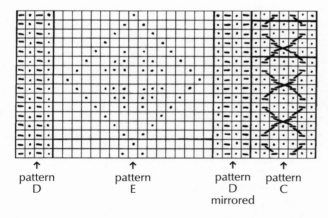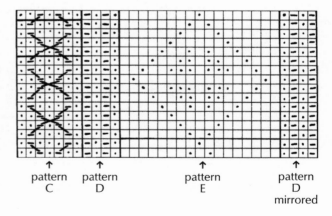

pattern D   pattern E   pattern D mirrored   pattern C   pattern C   pattern D   pattern E   pattern D mirrored

Patterns for the Woman's Bavarian Waistcoat are on pages 268 and 269.

On each front piece, the patterns from the center out are: C, D, E, D, A, then B (chart on opposite page) in the underarm area. Left and right sides mirror each other. Note in particular the subtle mirroring effects on pattern D.

Woman's Bavarian Vest

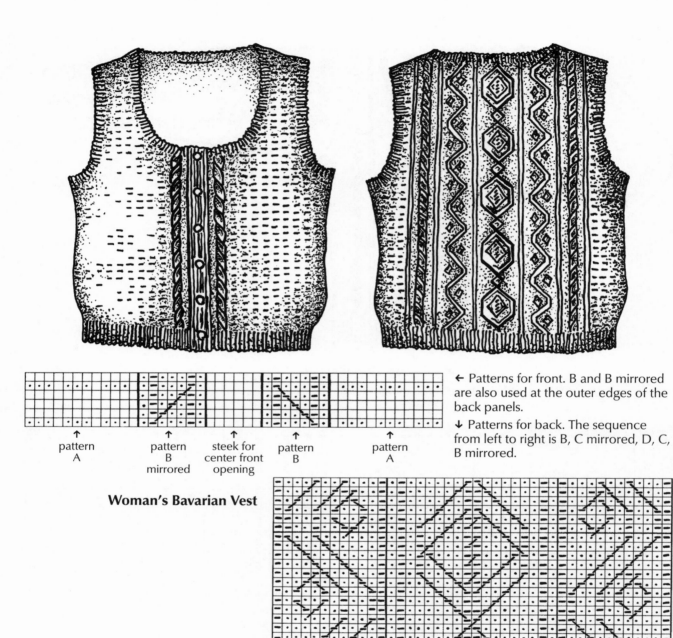

← Patterns for front. B and B mirrored are also used at the outer edges of the back panels.

↓ Patterns for back. The sequence from left to right is B, C mirrored, D, C, B mirrored.

↑ pattern A

↑ pattern B mirrored

steek for center front opening

↑ pattern B

↑ pattern A

Woman's Bavarian Vest

↑ pattern C mirrored

↑ pattern D (center)

↑ pattern C

Man's Bavarian Vests

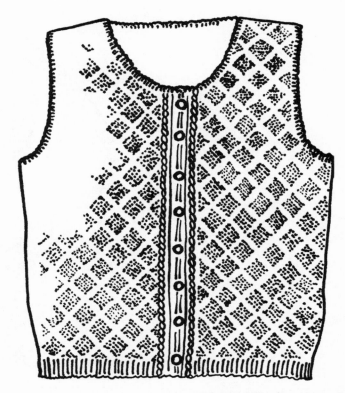

**Man's Bavarian
Vest 1**

Patterns for Man's Bavarian
Vest 1 are on this page.
Patterns for an alternative
vest are on page 274. The
structure shown follows Plan
14 (pages 110–11).

↑
pattern along
front openings

↑
side fronts
and back

Bavarian Cardigan

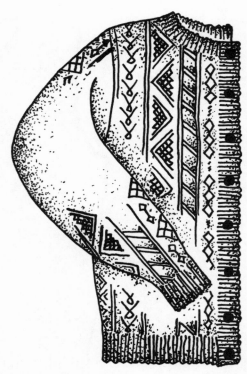

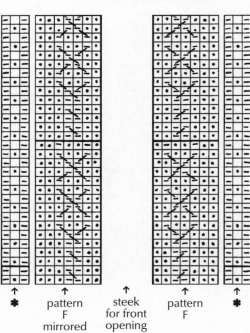

Bavarian Cardigan

Patterns on each front, starting at the side of the body, are E, ✳, D, ✳, C, ✳, B, ✳, F, mirrored across the front opening. Patterns across the back are E, ✳, D, ✳, C, ✳, B, ✳, A (at center back), and reverse (mirrored) from ✳ and B back to E.

A mirrored version of pattern B is on page 274. The structure shown here follows Plan 15 (pages 112–15).

The Bavarian Cardigan displays an abundance of traveling-stitch panels. Pattern A runs down the center back and along the top of each sleeve. The pattern marked ✳ repeats between all of the other panels.

The cardigan finishing combines several options. Cast on for the lower band and work the body. Pick up stitches and complete the neckband. Then pick up stitches along each front edge and work a ribbed band.

↑ ✳ ↑ pattern F mirrored ↑ steek for front opening ↑ pattern F ↑ ✳

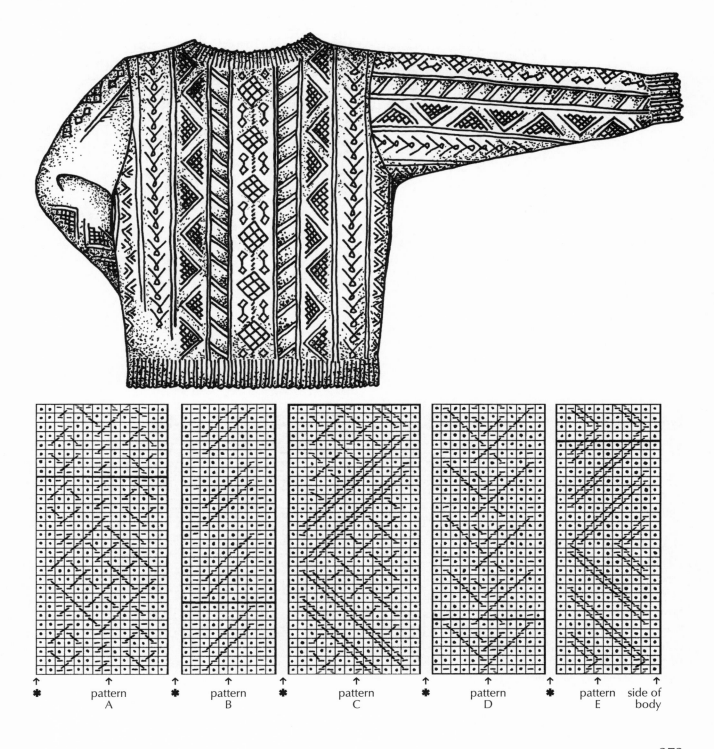

↑　　　↑　　　　↑　　　↑　　　　↑　　　↑　　　　↑　　　↑　　　　↑　　　↑　　↑
✻　　pattern　✻　　pattern　✻　　pattern　✻　　pattern　✻　　pattern　side of
　　　　A　　　　　　　B　　　　　　　C　　　　　　　D　　　　　　　E　　　body

Bavarian Cardigan

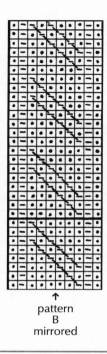

↑
pattern
B
mirrored

Man's Bavarian Vest 2

↓ These are patterns for an alternative design, similar to the one on page 271.

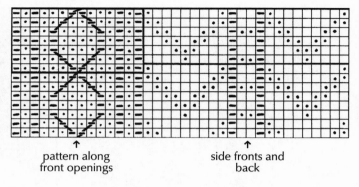

↑
pattern along
front openings

↑
side fronts and
back

Tyrolean Jacket 1

→ Patterns for fronts.

❧

On both Tyrolean jackets, use pattern A for sides, back, and sleeves.

❧

The bobble for both jackets is also the same.

Row 1: Purl in front and back of loop twice; turn.

Row 2: K4; turn.

Row 3: P4; turn.

Row 4: Slip 2nd, 3rd, and 4th stitches over 1st stitch, then slip 1st stitch to right needle.

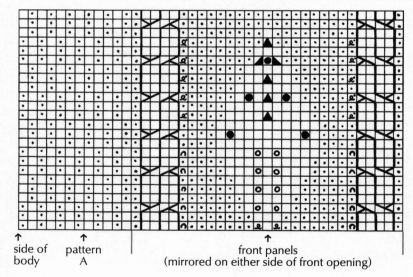

↑
side of
body

↑
pattern
A

↑
front panels
(mirrored on either side of front opening)

274

Tyrolean Jackets

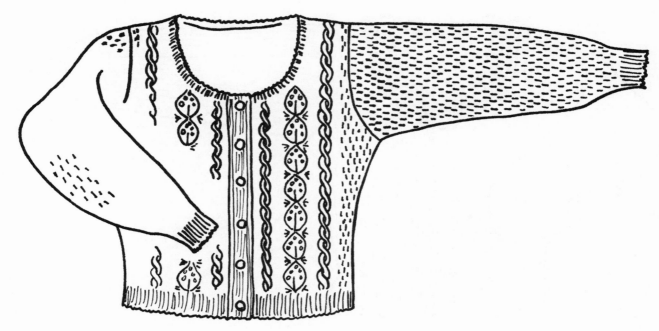

We also lack information about the origins of Tyrolean sweaters, but by the early twentieth century garments from the Tyrol incorporated cables and bobbles, instead of twisted traveling stitches. In this way, they resemble the work of Aran knitters. However, a unique feature of these garments is bits of embroidery—small flashes of color, like those you would expect to find in alpine meadows when wildflowers bloom. The embroidery embellishes and emphasizes the knitted-in patterns. Tyrolean sweaters, like Bavarian jackets, are close-fitting and waist-length, for the same reasons.

Patterns for Tyrolean Jacket 1 are on pages 274 and 275. Patterns for an alternative jacket are on page 277. The structure shown follows Plan 15 (pages 112–15).

Tyrolean Jacket 1

Chain-stitch embroidered details are added to the front panels at the locations indicated.

Berchtesgaden Sweater

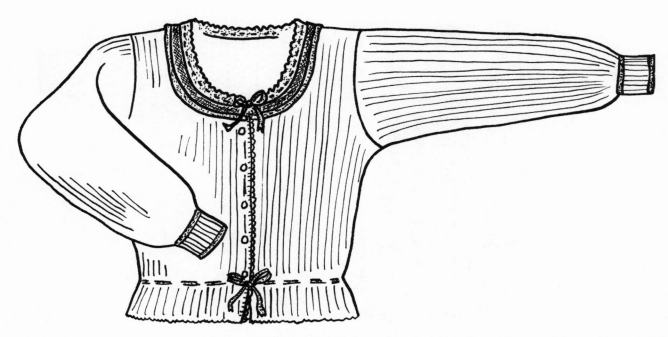

The Berchtesgaden sweater, a simple style, relies for its design interest on color contrast and lace edging, both located around the scoop neckline. The result is an understated, elegantly feminine garment. The body and sleeves are knitted in black, trimmed with vivid red and green. The snug fit of the body is accentuated by a drawstring that is laced through eyelets at the waist; the eyelets, located at 1-inch intervals, bracket the ribs. This combination forms a short peplum around the hips. Early examples of these garments were probably felted and cut to shape, with red and green accents covering the cut edges.

Today, the body and sleeves are knitted in a simple, twisted ribbing. Stitches picked up around the scoop neckline form the foundation for an insert that consists of two large tucks, which fold down like a narrow collar. One tuck is red and one is green. Each is worked in a different, simple, textured stitch, such as seed stitch, garter stitch, or reverse stockinette. A simple lace edging in black finishes the neckline, which is fitted with a drawstring. The front button overlaps are edged with picot crochet.

The body is increased at the underarm to form a short half-gusset beneath the shaped armhole. The sleeves, picked up and worked down from the armhole, require little or no reduction in circumference before they are gathered into the cuff. This gathering occurs when the excess fullness is decreased out all at once just before the cuff is worked. The twisted ribbing used in the body and sleeves reappears in the cuff, with an edging on each side worked in one of the contrasting colors. The texture of each edging strip coordinates with the tuck of the same color located at the neckline.

Berchtesgaden Sweater

→ All-over twisted ribbing used for body and sleeves.

→→ Lace edging used at neck, worked back and forth.

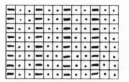

Cast on 5 stitches.

Row 1: K1, yarn-over twice, K2tog, yarn-over twice, K2.

Row 2: Slip 1 purlwise, P7.

Row 3: K8.

Row 4: Bind off 3 stitches purlwise, P5.

Tyrolean Jacket 2

→ Patterns for fronts.

↓ Embroidered details, formed with chain stitches at the locations indicated.

❧

On both Tyrolean jackets, use pattern A for sides, back, and sleeves.

❧

The bobble for both jackets is also the same; see page 274.

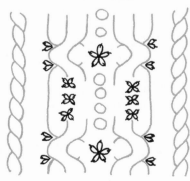

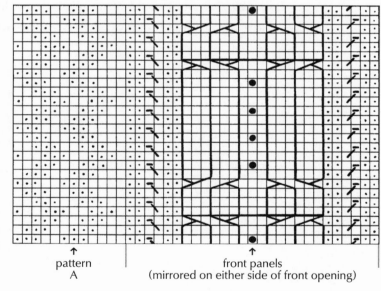

↑
pattern
A

↑
front panels
(mirrored on either side of front opening)

Geometric Patterning

Geometric patterns in knitting can be achieved through color contrast, directional knitting, or combinations of the two. These approaches have been used to make interesting folk sweaters. This chapter includes a simply elegant traditional sweater (the Danish Farmhand's Sweater) along with significant textural and color-management challenges: Argyle patterning and basketweave (also known as entrelac).

Basketweave receives extensive coverage here. Once you understand how it is structured, the technique is easy to work without any written instructions. It's far less complicated to do in the round than flat, although of course both options are possible. The detailed directions on pages 284–91 include information on the variations you will encounter.

Danish Farmhand's Sweater

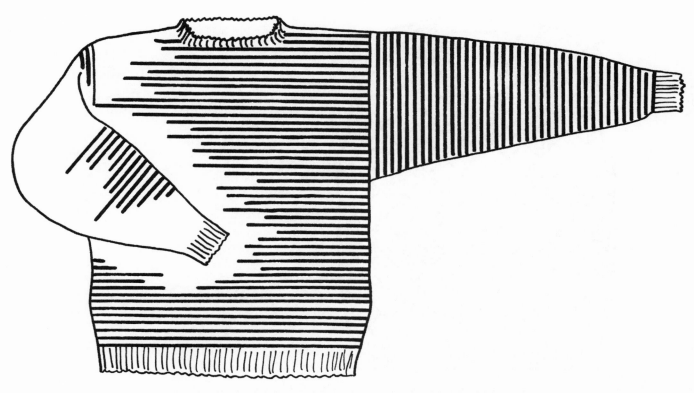

**Danish Farmhand's
Sweater**

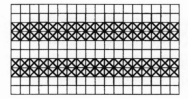

Narrow horizontal stripes of blue and white were fairly common in undershirts of the early nineteenth century, especially among Danish farmhands. These shirts were usually knitted in the round to the armhole. Then the work was divided, and front and back were worked separately to the neck. Shoulder straps were grafted together, a narrow neckband was applied, and the sleeves were worked from the shoulders to the wrists. These functional garments, snug in body and sleeve, were usually worn under a vest during working hours.

Here's a simple technique through which Danish knitters smoothed out the joins where the rounds meet and change colors. Knit the first stitch of each new stripe with both colors. Continue knitting around, completing the first row of the new stripe and the joining double stitch. Then carefully pull the strand of yarn from the previous stripe to hide it beneath the new color.

Scottish Argyle Vest

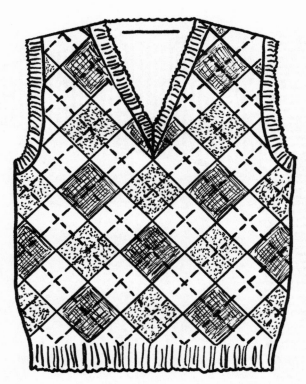

As so many other sweaters have been, the argyle sweater was adapted from a technique that first appeared in stockings. In Scotland, early leggings were made of woven fabric—tartan plaids, cut on the bias to improve the textiles' flexibility. Argyle knitting produces a pattern similar in appearance to bias tartan.

The argyle sweater is a product of the twentieth century. Argyle patterns are traditionally worked flat. Often only the sweater front is patterned. Argyle sweaters or vests have shaped armholes, and usually have V necklines.

Argyle knitting is not a color-stranding technique. The individual colors are instead held on, and manipulated with, butterflies or bobbins. The yarn for each block or section of color is drawn from a separate bobbin or ball of yarn. The unused color is not carried across the back of the fabric. When a section has been completed, its bobbin is left behind and a new bobbin is picked up. To avoid holes in the work, always pick

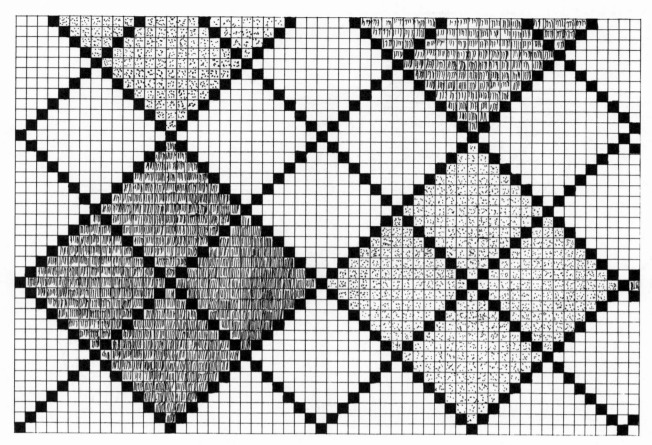

Scottish Argyle Vest

This pattern for argyle dicing includes three colors in the diamonds, plus a fourth color for the diagonals.

up the new color from beneath the completed color, so the two yarns interlock at the changing point.

A true argyle pattern has an overlying pattern of diagonal lines. The yarns for the diagonals must travel left and right across the diamonds. These yarns are managed in a different way. Because a pair of diagonals starts from a single point, wind a small butterfly at each end of a length of yarn. Begin the first stitches of the diagonal with the center of the strand; this allows the diagonal to move both right and left from the same initial point.

If you work in the Scottish way, you will need to seam the pieces. But if you borrow an intarsia technique from Eastern Europe (pages 206–07), you can make the ultimate, seamless argyle vest or sweater!

Finnish Basketweave Sweater

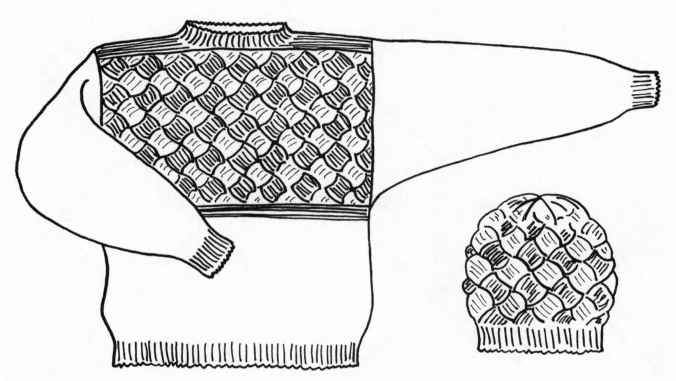

The basketweave yoke on this sweater has been set off by rows of garter stitch at its lower edge and in the shoulder area. Basketweave is easiest to work on sweater plans with straight armholes.

This geometric type of knitting, found across Scandinavia, resembles woven basketry (when seen from a distance!). It was popular for caps, mittens, and the leg portions of socks, and occasionally also was used to make waistcoats. This type of work, today known most often by its French name, *entrelac,* was particularly striking in Finland, where it was worked in dramatically contrasting red and black.

Even before I became passionate about ethnic stockings, I was blown away by a pair of entrelac knee socks at the Vesterheim Norwegian-American Museum, in Decorah, Iowa. The stitches were almost invisible and the units appeared almost perfectly square. The fabric looked like ribbons woven together on the diagonal. They retained the contour of the leg, even though there was no shaping: just the highly elastic structure.

Basketweave can be easily added to a sweater design. It is particularly effective in the yoke; an entire sweater can be a little overwhelming if the units are large or the colors contrast sharply.

Basketweave or entrelac

Like other folk-knitting techniques, basketweave has a logical structure. Once you understand how it is constructed, you will be able to tell what step comes next simply by looking at your knitting, and you will be able to leave written instructions behind.

Working in small sections requires a lot of turning from knit to purl and back again. Again, knitting in reverse greatly simplifies this process! When picking up stitches, pick them up so that they form knit loops on the face side of the fabric. Depending on your yarn, needles, or proficiency level, you may want to use a crochet hook to pull each loop through.

When selecting your needle size, keep in mind that the structure works best when it is not tensioned too loosely. In addition, the elasticity of basketweave is not the same as for stockinette—and you will want to avoid seams in basketweave areas. If you knit a garment that combines basketweave with stockinette and block it flat, the basketweave sections will ripple. To avoid this, plan ahead and determine your gauge for both the basketweave pattern and for stockinette. Accommodate the difference between the two by adjusting your stitch count (or changing needle sizes) when you move from one section to the other. Notice the garter stitch on each side of the basketweave section on the sweater in the drawing. This makes it easy to adjust the stitch count before starting the pattern and eliminates the need for an unsightly seam at the shoulders.

Basketweave can be worked round or flat. For working in the round, you need to understand how to construct the basic squares, as well as the base and finishing rows of horizontal large triangles (the size of a half-square). For working in flat pieces, you need to be able to make one or two additional types of units: vertical large triangles (half-squares) to complete the sides of every other row and, in some instances, small triangles (quarter-squares) at the ends of the finishing row.

If you want to become thoroughly familiar with basketweave before adding it to a garment, knit two samples in the technique, one in the

Direction of knitting progress for basketweave.

round and one flat. With yarn that works up at a gauge of about 5 stitches to the inch and appropriately sized needles, you can cast on 36 stitches for each sample (6 units as described below). Start with the circular sample, which is easier. You can knit it on double-pointed needles (or an 11-inch circular one). Work the flat sample on straight needles. On each sample, knit a row or two of ribbing before beginning the basketweave.

Setting up basketweave: round or flat

To set up the work for either round or flat knitting, construct a base round (circular) or row (flat) of triangles above the ribbing or welt. Each unit must consist of an even number of stitches, and the total number of stitches in the garment must be evenly divisible by the unit number. The number of *rows* in each individual unit is twice the number of *stitches* in the unit (one of these rows may consist of the picked-up stitches at the start of the unit).

Thus, if a unit contains 6 stitches it will consist of 12 rows when completed, and the total number of stitches over which the patterning is worked must be evenly divisible by 6 (for example, 54 or 72 or 144). All of the examples are based on 6-stitch units.

Base round of triangles

Repeat the following sequence:

Row 1: K2, turn	Row 6: P4, turn.
Row 2: P2, turn.	Row 7: K5, turn.
Row 3: K3, turn.	Row 8: P5, turn.
Row 4: P3, turn.	Row 9: K6.
Row 5: K4, turn.	

Each short *knit* row in the sequence (after the first one) works across the stitches worked in the previous two rows and adds one stitch from the final row of the ribbing or welt.

Repeat this sequence for each triangle across the round. For each subsequent triangle, the first K2 follows the K6 of the previously completed triangle. At the end of the last unit, you will have completed the K6 of the final row. Your next step depends on whether you are working in the round or on flat pieces.

Basketweave in the round

In the base round, the triangles form with the work proceeding in the standard direction, from right to left. As you attach the first round of squares, the squares will form in the opposite direction (left to right) around the tube of fabric. The direction reverses in this way with each following round of squares.

First round of squares

Squares form from left to right.

The *first square* shifts the direction of the work and is slightly different from the remaining squares in the sequence. The working yarn is located at the point of the V between the first and last triangles that you worked on the base stitches. On one side you have 6 open stitches; on the other side, you have a selvedge. That is the edge you want.

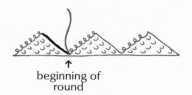

↑
beginning of
round

Pick up 6 stitches along the selvedge of the triangle.

Row 1: P5, P2tog, turn. (The second stitch in the P2tog is the first available stitch from the next triangle.)

Row 2: K6, turn.

Alternate rows 1 and 2 until all the stitches from the next triangle have been included in a P2tog. The sequence ends with row 1; the first square is complete. Turn the work at the end of the final row. You are now in position to pick up stitches along the next triangle.

The *second and following squares* in this round are worked as follows:

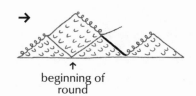

→

↑
beginning of
round

Pick up 6 stitches along the adjacent selvedge.

Row 1: K6, turn.

Row 2: P5, P2tog, turn. (The second stitch in each P2tog is the first available stitch from the next triangle.)

Alternate rows 1 and 2 as before until this square has been completed. End with row 2. The turn at its end will put you in position to pick up stitches for the next square.

Continue around.

Second round of squares, and all even-numbered rounds

Squares form from right to left.

The *first square* shifts the direction of the work and is slightly different from the remaining squares in the sequence. The working yarn will be at the bottom of a V between the first and last squares worked on the previous round.

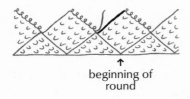

beginning of round

Pick up 6 stitches along the adjacent edge (this will be a selvedge on the first square from the previous round), from base to tip.

Row 1: K5, SSK, and turn. (The SSK will include one stitch from the last square worked on the previous round).

Row 2: P6, turn.

Alternate rows 1 and 2 until all the open stitches along the last square's edge have been worked. The sequence ends with row 1.

The *second and following squares* in this round are worked as follows:

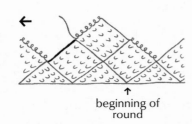

beginning of round

Pick up 6 stitches along the adjacent selvedge.

Row 1: P6.

Row 2: K5, SSK, and turn.

Alternate rows 1 and 2 until all 6 open stitches in this set have been worked. The sequence ends with row 2, without a turn.

Continue around.

Third round of squares, and all other odd-numbered rounds

Follow the instructions for the first round of squares, but instead of joining to the triangles you will join to the edges of the squares of the previous round.

Completing the section of basketweave

Continue in this manner until you've reached the desired depth of fabric.

Work a final row of triangles, rather than squares, to produce a flat upper edge on the fabric. This final round of triangles can be worked as an even- or odd-numbered round. Then bind off the edge, or resume working stockinette or garter stitch.

To work the final triangles, leave one stitch unworked at the edge of every second row, reducing the stitches by half—back to the original number on the needles before you began the baketweave section. The example given here involves an odd-numbered round (follows completion of an even-numbered round of squares).

The *first triangle* shifts the direction of the work and is slightly different from the remaining triangles in the sequence.

Pick up 6 stitches along the adjacent selvedge.

Row 1: P5, P2tog, turn.	Row 7: P2, P2tog, turn.
Row 2: K5, turn.	Row 8: K2, turn.
Row 3: P4, P2tog, turn.	Row 9: P1, P2tog, turn.
Row 4: K4, turn.	Row 10: K1, turn.
Row 5: P3, P2tog, turn.	Row 11: P2tog, turn.
Row 6: K3, turn.	

The *second and following triangles* in this round are worked as follows:

Pick up 6 stitches along the adjacent selvedge.

Row 1: K6, turn.	Row 7: K3, turn.
Row 2: P5, P2tog, turn.	Row 8: P2, P2tog, turn.
Row 3: K5, turn.	Row 9: K2, turn.
Row 4: P4, P2tog, turn.	Row 10: P1, P2tog, turn.
Row 5: K4, turn.	Row 11: K1, turn.
Row 6: P3, P2tog, turn.	Row 12: P2tog, turn.

Continue around.

Basketweave in flat pieces

If you're working flat, you will need to produce a vertical large triangle (half-square) at each edge on every other row of squares. Here's one way to accomplish that. *Inc 1* here means knit into both the front and the back of the stitch.

First row of squares, and all other odd-numbered rows

Initial large triangle (half-square):

When you finish the base row of triangles, cast on 1 stitch (backward-loop cast-on) and turn.

Row 1: P2tog, turn. (The second stitch in each P2tog is the first available stitch from the next triangle.)

Row 2: Inc 1, turn.

Row 3: P1, P2tog, turn.

Row 4: K1, inc 1, turn.

Row 5: P2, P2tog, turn.

Row 6: K2, inc 1, turn.

Row 7: P3, P2tog, turn.

Row 8: K3, inc 1, turn.

Row 9: P4, P2tog, turn.

Row 10: K4, inc 1, turn.

Row 11: P5, P2tog, turn.

You can skip the cast-on of 1 stitch at the beginning of the initial large triangle. In that case, row 11 will be P6, turn. The sequence with the extra cast-on stitch produces a smoother edge on the fabric; the sequence without it is easier to remember.

The *full squares* in this row are worked as follows:

→

Pick up 6 stitches along the adjacent selvedge.

Row 1: K6, turn.

Row 2: P5, P2tog, turn. (The second stitch in each P2tog is the first available stitch from the next triangle.)

→

Alternate rows 1 and 2 as before until this square has been completed. End with row 2. The turn at its end will put you in position to pick up stitches for the next square.

Continue until you reach the other side.

Final large triangle (half-square):

Pick up 6 stitches along the adjacent selvedge.

Row 1: K6, turn.

Row 2: P4, P2tog, turn.

Row 3: K5, turn.

Row 4: P3, P2tog, turn.

Row 5: K4, turn.

Row 6: P2, P2tog, turn.

Row 7: K3, turn.

Row 8: P1, P2tog, turn.

Row 9: K2, turn.

Row 10: P2tog, turn.

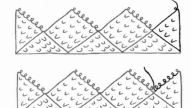

Slip 1 remaining stitch to working (righthand) needle and pick up 5 additional stitches along the selvedge just formed, then proceed to row 1 of either *second row of squares* (below) or *completing the section of basketweave* (next page).

Second row of squares, and all other even-numbered rows

The squares in even-numbered rows are all worked as follows:

Pick up 6 stitches along the adjacent selvedge (note that on the first square, 1 stitch will be on the needle as you start, so you will pick up 5 additional stitches along the selvedge).

Row 1: P6.

Row 2: K5, SSK, and turn.

Alternate rows 1 and 2 until all 6 open stitches in this set have been worked. The sequence ends with row 2, without a turn. Continue across.

Completing the section of basketweave

As on the circular version, work a final row of triangles to produce a flat upper edge on the fabric.

This is easiest to accomplish on an even-numbered row (following an odd-numbered row of squares). In this case, only one type of triangle needs to be inserted in the gaps, and all of the triangles in the row are worked in the same way:

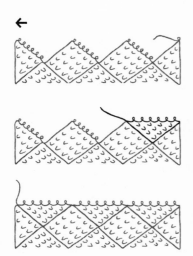

Pick up 6 stitches along the adjacent selvedge.

Row 1: P6, turn.	Row 7: P3, turn.
Row 2: K5, SSK, turn.	Row 8: K2, SSK, turn.
Row 3: P5, turn.	Row 9: P2, turn.
Row 4: K4, SSK, turn.	Row 10: K1, SSK, turn.
Row 5: P4, turn.	Row 11: P1, turn.
Row 6: K3, SSK, turn.	Row 12: SSK, turn.

If the length of your fabric requires that you work this final series of triangles as an odd-numbered row (following an even-numbered row of squares), you will need to insert larger triangles (half-squares) on the inside gaps, but you will also need to make smaller triangles (quarter-squares) at the ends of the row. Here's how:

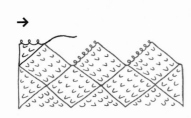

Initial triangle (quarter-square):

Row 1: P2tog, turn.	Row 6: K2, turn.
Row 2: Inc 1, turn.	Row 7: P1, P2tog, turn.
Row 3: P1, P2tog, turn.	Row 8: K1, turn.
Row 4: K1, inc 1, turn.	Row 9: P2tog, turn.
Row 5: P2, P2tog, turn.	

For this unit, 3 open stitches remain on the needle (half the number in a full unit).

The *full triangles* in this row are worked as follows:

Pick up 6 stitches along the adjacent selvedge.

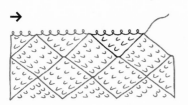

Row 1: K6, turn.	Row 7: K3, turn.
Row 2: P5, P2tog, turn.	Row 8: P2, P2tog, turn.
Row 3: K5, turn.	Row 9: K2, turn.
Row 4: P4, P2tog, turn.	Row 10: P1, P2tog, turn.
Row 5: K4, turn.	Row 11: K1, turn.
Row 6: P3, P2tog, turn.	Row 12: P2tog, turn.

Continue across the flat fabric.
Final triangle (or quarter-square):

Pick up 6 stitches along the adjacent selvedge.

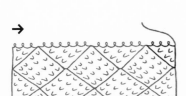

Row 1: K6, turn.	Row 4: P2, P2tog, turn.
Row 2: P4, P2tog, turn.	Row 5: K2, turn.
Row 3: K4, turn.	Row 6: P2tog, turn.

For this unit, 3 open stitches remain on the needle (half the number in a full unit).

Bind off, or return to regular knitting.

Crochet-Enhanced Knits

I n crochet, as in knitting, there are differences between the Eastern and Western approaches. In knitting, the end product is the same; in crochet, the end products are decidedly different. The Eastern techniques are known by many names, including *Bosnian crochet* and *shepherd's knitting,* as well as simpler terms, like *hooking* and *looping.*

Why would a knitter care about this form of crochet—other than to be mildly curious about the English name, *shepherd's knitting?* I can think of two good reasons: its history intersects with that of our craft, and it has been used through history and in many countries as a strong complement to knitted construction.

Eastern and Western crochet

In Eastern crochet, the slip stitch is the basic unit of construction. In the West, we most often employ the slip stitch in two ways, neither of which involves the construction of cloth. In crochet, we use slip stitches to get from one place to another. We also use slip-stitching as a supplementary technique to make tidy edges on knitted or woven fabric. The fabric produced by the Eastern techniques is solid, unlike the openwork crocheted cloth familiar to the Western world. Western crochet emphasizes textural patterns, sometimes made more complex through the use of color. In Eastern fabrics, the texture remains relatively consistent and most of the designs are produced with color patterning.

Because the loops of the slip stitches in Eastern crochet advance in one direction (from right to left when worked right-handed, or left to right when worked left-handed), the pattern and fabric

↑ Forged hooks have been favored in Central Asia.

→ Hooks made from spoon handles have been favored in Scandinavia.

The slip stitch is the main structural component of Eastern crochet, augmented by limited use of single crochet. This style of work goes by many names, including *shepherd's knitting* from the north of Scotland and *Bosnian crochet,* from the French description of the work typical of Eastern Europe.

I use *shepherd's knitting* to describe slip-stitch crochet worked through the lower (front) side of the chain head, because the back of the work looks like true knitting spiraling around the circular structure. The V that looks like a knit stitch lies on its side because it is the alignment of the upper half of the chain head.

I use *Bosnian crochet* to describe slip-stitch crochet worked through the upper (back) of the chain head, leaving the lower (front) half exposed on the surface; this is the recognized terminology used in Western cultures.

Shepherd's knitting or Bosnian crochet?

Shepherd's knitting

The hook passes through the lower (front) half of the chain head. The yarn passes over the hook from back to front and is drawn through the two loops on the hook (the working loop from the last stitch and the chain-head loop) to form a new working loop.

Bosnian crochet

The hook passes through the upper (back) half of the chain head. The yarn passes over the hook from back to front and is drawn through the two loops on the hook (the working loop from the last stitch and the chain-head loop) to form a new working loop.

---

are decidedly biased. Because the design depends upon the positions of the loops and the ways they are worked (with options I'll explain in a moment), the work must proceed in only one direction. Thus Eastern crochet is considered a circular technique, suitable for making accessories, especially socks, mittens, and bags, although the cloth produced with this technique can be cut and bound. Usually this is done to make vests.

Eastern crochet is most often worked with a short, flat hook, often made from a spoon handle or from heavy forged wire with a wide handle spiraling out toward a flattened hook. The shaft is angled, and determines the size of the completed loop. Because the hooks are handmade, no two are identical. The flat hook is important. It slips easily into the middle of a chain head. The familiar round hook does not separate the lower and upper halves of the chain head as neatly, especially when the hook needs to work around the lower side of the chain head.

There are no commercially available hooks for Eastern crochet at the time of this publication. In lieu of finding someone to handcraft a suitable tool, I suggest altering a standard Western crochet hook. A size that corresponds to your knitting needle should work for gauge. With a fine file, flatten the two sides of the hook, angled toward a narrow top. The flat area should be about 1 inch long. The front of the hook should be

Modified Western-style hook

Crochet hook seen from front (left pair) and side (right pair). In each pair, the standard hook is on the left and the modified, Eastern-style shape is on the right.

filed toward a point at the top. I have even used a fingernail file to shape an aluminum crochet hook.

The uses of the loop

In crochet, one loop remains on the hook at the completion of each stitch. Each completed stitch has an interlocked loop at its top, which I call the *chain head*. The chain head has a *lower (front) side* and an *upper (back) side*. Each new stitch is worked through a chain head from the previous round—and herein lies another structural difference between the Eastern and Western approaches to crochet. In the West, we draw the new loop under *both* sides of the chain head. In the East, the new loop is pulled under either the front or the back half of the loop.

The revelation of shepherd's knitting

When a new loop is worked around the *lower, front half* of the chain head, few people even recognize the structure as crochet. I first encountered this technique through some awesome socks from Central Asia. As a knitter, I learned with pure delight that the English translation of the name for the process is *shepherd's knitting*.

I have to believe that the English terminology comes from the appearance of the fabric. On the face, it looks like a form of needlework. On the back, it looks like spiraling stockinette stitches. When a stitch is formed,

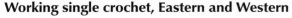

Working single crochet, Eastern and Western

Western-style single crochet

The Western-style single crochet is worked by first drawing a loop under *both* sides of the chain head and then drawing another loop through the two loops on the hook.

Eastern-style single crochet

The Eastern-style single crochet is traditionally used only in Bosnian crochet, not shepherd's knitting. It is worked by first drawing a loop under the upper (back) side of the chain head and then drawing another loop through the two loops on the hook.

When you work colored patterning in either style, the last loop in a color area must be worked in the *new* color if the color being dropped is not to advance to the left as the working loop for the next stitch.

In the Middle East and much of Eastern Europe, the loop in single-crochet work advances to the left. This produces what I call a stained-glass look.

In Scandinavia, the new color in a single-crochet sequence is used to form the final loop in a section and the resulting colored pattern is therefore clearly defined and in sharp focus.

the yarn pulls up the front side of the chain head and leaves its two ends exposed on the face of the fabric as small, vertical "blips" of yarn. The knitted appearance on the back occurs because the upper half of the chain head is pushed to the back and left exposed, creating what appears to be the V of a knit stitch, lying on its side.

Bosnian crochet

When a new loop is worked around the *upper, back half* of the chain head, most people recognize the resulting fabric as Bosnian crochet. The surface consists of short, horizontal floats of yarn, produced by the lower (front) sides of the chain heads. Designs may be patterned with color or texture. In the latter, designs are formed by working around the upper or lower side of each chain head, according to a patterning sequence. This produces a pattern of floats against the plain ground.

When symmetrical, colored patterning is deemed necessary, single crochet is incorporated and each stitch is worked around the upper (back) half of a chain head. This is often used as a design element on otherwise knitted, color-stranded socks from the region west of the Black Sea.

The reach and impact of Eastern crochet styles

We can follow the spread of shepherd's knitting from Central Asia to the Middle East and the Balkan states, then north through Eastern Europe via the old overland trade routes, then west along the waterways through Scandinavia and the North Sea Islands. Bosnian crochet traveled much the same route, from Turkey and the Balkan states north to Finland.

Shaping Eastern crochet

An increase is worked in the form of a chain stitch that presents itself as a new stitch on the next round.

Decreases result when two chain-head loops are worked together to remove one stitch; the order in which the stitches are entered depends on which side of the chain head is being worked.

Shepherd's knitting decrease

Enter the first chain head, then the second one, drawing the yarn through these two loops on the hook and the working loop from the last stitch.

Bosnian crochet decrease

Enter the second chain head, then the first one, drawing the yarn through these two loops on the hook and the working loop from the last stitch.

295

In garments along these routes, from footwear in Turkey to sweaters in Finland, we can find knitting enhanced with this form of crochet, and we discover patterns that have a symmetry not possible with the slip stitch. Single crochet, worked in the Bosnian style, produces straight edges on the cloth and vertically aligned patterns. The work must remain circular or, if it is worked flat, the yarn must be broken off at the end of each row and rejoined at the beginning of the next row.

In the southern parts of the geographic region where this work occurred, the chain head advances to the left before the color change, breaking the edges of the color pattern with horizontal floats that extend beyond the design. In the northern parts of the region, the new color is pulled through the last loop, to keep the color pattern in sharp focus.

Finnish Knit/Crochet Sweater

Patterns for sleeves.

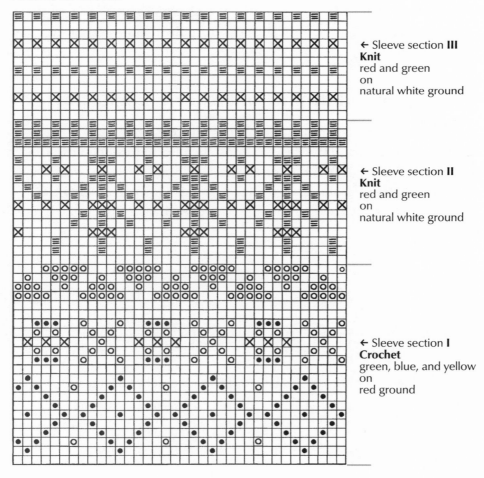

← Sleeve section **III**
Knit
red and green
on
natural white ground

← Sleeve section **II**
Knit
red and green
on
natural white ground

← Sleeve section **I**
Crochet
green, blue, and yellow
on
red ground

I have found intriguing references to a number of traditional Finnish sweaters, including what is referred to as the "all-time favorite" Jussi, the Voyri, the Pirttikyla, and the reputedly "popular" Northern Lights sweaters. I have not found examples of any of these garments, so it's not clear what techniques they incorporated or what their designs were like.

Yet I have discovered one treasure. The traditional sweaters of the Korsnäs district of Finland, which date back to the 1800s, show the exciting results that can come from combining knitting with Bosnian crochet. If the Korsnäs sweater is any indication of traditional Finnish garments, those yet to be seen must be magnificent.

Several items in the bibliography contain information on Eastern crochet styles, including bits and pieces in some of the Scandinavian books.

Peter Collingwood's *The Maker's Hand* and John Gillow and Bryan Sentance's *World Textiles* contain glorious, inspiring pictures.

For technique, see the *Spin-Off* articles that John Yerkovich and I wrote, as well as the brief coverage in Lis Paludan's *Crochet: History and Technique.*

Finnish Knit/Crochet Sweater

Patterns for cuffs.

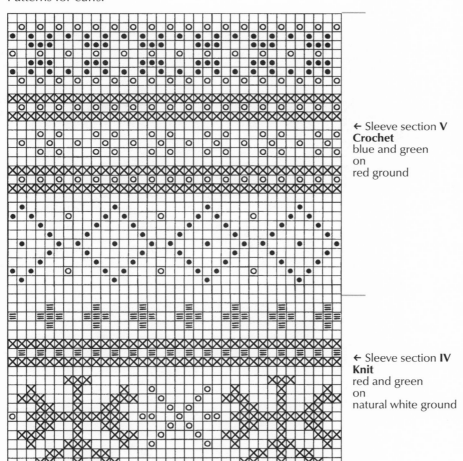

← Sleeve section **V**
Crochet
blue and green
on
red ground

← Sleeve section **IV**
Knit
red and green
on
natural white ground

Finnish Sweater Combining Knitting and Crochet

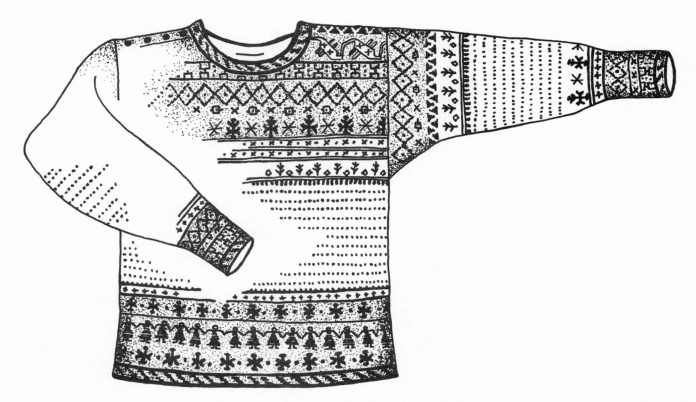

This style of sweater displays a wonderful combination of techniques and colors. The traditional colors are red, natural white, medium green, sky blue, and muted yellow. The garment plays crocheted sections with red backgrounds against knitted portions with white backgrounds. The crocheted portions include the body's lower section and upper yoke and the sleeves' cuffs and upper arms. Stockinette forms the middle portions of both body and sleeves. The sections reverse their order on sleeves and body, around a main section of stripes on each garment piece. The end result is worth all those ends on the yoke!

The body and sleeves are divided into five design sections. Starting at the bottom of the body and the tops of the sleeves, these include:

Patterns for the Finnish Knit/Crochet Sweater are on pages 296, 297, and 300–02.

I. Single-crocheted, with large motifs on a red background. There are two or three colors per row, and the dominant contrasting color is the medium green. Begins with optional slip-stitch edging.

II. A narrow knitted section, with small red and green motifs on a natural white background. There are usually two, occasionally three, colors per row.

III. A wide knitted section of stripes: two white rows, then one row of alternating white and red stitches, two white rows, then one row of alternating white and green stitches. The colored stitches in the alternating rows can be stacked above each other or offset.

IV. Another small, knitted section, with patterning similar but not identical to that in section II. The background is again white. On the body, this section must be divided, because it extends into the straight division for the armholes for a short distance.

V. A second wide, single-crocheted section, worked on a red background, with patterning similar in proportions to that in section I. On the body, this section must be worked flat to accommodate the armholes. The working strand must be broken off at the end of each row and rejoined again at the opposite edge to start the next row. Ends with optional slip-stitch edging.

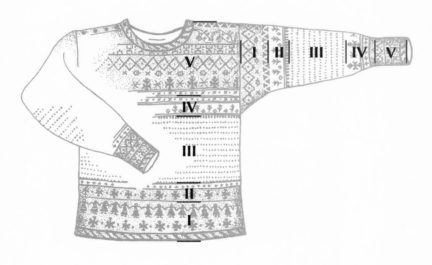

Because the crocheted yoke is not as elastic as knitted fabric would be, older sweaters had deep crewnecks. Often a buttoned placket was placed at the center front or on the left shoulder. Modern versions usually have wider, but still deep, crewnecks that eliminate the need for a placket.

Edges, including neck bands, can be finished with multiple rounds of patterned slip-stitch crochet. On a sweater with a buttoned placket, the neck band and placket need to be single-crocheted instead of slip-stitched, so the overlapping ends will have straight edges.

Finnish Knit/Crochet Sweater

Patterns for lower body.

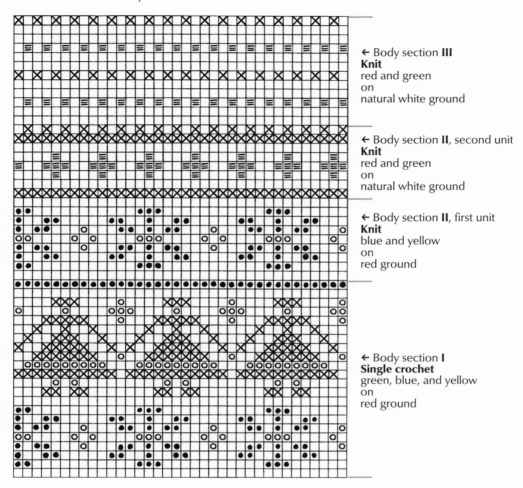

← Body section **III**
Knit
red and green
on
natural white ground

← Body section **II**, second unit
Knit
red and green
on
natural white ground

← Body section **II**, first unit
Knit
blue and yellow
on
red ground

← Body section **I**
Single crochet
green, blue, and yellow
on
red ground

Optional slip-stitch edging

What appear to be vertical lines
will have a bias slant.

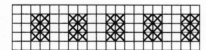

Crochet
green
on
red ground

Before you embark on a project that blends knitting and crochet so closely, explore *your* gauge with *your* yarns in both techniques.

First determine your knitting gauge and preferred needles. Then determine which size crochet hook will let you move from one technique to the other while keeping the transition areas smooth.

Start testing with a crochet hook that corresponds to your knitting needles' measurement. This is easiest to determine according to metric designations. If you are on 3.5mm needles, try a 3.5mm

Finnish Knit/Crochet Sweater

Patterns for middle of body.

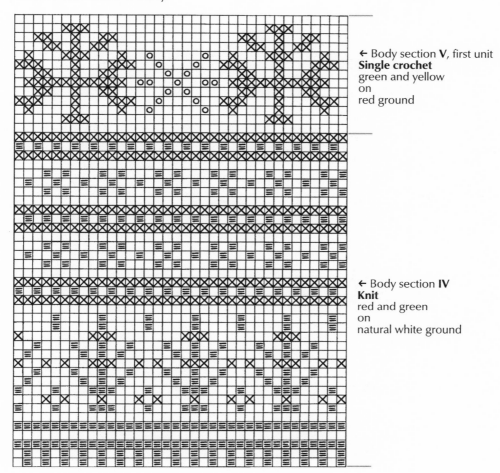

← Body section **V**, first unit
Single crochet
green and yellow
on
red ground

← Body section **IV**
Knit
red and green
on
natural white ground

Color key

ground, either red or natural white, as noted
red (when on white ground)
green
blue
yellow

hook. However, you may crochet either more loosely or more tightly than you knit, so be prepared to experiment until you get the right combination. To shift from crochet to knit, pick up and knit stitches through the crochet loops. The appearance of the transition will be affected by whether you pick up through the lower (front) half of the chain head, the upper (back) half of the chain head, or under both sides of the chain head.

To shift from knit to crochet, work a row of slip stitch through the loops of the knit stitches.

Finnish Knit/Crochet Sweater

Patterns for upper body
(completion of yoke).

← Body section **V**, second unit
Single crochet
green, blue, and yellow
on
red ground

Color key

☐	ground, either red or natural white, as noted
☰	red (when on white ground)
☒	green
●	blue
○	yellow

Bibliography

The works listed here have been published in many different countries and languages. Because of their abundance of charted patterns, they can provide a lot of useful information even if you can't read the text, and sometimes the businesses that import books provide partial or full translations as a service to their customers.

Abbey, Barbara. *The Complete Book of Knitting.* New York: Viking, 1971.

———. *Susan Bates Presents 101 Ways to Improve Your Knitting.* New York and London: The Studio Publications, 1949. This book may be small, but it's a gem.

Almay, Mirja, Marketta Luutonen, and Kyllikki Mitronen. *Sydämenlämmittäjä ja tikkuripaita: perinteisiä neuleita Suomesta ja Eestistä.* Helsinki: Kustannusosakeyhtiö Tammi, 1993. English summary translated by Raili Kannel.

Bøhn, Annichen Sibbern. *Norwegian Knitting Designs.* Oslo: Grøndahl, 1975. This is a revised English version of *Norske strikkemønstre.*

Breivik, Olga Marie, Aud Lysberg, Torun Selstad, Anne-Catherine Sundt, Torild Finsrud Velure, and Vigdis N. Westgaard. *Fanatrøyer* (Fana Sweaters). Bergen: Eide Forlag, 1998. Includes English translation by Judith Mercer Cabot.

Christoffersson, Britt-Marie. *Swedish Sweaters: New Designs from Historical Examples.* Translated by Gunnel Melchers. Newtown, Connecticut: Taunton Press, 1990.

Collingwood, Peter. *The Maker's Hand: A Close Look at Textile Structures.* London: Bellew, 1998. Pages 34–39 show Eastern-style crochet.

Compton, Rae. *The Complete Book of Traditional Knitting.* New York: Scribner, 1983.

Dale Yarn Company. *Knit Your Own Norwegian Sweaters: Complete Instructions for Fifty Authentic Sweaters, Hats, Mittens, Gloves, and Caps.* New York: Dover, 1974.

Dandanell, Birgitta, and Ulla Danielsson. *Twined Knitting: A Swedish Folkcraft Technique.* Translated by Robin Orm Hansen. Loveland, Colorado: Interweave Press, 1989. This is an English version of *Tvåändsstickat.*

Debes, Hans M. *Føroysk bindingarmynstur.* Tórshavn, Færoe Islands: Føroysk Heimavirki, 1983.

Don, Sarah. *The Art of Shetland Lace.* London: Bell and Hyman, 1984.

———. *Fair Isle Knitting: A Practical Handbook of Traditional Designs.* London: Bell and Hyman, 1982.

Edmondston, Eliza. *Sketches and Tales of the Shetland Islands.* Edinburgh: Sutherland and Knox, 1856.

Director of Random Keyboard Input and Typographic Irregularity

Erlbacher, Maria. *Überlieferte Strickmuster aus dem Steirischen Ennstal.* 3 volumes. Trautenfels: Landschaftsmuseum, 1986. Austrian/Bavarian twisted-stitch patterns.

Fanderl, Lisl. *Bäuerliches Stricken 1: Alte Muster aus dem alpenländischen Raum.* Rosenheim: Rosenheimer, 1994.

———. *Bäuerliches Stricken 2.* Rosenheim: Rosenheimer, 1992.

———. *Stricken 3: 165 Muster aus Aus Bauern- und Bürgerhäusern.* Rosenheim: Rosenheimer, 1983.

Fatelewitz, Madelynn. "Knitting in the North Atlantic." *Threads* no. 16 (April/May 1988): 50–53.

Fee, Jacqueline. *The Sweater Workshop: Knit Creative Seam-Free Sweaters on Your Own with Any Yarn.* Second edition. Camden, Maine: Down East Books, 2002.

Gainford, Veronica. *Designs for Knitting Kilt Hose and Knickerbocker Stockings.* Edinburgh: Scottish Development Agency, 1978. Revised edition: Pittsville, Wisconsin: Schoolhouse Press, 1995.

Gibson-Roberts, Priscilla A. "Old World Crochet: A Brief History." *Spin-Off* 25, no. 2 (Summer 2001): 54–56.

———. *Salish Indian Sweaters: A Pacific Northwest Tradition.* Saint Paul: Dos Tejedoras Fiber Arts Publications, 1989.

Gillow, John, and Bryan Sentance. *World Textiles: A Visual Guide to Traditional Techniques.* New York: Little, Brown, 1999. Pages 43–45, "Netting, Linking and Looping," concern old-world crochet.

Guðjónsson, Elsa E. *Notes on Knitting in Iceland.* Fourth edition, revised. Reykjavík: National Museum of Iceland, 1983.

Häglund, Ulla, and Ingrid Mesterton. *Bohus Stickning.* Uddevalla, Sweden: Bohusläns museums förl., 1999.

Hartley, Marie, and Joan Ingilby. *The Old Hand-Knitters of the Dales.* Clapham, England: Dalesman, 1969. Reissued 1991, 1996.

Harvey, Michael, and Rae Compton. *Fisherman Knitting.* Shire Album 31. England: Shire Publications, 1978.

Hinchcliffe, Frances, and Santina Levey. "Glove, Cap, and Boot-Hose." *Crafts,* no. 57 (July/August 1982): 33–40.

Hollingworth, Shelagh. *The Complete Book of Traditional Aran Knitting.* New York: Saint Martin's Press, 1982.

Johansson, Britta, and Kersti Nilsson. *Binge: en halländsk sticktradition.* Stockholm: LT, 1980.

Keele, Wendy. *Poems of Color: Knitting in the Bohus Tradition.* Loveland, Colorado: Interweave Press, 1995.

Kiewe, Heinz Edgar. *The Sacred History of Knitting.* Second edition. Oxford: Art Needlework Industries, 1971.

Klift-Tellegen, Henriëtte van der. *Knitting from the Netherlands: Traditional Dutch Fishermen's Sweaters.* Translated by Marianne Wiegman. Asheville, North Carolina: Lark Books, 1985. This is an English version of *Nederlandse visserstruien.*

Krassnig, Griseldis. *Wir Stricken Tiroler Trachtenjoppen.* Innsbruck: Fernschule der Landwirtschaft, n.d.

Lane, Barbara. "The Cowichan Knitting Industry." *Anthropology in British Columbia,* no. 2 (1951): 14–27.

LeCount, Cynthia Gravelle. *Andean Folk Knitting: Traditions and Techniques from Peru and Bolivia.* Saint Paul: Dos Tejedoras Fiber Arts Publications, 1990.

Lind, Vibeke. *Knitting in the Nordic Tradition.* Translated by Annette Allen Jensen. Asheville, North Carolina: Lark Books, 1984. This is an English version of *Stik med nordisk tradition* (København: Høst, 1982).

Luutonen, Marketta. *Korsnäsin Kuviolliset Villapaidat.* Helsinki: Kolmas Pianos, 1987.

McGregor, Sheila. *The Complete Book of Traditional Fair Isle Knitting.* New York: Scribner, 1982.

———. *The Complete Book of Traditional Scandinavian Knitting.* New York: Saint Martin's Press, 1984.

———. *Traditional Knitting.* London: B. T. Batsford, 1983.

Meikle, Margaret. *Cowichan Indian Knitting.* Museum Note Number 21. Vancouver, British Columbia: U. B. C. Museum of Anthropology, 1987.

———. "The Cowichan Knitting Industry." Paper presented to the Native American Art Studies Association, September 1983.

Morgan, Gwyn. *Traditional Knitting Patterns of Ireland, Scotland, and England.* New York: Saint Martin's Press, 1981.

Norbury, James. *Traditional Knitting Patterns, from Scandinavia, the British Isles, France, Italy, and Other European Countries.* New York: Dover, 1973.

Nylén, Anna Maja. *Swedish Handcraft.* Translated by Anne-Charlotte Hanes Harvey. New York: Van Nostrand Reinhold, 1977.

Pagoldh, Susanne. *Nordic Knitting: Thirty-One Patterns in the Scandinavian Tradition.* Translated by Carol Rhoades. Loveland, Colorado: Interweave Press, 1991. This is an English version of *Stickat från Norden.*

Paludan, Lis. *Crochet: History and Technique.* Loveland, Colorado: Interweave Press, 1995. Pages 286–87, "Shepherd's Knitting."

Pearson, Michael. *Michael Pearson's Traditional Knitting: Aran, Fair Isle, and Fisher Ganseys.* New York: Van Nostrand Reinhold, 1984.

Reynolds Lopi. New York: Reynold Yarns/Alafoss of Iceland, 1983.

Rutt, Richard. *A History of Hand Knitting.* London: B. T. Batsford, 1987. Reissued: Loveland, Colorado: Interweave Press, 2003.

Smith, Mary, and Chris Bunyan. *A Shetland Knitter's Notebook: Knitting Patterns and Stories.* Lerwick, Scotland: The Shetland Times, 1991.

Smith, Mary, and Maggie Liddle. *A Shetland Pattern Book: Knitting Designs.* Eleventh revised edition. Lerwick, Scotland: The Shetland Times, 1992.

Strikke, hekle, binde. Oslo, Norway: Landbruksforlaget, 1989.

Sundbø, Annemor. *Everyday Knitting: Treasures from a Ragpile.* Translated by Amy Lightfoot. Kristiansand, Norway: Torridal Tweed, 2000. This is an English version of *Kvardagsstrikk.*

————. *Setesdal Sweaters: The History of the Norwegian Lice Pattern.* Translation by Amy Lightfoot. Kristiansand, Norway: Torridal Tweed, 2001. This is an English version of *Lusekofta fra Setesdal: Setesdalskofta i strikkehistoria* (Kristiansand, Norway: Nordic Academic Press, 1998).

Thomas, Mary. *Mary Thomas's Book of Knitting Patterns.* New York: Dover, 1972.

————. *Mary Thomas's Knitting Book.* New York: Dover, 1972.

Thompson, Gladys. *Patterns for Guernseys, Jerseys, and Arans: Fishermen's Sweaters from the British Isles.* Third revised edition. New York: Dover, 1971.

Traditional Knitting with Wool. Melbourne: Australian Wool Corporation, 1982.

Turnau, Irena. *History of Knitting before Mass Production.* Translated by Agnieszka Szonert. Warsaw: Institute of the History of Material Culture, Polish Academy of Sciences, 1991. This is an English version of *Historia dziewiarstwa europejskiego do poczatku XIX wieku.*

————. "The Knitting Crafts in Europe from the Thirteenth to the Eighteenth Century." *The Bulletin of the Needle and Bobbin Club* 65, nos. 1 and 2 (1982): 10–42.

Walker, Barbara G. *Charted Knitting Designs: A Third Treasury of Knitting Patterns.* Pittsville, Wisconsin: Schoolhouse Press, 1998.

————. *A Treasury of Knitting Patterns.* Pittsville, Wisconsin: Schoolhouse Press, 1998.

Wright, Mary. *Cornish Guernseys and Knit-Frocks.* Penzance, Cornwall: Alison Hodge; London: Ethnographica, 1979.

Yerkovich, John. "Old World Crochet Bags: Delightful Bags to Carry Small Treasures." *Spin-Off* 25, no. 2 (Summer 2001): 57–60.

Zimmermann, Elizabeth. *Knitting Workshop.* Pittsville, Wisconsin: Schoolhouse Press, 1981.

Abbreviations

K	knit
K2tog or K3tog	knit two or three stitches together
M1R	make-one raised
P	purl
P2tog or P3tog	purl two or three stitches together
S1 or S2	slip one or two stitches
S1, K1, PSSO	slip one, knit one, pass slipped stitch over
SSK	slip, slip, knit
SSP	slip, slip, purl

Quotations

Index

Colophon

Special thanks to the designers of the fonts and the programs that made creating this complex book a joy.

In selecting fonts, we aimed first for legibility, then for aesthetics, determined not to sacrifice either. All of the fonts are contemporary faces with classic grace. They handled our linguistic requirements with ease. Long after we had chosen, we discovered that their stories and histories suit this work as much as their letterforms do. Their designers live in the United States, Germany, Canada, and Hungary. The synergy resonates at many levels.

The body type is **Warnock,** designed by Robert Slimbach (2000, Adobe). It is named after John Warnock, the co-founder of Adobe Systems. Once we discovered Warnock, the page layouts acquired the personality we sought. The primary text is set at 11.5/15.5. ❖ Most of the display type is **URW Alcuin,** designed by Gudrun Zapf von Hesse (1991, URW++). Her calligraphic sensibilities strongly influenced this face. ❖ The sans serif type used for the captions and callouts is URW Classico, designed by Hermann Zapf (1990, URW++). He's a well-known designer and the

husband of Gudrun Zapf von Hesse. ❖ The small arrows come from FF Dingbests, by Johannes Erler (FontFont). ❖ On the cover, the "handwritten" font is *Rodin*, designed by Denis Kegler and created in association with the Philadelphia Museum of Art (1997, P22). The flower on the spine is part of Alien Ornaments, designed by Amondó Szegi (2000, T.26). ❖ On the title page, the modern-medieval face is Tyndale, designed by Ted Staunton (2002, P22/International House of Fonts). It's named for William Tyndale (c. 1494-1536), an Englishman who translated the Bible so common folk could read it. ❖ Finally, the words *Nomad Press* occasionally appear in Pan-Am, designed by Christina Torre and Richard Kegler (2000, P22). It's based on lettering used for a variety of printed ephemera at the 1901 Pan American Exhibition.

We processed Priscilla's original pen-and-ink drawings of the sweaters and charts with Photoshop 7 and assembled the book in InDesign 2.

This array of wonderful tools seasoned our long hours of work with a lot of pleasure.